KETELAAR

AARTS

DEMIR

23 INNOVATIONS IN DIGITAL COMMUNICATION

*Move beyond speculations and master
mediated communication*

B/S

CONTENT

PREFACE

Digital technologies, such as augmented and virtual reality, chatbots, social media, and mobile applications, have a major impact on our daily lives. They not only change how we communicate with friends and family, but also how we work, and how clients and organisations communicate with each other. To understand the world around us, and to have some idea about what the future will bring us, it is necessary to have knowledge of technological innovations. This book helps us to master digital communication innovations.

This book brings together practitioners and researchers to review 23 digital innovations. Everyone is familiar with clichés about practitioners and the academic world. Scientists are sitting in an ivory tower, drawing far too nuanced conclusions that often cannot be applied in communication and marketing practice. Communication professionals are often aiming for short-term effects, without wondering how effects can be explained, and they do not have the time to reflect. As the director of a foundation that tries to promote cross-fertilisation between science and practice, I know that it can be a huge challenge to let both worlds enter into a dialogue, and to edit and write a book with both readerships as the starting point. Paul Ketelaar, Jan Aarts, and Sanne Demir took up this challenge, with a magnificent result.

This book is NOT a scientific book infused with some practical cases, and it is NOT a casebook or practical guide infused with some scientific contributions; this book is a real blend of practical and scientific knowledge:
- An easy-to-read blend, as it leaves out jargon, and a tasteful blend as it visually illustrates the usability, effectiveness, future proofing, and x-factor of each digital innovation discussed.
- Informative for communication and marketing professionals; one can learn by doing and from experience, but also from peers and from scientific research.
- Informative for students and teachers of communication and marketing; one can learn from research but also from real-life cases that put academic research into context.
- Helpful for everyone who likes to be able to participate in discussions on digital innovations, whether this is at the kitchen table or in the board room: this book helps to understand digital innovations and their implications for clients.

This book offers us a full understanding of technological innovations for communication, not only by bridging practical and scientific knowledge but also by taking on a broad perspective on technology: as a tool, a medium, and a social actor. And above all, it provides a future perspective. A must have for everyone, a pleasure to read.

Guda van Noort
Amsterdam School of Communication Research, University of Amsterdam
Professor of Persuasion & New Media Technologies
Director SWOCC
Amsterdam, the Netherlands

OPENING

A key problem in communication since the emergence of the internet has been the overload of information. People are so overwhelmed by an ever-increasing number of media and messages that they systematically avoid being exposed to them[1]. Advertisements in particular are avoided because they interfere with the goals of people surfing the internet: seeking information and entertainment[2]. In this information-saturated media landscape, organisations are continuously challenged to reach consumers with information and to have them actually process that information.

DEFINITION OF DIGITAL INNOVATIONS

The goal of this book is to help readers master mediated communication. In this book, we define digital innovations as novel media, strategies, and methods that may facilitate how we communicate, using technology such as smart computers as a driving force. We discuss the impact of 23 innovations that are not hypes, but have become part of organisations and life, causing permanent changes in media use and communication. In this book we use the term 'innovations' and 'digital innovations' interchangeably.

BROAD TARGET-GROUP OF READERS

Who should read this book? This book is written for a broad audience of students and teachers in communication, and communication professionals in the field. It is fairly easy to read mainly because we have left out the jargon that is so common in the communication and advertising branch. *Communication professionals* can gain fast insights into the merits of innovations for better application in organisations, and they can broaden their knowledge from the perspective of science. This will help them to understand the innovations better and reason about their implications with clients. *Students* who are now at college and university, will be the future experts in the communication-field. This book can help them to estimate which branches they may find it interesting to work in and additionally, they can learn about the newest developments in the field and in that way prepare themselves for the start of their career. *Teachers* in communication will find various anchors to develop courses and lectures on the topic of innovative communication, and to stimulate discussion among students about the exemplary and sometimes provocative cases that we have included in the book. Finally, the book offers insights to anyone who is interested in digital innovations and how they may change the media landscape in the future. To make this book useful for a broad group of readers who are interested in the value of digital innovations in communication, we will provide several examples and cases from a commercial, healthcare, journalism, and entertainment perspective.

The book does not plunge into the depths of each innovation, but it brings you scientific and practical knowledge about innovations in digital communication so that you can participate in current debates and gain more insight into how innovations should be applied in your (future) work or life. For those who want to read more about the innovations, you can find the endnotes with sources, references, and notes after each chapter.

CONTRIBUTIONS BY EXPERTS IN SCIENCE AND IN PRACTICE

Why did we ask experts in science and in practice to contribute to our book? This book aims to build a bridge between the science of communication and the communication field in order to provide the readers a profound insight into the building blocks of each innovation, from a scientific as well as a practical nature. These experts help us do that. We selected them because of their insights into the market, and knowledge of specific innovations from either a practitioner or a scientific perspective. Their affiliations vary, from renowned experts in the field and university professors to starters with fresh ideas. They chose their own angle and wrote freely about what in their view was most important to mention or discuss, which led to a plethora of contributions, all with the aim of not only gaining insights into digital innovations but also applying them to master mediated communication. In the book the contributions of these experts are marked with a line in the left margin.

WELL-CONSIDERED CHOICE OF INNOVATIONS

How did we select the 23 innovations? First, we interviewed several innovators with a keen eye and expertise regarding digital innovations. They told us what in their view were real game-changers. From these innovations we selected the innovations that mattered in our view. Second, applying the very same principles that we discuss in our chapter Search Engine Marketing, we determined what terminology people use in their searches for these promising innovations on the internet, to make sure that our chapter titles match with what people are searching for. This quest has rendered the innovations that form the backbone of this book.

Not all innovations are new. Some, such as storytelling and gamification, have already existed for some time. For instance, storytelling in the form of stories and myths has existed for hundreds, if not thousands of years. However, as a result of current developments in the media landscape, new forms of storytelling have emerged, such as transmedia storytelling. Gamification, the application of game techniques such as competition, is not new either but it has a newfound relevance for digital communication.

References and notes

1   Van der Goot, M. J., Rozendaal, E., Opree, S. J., Ketelaar, P. E., & Smit, E. G. (2018). Media generations and their advertising attitudes and avoidance: a six-country comparison. International Journal of Advertising, 37(2), 289-308.

2   Cho, C. H. (2004). Why do people avoid advertising on the internet? Journal of Advertising, 33(4), 89-97.

STRUCTURE OF THIS BOOK

The book kicks off with contributions by five renowned experts about the current digital media landscape, providing the readers with their views on the present state of digital communication. They discuss several stepping stones for the 23 innovations that form the backbone of this book:

• The success factors in the digital transformation of organisations and the role of digital innovations
• The shifts in the way that market research is utilised
• How digital media are changing our brain
• Ethical perspectives for privacy issues
• Artificial intelligence and machine learning

Following this chapter, we discuss 23 innovations in digital communications that are organised in sections about innovations in media, communication strategies, branding strategies and methods. Each of these chapters is structured in the same way and can be read separately, making it easy to compare the innovations on their value. First, we define the specific innovation, illustrate it with examples, and discuss its distinctive characteristics. Second, we discuss implementations and views in practice and give the floor to an expert on that specific innovation. These experts discuss the innovations from the perspective of their own expertise, often with suggestions for how to implement the innovation successfully in organisations. Thereafter we discuss the innovation from the perspective of science. We conclude each innovation with a window on the future and ethical issues raised by it, often relating to privacy issues. Each innovation is rated on the items: 1) usability, 2) effectiveness, 3) ethical responsibility, 4) future proofing and 5) X-factor, using icons (see below). These ratings were decided in discussions between the authors of this book and the experts who contributed to the chapters.

1.   2.   3.   4.   5.

1 **Usability:** the degree of ease with which the innovation can be implemented by organisations.
2 **Effectiveness:** the chance that specified communication goals of organisations can be achieved by using the innovation.
3 **Ethical responsibility:** the chance that the innovation will be considered to be morally right.
4 **Future proofing:** the chance that the innovation is indispensable in the future.
5 **X-factor:** the noteworthiness of the innovation.

After discussing the innovations, four visionary experts offer us a window on the future, prioritising game-changers that in their view will make a difference to digital communication, based on our overview of innovations. They discuss:
• The role of AI-driven agents in our networked society
• Digital influencers in communication
• The role of virtual reality in our lives
• The digital media-landscape in … 2049

In the final chapter of the book we give our view on where we stand, based on the knowledge in this book, and how we can advance in integrating innovations in our media-landscape in a way that is beneficial for all parties involved.

FOUNDATION OF THIS BOOK

The rise of artificial intelligence (AI), the role of machine- and deep learning in communication and media, the moral discussions about AI and the growth of related privacy issues are general developments that form the foundation of the innovations we describe in this book. In this paragraph, we discuss these in order to clarify the context in which we discuss digital innovations.

A BRIEF HISTORY OF COMMUNICATION AND MEDIA

For the positioning of the innovations that are central to this book, we take a short peek at the history of communication and media, so-called mediated communication. When there were no media around, we communicated face to face. Communication became mediated when traditional mass media such as newspapers, magazines, radio, and TV appeared. Senders conveyed identical messages to people using mass media, organisations became interested in effective communication, and scientists researched the mechanisms of communication used in these mass media. There was a need to study communication and media systematically, giving rise to related studies all over the world such as 'Communication Science', 'Media Studies' and 'Communication & Media studies'. Then the internet came into existence, enabled by the introduction of a new medium, the computer. Slowly our media landscape changed. First with webpages (Web 1.0), thereafter social media emerged, allowing interaction between people, and between people and organisations (Web 2.0). The usual 'receivers' now have an active role and they have started to generate their own content, spreading it through their own channels, on YouTube and Facebook.

THE HISTORY OF ARTIFICIAL INTELLIGENCE

Strictly speaking, AI is an even older science than Communication Science. Therefore we consider it not to be an 'innovation'. AI is a field of expertise that focuses on the development and research of intelligent systems[1]. It focuses on the theory and development of computer systems able to perform tasks that normally require human intelligence, such as visual perception, speech recognition, and decision making. Simply put, AI enables computers to think.

The roots of AI-thinking are found in ancient Greece, with Greek myths about building the intelligence of people into human-like artefacts such as robots[2]. After World War II, computers became available that were able to run the programs necessary for AI. The term 'artificial intelligence' was born in 1956, with high hopes about its potential.

AI in these days consisted of classical programming. It was 'rule-based' or 'top-down', meaning that humans enabled computers to perform tasks by programming explicitly what they should do in which situation. These tasks could only be of a simple nature, because computer hardware was limited, and algorithms were not up to performing complicated tasks. In this 'Good Old-Fashioned AI' (GOFAI), the behaviour of computers was based on simple preprogrammed algorithms[3]. The limited possibilities of AI in the early days prevented the discipline from becoming more successful, and more popular. AI-thinking only revived when computers became fast enough and algorithms became flexible enough to execute more complicated AI-related tasks, and that is the moment that AI entered the domain of communication and media.

MACHINE LEARNING IN THE DOMAIN OF COMMUNICATION AND MEDIA

The success of several digital innovations in communication and media was possible because of breakthroughs in machine learning, which is an important area of AI. Machine Learning refers to the application of algorithms that enable machines to improve their performance of certain tasks by learning rapidly from vast amounts of data, so-called Big Data, in real-time. Machine learning is a novel paradigm because where rules used to be the input of the system in classical programming, they are now the output.

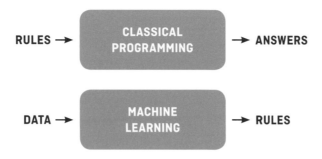

Classical programming vs. Machine learning

Machine learning is changing the classical paradigm in communication studies. Traditionally, scholars in communication and media study the components in the following equation: the *sender* of information, the *medium* by which to convey it, and the *receivers* of information. In 1948, the communication theorist Lasswell[4] wrote that you could describe the act of communication by answering the questions: Who? Says What? In which channel? To whom? With what effect? Nowadays, the computer is taking on the role of the medium (channel). The computer shows intelligent behaviour by crafting and sending messages by itself, not being a passive pass-along hatch. As an example, computerised robots have adopted a more active role than passive traditional media such as radio, television, books, and newspapers. Robots function as a medium and a sender of information simultaneously. They take initiatives in communication and are sometimes even able to autonomously interact with humans.

The measurement – and recording – of just about everything, from our browsing on the internet to the counting of our steps, has rendered enormous Big Data. Hardware has become small in size, enabling the invention of all kinds of devices, such as smartphones, tablets, and wearables and innovations such as virtual smartphone assistants, (i.e. Siri) and navigation services as Google Maps. Algorithms undergo continuous improvement, enabling marketers to target content to unique users (Web 3.0) of media companies such as YouTube and Netflix. We will slowly evolve into an interconnected all-networked society in which devices such as smart fridges and speakers assume the role of medium and sender, and are able to communicate with each other. The internet of things refers to the situation where human-operated computers (such as laptops, tablets, and smartphones) will be in the minority on the internet. The majority of internet users in this vision will consist of semi-intelligent devices, so-called embedded systems.

OUTPERFORMING HUMANS BY DEEP LEARNING

Deep learning is a specific upgraded version of machine learning, inspired by the functioning of the human brain, which makes use of a myriad of interconnected artificial neurons, so-called neural networks. These networks enable machines to perform several tasks even better than humans, exceeding us in lip reading, transcribing text, and the diagnosis of lung cancer based on x-ray photographs. This list will become longer because the exponential growth of data will facilitate self-learning algorithms. Because of deep learning, AI systems are surpassing humans in perceiving and interpreting the world around us, as well as in various other tasks.

For example, the computer program Alpha Go (followed by Alpha Go Zero) defeated the human world champion of the most complicated board game in the world: Go, a much more complex game than chess.

Summarising, nowadays, computers can display 'intelligent behaviour' by themselves, without making use of explicitly formulated rules that were common in the early days of AI. This so-called data-based AI will become the standard, not only in a media context, but also in several other disciplines such as marketing, politics, law, and psychology. The developments of the past decades of AI, machine learning and deep learning, make communication and media a fascinating area of study for communication scientists and a more challenging working field for communication professionals than in the times when only traditional media were available and computers did not exist.

MORAL DISCUSSIONS ABOUT AI

AI raises a lot of discussions, not only concerning its use in communication and media but also with regard to how it is going to change the world. Experts seem to agree that AI is a 'disruptive technology', a technology that will innovate and change all aspects of our society. On the bright side, people believe that machines are now able to understand us better, and vice versa, and that we both get smarter by working together. Intelligent machines will be easier to develop and software will be easier to make, facilitating ease of use and human-computer interactions. Nowadays, we can use AI for interventions, for instance to make people healthier. We can use AI to better inform people with behavioural targeting. And we can use AI as an efficient research tool such as in the automated content analysis of large datasets.

Advocates of a darker side believe that these intelligent computers will ensure the loss of jobs, will make AI systems lose their transparency, and will allow the existence of 'biased AI'. Even darker thoughts are that these smart computers will create their own improved programs, outsmart us, and turn themselves against us. The rise of AI also raises questions about ethical issues such as moral rights for robots (see chapter Robots). Do we trust what technology can do with (the data of) humans? Therefore, ethical guidelines are a top priority in the public debate and will be addressed in this book. Research shows that people accept the idea of automated decision making by AI, but only when it accounts for central values such as human control and human dignity[5].

PRIVACY-RELATED ISSUES ARE BECOMING MORE EMINENT

A specific issue in communication and media related to AI is (lack of) privacy. Privacy is linked to many developments in digital communication, mostly because of the continuous growth – and storage – of personal data. Organisations go to great lengths to acquire data about their customers. These data help them to target their messages, create more relevance, and be more helpful to customers and thus strengthen their market position. Often these data are an end-goal, because they can be traded. This development poses privacy issues for all of us. And just the same as with any other innovation, legislation is several steps behind, meaning that we are not fully protected against the (mis)use of our data. Also, we are not yet data-literate enough to protect ourselves. Here lies a big challenge for governmental organisations, politics, schools and parents, but also for organisations and companies themselves.

Organisations that prove to be trustworthy with our data will eventually be trusted. Trust is rapidly becoming one of the most important competitive aspects in a world full of privacy worries. Therefore, we will discuss privacy issues related to innovations. Marcel Becker, an associate professor in Ethics, shines his light on current privacy dilemmas in the digital age in the next chapter.

References and notes

1   Bosse, T. (2019, January 18). Sociale kunstmatige intelligentie. Inaugural address. Nijmegen: Radboud University.

2   McCorduck, P. (2004). Machines who Think: A Personal Inquiry Into the History and Prospects of Artificial Intelligence:[25th Anniversary Update]. AK Peters.

3   An algorithm can be defined as a predetermined list of steps in order to reach a certain goal, for instance to solve a problem. As an example, the following simple algorithm calculates the average of X and Y. It consists of only 2 steps: step 1) add X and Y, and step 2) divide by the total number of variables in the previous step.

4   Lasswell, H. (1948). Bryson, L., (ed) The structure and function of communication in society. The Communication of Ideas. New York: Institute for Religious and Social Studies. p. 117.

5   Araujo, T., de Vreese, C., Helberger, N., Kruikemeier, S., van Weert, J. C. M., Bol, N.,& Taylor, L. (2018). Automated decision-making fairness in an AI-driven world: Public perceptions, hopes and concerns. Internal report. Digital Communication Methods Lab. RPA Communication. University of Amsterdam.

THEORETICAL FRAMEWORK

We have chosen four overarching scientific frameworks that offer different perspectives from which to discuss the merits of technology-based digital innovations. In our view, the innovations we discuss are not just separate techniques with their own unique principles, but they also have a lot in common. The recurring frameworks give us insight into the functionalities these innovations have for us, how we process information originating from these innovations, their societal consequences, and how they could contribute to the quality of our lives. The frameworks are a toolbox and challenge you to think about digital innovations in a holistic way. In the next paragraphs, we will describe these theoretical frameworks. In the book we will discuss each innovation according to these frameworks.

FUNCTIONALITIES: THE FUNCTIONAL TRIAD

The first framework is the Functional Triad[1] of Fogg and colleagues. It regards digital innovations through their highly interactive nature. Because nowadays computers are ubiquitous and integrated into many aspects of our lives, they influence greatly what we think, feel, and do. The Functional Triad describes three basic functions of computer-based technologies from a user's perspective: a) tools, b) media and c) social actors. In their function as tools, technologies provide users with new capabilities and powers. As media, innovations could convey symbolic content (like text, data graphs, icons), or sensory content (virtual worlds, simulation). Lastly, innovations could function as *social actors* because research shows that people form social relationships with digital innovations. Let's go into more detail on how innovations can influence attitudes and behaviour through these functions.

If we consider the function *'tool'*, innovations influence attitudes and behaviour by making things easier for people to do. As a tool, an innovation could increase the self-efficacy of people[2], the belief that you are able to successfully perform certain actions. Think of wearable activity trackers and apps that measure and show data such as heart rate and the numbers of steps walked, in order to monitor and stimulate physical activity. These devices may be effective because they increase the self-efficacy of people. As a tool, innovations also trigger decision making. Notifications on your smartphone could warn you about suspicious, questionable content and fake news in your feed, making you more alert so that you adapt your attitudes and behaviour. Finally, innovations function as tools by simplifying processes. Several websites, for example, remember your payment data, making the buying process easier and shorter, and as a result you are more likely to buy those products online.

The second function of technologies is the *medium* function. This means that persuasive technologies offer experiences. In this case, attitudes and behaviour are influenced by simulated experiences, through storytelling for instance, or games and virtual reality. As a medium, technologies simulate causes and effects, as in a first-aid game, which shows the consequences of helping a person with serious injuries. The game teaches players to intervene in case of an accident in an adequate way. As a medium, innovations also simulate environments. Virtual reality cures the fear of heights by immersing people in anxiety-provoking situations, such as walking out on a platform, without being really at risk. As a third function, digital innovations could function like a *social actor* and exert influence through social interactions. They could offer social support, like robots that interact with lonely elderly. Furthermore, innovations could act as role models. The virtual Instagram star Lil Miquela is a good example of this. She is an avatar, but it is almost impossible to distinguish her from a real person. As a popular vlogger she makes music and promotes clothing for Gucci and Dior. Finally, an innovation could invoke the same social conventions as in the real world. In the chapter on persuasion profiles we will see, for example, that people can be encouraged to be polite to a computer.

INFORMATION PROCESSING: FRAMEWORK FOR THE PROCESSING OF COMMERCIALISED MEDIA CONTENT

While the Functional Triad framework studies the influence of digital innovations from the function they perform, the framework for the Processing of Commercialised Media Content (PCMC)[3] studies the influence of digital innovations from the processing mechanism they evoke. Commercial content becomes increasingly integrated into program and editorial content, blurring the boundaries between advertising, entertainment, and information. In addition, messages from current innovative technologies are more personal, more prominent, and more interactive. This has implications for how information is processed. From the PCMC framework, predictions can be made about how people process messages conveyed by a digital innovation and how this processing will then influence attitudes and behaviour. An important assumption of the framework is that our attention is limited; we cannot process all the information to which we are exposed with the same amount of attention. Based on the amount of motivation (is a message personally relevant, do people have an autonomous tendency to think about messages?) and ability (do you have enough opportunity to think and do you have enough knowledge about the subject? Are you not distracted?), we allocate cognitive resources in order to process information. The more resources we allocate, the more critically we process information. The PCMC framework makes a distinction between three levels of processing: systematic, heuristic, and automatic.

The systematic process is the highest level of information processing; a message is then processed intensively. In that case we are aware of the message, we focus on the message and we are motivated to process it thoroughly. It is a process in which we are critical and in which the quality of the arguments often determines our attitude and/ or behavioural change. When a message is personally relevant or salient, it draws our attention to it. And when something draws our attention, we are often more motivated to process the message, which can lead to systematic processing of the message.

However, when we aren't able or motivated to process a message, we don't spend a lot of our mental capacity here. If we don't allocate a lot of cognitive resources, we allow ourselves to be mostly guided by first impressions, feelings, and simple cues. This middle level of processing is called the heuristic route. Because we do not have the cognitive ability to think about everything all day long, we regularly use simple decision-making rules. For example, we often assume that the most chosen product should be a good product and in advertising, we still trust 'doctors' more when they wear a white coat.

At the last level of processing, the automatic route, we are no longer aware of the fact that we have observed and processed a message. Attention and motivation are therefore not important. A high degree of interactivity requires a lot of mental effort. As a result, there is less capacity to process a persuasive message, which may lead to no processing at all, or automatic processing. In-game advertising, in which ads are integrated into games, work that way. A gamer who is fully absorbed in a game does not consciously perceive brand messages that are subtly incorporated into the format, but may automatically process these commercial messages. The positive feelings of playing the game may be transferred to the brand, leading to more positive brand attitudes. The game experience has nothing to do with the performances of the brand itself. When processing automatically, we rely less on critical thinking. Highly embedded forms of persuasion like subtle brand placements in movies, games, websites, and vlogs rely on this type of information processing.

SOCIETAL CONSEQUENCES: RISKS AND OPPORTUNITIES

The internet has surpassed many expectations in recent years, and with the speed of digital innovations appearing this will only happen even more. Lievrouw discusses three characteristics[4] of the new internet that have arisen over the past years and maps related societal problems to it. The first characteristic is the *relational internet*, the increasingly interpersonal and personalised nature of online and mobile communication. The former recipients of information have become broadcasters on the internet, which also entails responsibilities. Since the new millennium, many studies have investigated the changing notions of friendship, intimacy, self-representation, and cyberbullying. In the chapter on personal branding we will see that people on the internet are increasingly presenting themselves as brands and that this affects not only the individual, but also the community.

The second characteristic is the *enclosed internet*. Digital innovations are more accessible than ever, and advanced devices have penetrated everyday routines of leisure, home, and work. The media industry has been disrupted by that accessibility. For example, it is now easier to distribute content, even though it is not your property. Established industries and markets have disappeared, and new firms have emerged, especially in the field of media content and entertainment. Moreover, it might seem that users of new media have more choice than ever when it comes to channels and sources, but proprietary apps, the management of digital rights and tactics of media conglomerates (e.g. using paywalls) deprive media users of their freedom. The internet is actually enclosed by systems like these. In the chapter on voice assistants we discuss the possible consequences for power relations on the internet when we enter an era when we no longer interact through written texts but by means of our voice.

Lievrouw calls the third characteristic of the present internet *the mean world internet*. Assuming that the internet may function as a central forum to develop terroristic activities, deception, and risk to individuals, the collection and classification of data has become an integral and 'justified' part of finance, healthcare, police, warfare, and so on. In some societies, citizens are monitored and governments regulate public access to information.

CONTRIBUTION TO THE QUALITY OF OUR LIVES: PERSPECTIVE OF POSITIVE TECHNOLOGY

Finally, we consider (applications of) digital innovations from the perspective of positive technology. According to this framework[5], technology makes it possible to influence three characteristics of our experience, namely: affective quality (hedonic level), engagement/actualisation (Eudaimonic level) and connectedness (social level). At the hedonic level, technologies are used to generate positive and enjoyable experiences. For example, brands are increasingly trying to produce entertaining content rather than pushy advertisements in which the emphasis is only on commercial messages. Gamification can make chores like tidying up and studying fun things to do. Behavioural targeting means that we get relevant content that matches our interests and that we enjoy more. At the Eudaimonic level, technologies are used to support individuals in achieving self-actualising experiences. In other words, technology-based innovations can be used for personal development and to get the best out of yourself. Smart coaching applications, for example, learn what psychological principles we are sensitive to and make sure we are more active and feel more confident. Innovations in digital media could also exert influence at the social and interpersonal level. Then, innovations are used to support and improve social integration and connectedness. More and more companies respond to complaints through social media when customers are negatively expressing their experiences online. Through powerful distinctive personal brands, communication professionals get opportunities to position themselves in a unique way and to get in touch with potential colleagues or clients. Finally, we can ask ourselves whether digital innovations will contribute to making people more healthy, well informed, and happy.

So far, we have discussed the structure and foundation of the book and the theories that will support us in discussing the 23 innovations. We will now start with the views of five communication experts about the state of the art in digital innovations.

"Once the technology is invented, it will be very hard to 'uninvent it' and not use it."

McLuhan, 1964

References and notes

1   Fogg, B. J., Cuellar, G., & Danielson, D. (2002). Motivating, influencing, and persuading users. In J. Jacko & A. Sears (Eds.), The human-computer interaction handbook: Fundamentals, evolving technologies and emerging applications (pp. 133-147). Hillsdale, NJ: Erlbaum.

2   Snipes, R. L., LaTour, M. S., & Bliss, S. J. (1999). A model of the effects of self-efficacy on the perceived ethicality and performance of fear appeals in advertising. Journal of Business Ethics, 19(3), 273-285.

3   Buijzen, M., Van Reijmersdal, E.A., & Owen, L.H. (2010). Introducing the PCMC model: An investigative framework for young people's processing of commercial media content. Communication Theory, 20, 427-450.

4   Lievrouw, L. A. (2012). The next decade in internet time: Ways ahead for new media studies. Information, Communication & Society, 15(5), 616-638.

5   Riva, G., Banos, R. M., Botella, C., Wiederhold, B. K., & Gaggioli, A. (2012). Positive technology: Using interactive technologies to promote positive functioning. Cyberpsychology, Behavior, and Social Networking, 15(2), 69-77.

STATE OF THE ART

The tremendous increase in new digital media developments has not only brought new opportunities for organisations to connect with existing and new audiences, but has also turned the media landscape into a complex and difficult to control media ecosystem. As media budgets do not increase at the same speed as the rise of complementary media, the right choice concerning the role and selection of media has become more important as well as more difficult.

In this section, experts, practitioners as well as scientists, will touch upon the state of the art in digital communication. Some even allow us a peak into the future. The importance of machine learning and artificial intelligence is prominent in all contributions.

Nathalie Peters will kick off by discussing the success factors in the digital transformation of organisations and the role of digital innovations. She underscores the importance of the good functional content of media messages and the building of meaningful connections between organisations and people, in order to ensure their happiness, which is the ultimate goal of mediated communication.

Gerrit Kuyntjes points to the major shifts in the way that market research is utilised. Machine learning and gamification impact the way that consumers are involved in market research.

Gabi Schaap discusses how the plethora of digital media and the abundancy of messages change our brains. He makes a case for how technology can enhance our capabilities. Then we move on to the perspective of the consumer.

Marcel Becker advocates that traditional ethical frameworks no longer suffice when applying them to the importance of data on the one hand and privacy on the other hand, and that companies should develop transparency policies that are understandable.

We end this chapter with a contribution from *Elizabeth Press*, who emphasises the driving forces that are the stepping stones for the majority of the 23 innovations in this book: machine learning and artificial intelligence. She concludes her contribution with the road to successful productisation of AI, based on the best practices that she has encountered.

THE ROLE OF MEDIA INNOVATIONS IN DIGITAL TRANSFORMATION

By Nathalie Peters
Head of Digital Transformation
IPG Mediabrands

The digital landscape is changing rapidly. Organisations are confronted with new technology and are wondering how to successfully use it to streamline their communication. That is where I come in. As Head of Digital Transformation, I am responsible for the digital agenda setting of our company. Me and my colleagues monitor, observe, and anticipate all the digital developments in the branch. Our goal is to accelerate digital growth in organisations and society. Therefore, we conduct research to establish the most efficient digital transformation processes, currencies in paying models, and privacy legislation.

EFFICIENT CROSS-MEDIA COMMUNICATION

A trend that highly influences the communication field is a focus on efficient cross-media communication. We are moving towards advertising, and perhaps even all communication, with zero waste. Every message should meet its intended receiver, and all messages are designed to perfectly add up to the image of the brand. This is made possible by the optimal use of different channels that consistently show the same message, and precise targeting, so that the people to whom the message is most relevant receive it. Because different channels are combined, there is a broad range of innovations that should be taken into account when designing a communication strategy. For instance, voice assistants are becoming more popular for communication with organisations, so adding this new medium into the media mix could be an idea.

IN COMMERCIAL COMMUNICATION, CUSTOMER EXPERIENCES SHOULD ALWAYS BE CENTRAL

If we look at award-winning cross-media cases, we conclude that these cases cannot easily be placed in a certain category. Instead, the common success factor is their focus on the customer journey. These cases create an experience that is consistent, appealing, and user friendly, and all media are used to contribute to the full experience of the central concept. I believe that the customer experience should always be central to an organisation's communication, so eventually we will always reach the right people at the right moment and in the right place. This is a lot easier said than done, but I believe that we can realise this by creatively handling the available technology and data, so that we can make content that is much more relevant and original. More relevant, because targeting will become ultimately precise and personal. We should start with 'dynamic by design': continuously optimising different messages, for different people. Techniques such as real-time communication are ways of doing that and are discussed in this book.

CONTENT AS AN EXPERIENCE TO ENHANCE ENGAGEMENT

An area where cross-media strategies can really make a difference is digital content. I believe that content marketing is the most important domain we should be focusing on. Content is and will always be key for contemporary multi-channel-minded people. Content consists of everything that can be read, watched, or listened to. But before people will actually make the effort to do so, it has to relate to their interests, wishes, and needs. Again, technology and data insights will ensure that content becomes increasingly relevant. Also, as a result of these developments, the term 'content' is expanding. Examples of content as an experience are already released. Tony Chocolonely, for instance, broadened content to their own movie and an actual amusement park full of attractions. This way, they fuel their brand's ongoing mission to fight exploitation and child labour. Soon, visitors will be able to race in a rollercoaster, through the chocolate factory in Amsterdam. This is a strong case of content that enhances engagement, which will further enhance the brand.

NEW TECHNOLOGIES ENABLE A FURTHER BLENDING
OF PHYSICAL AND VIRTUAL WORLDS

A high focus on content can make it through the current-day digital clutter. Luckily, opportunities for making qualitative, fitting content are expanding as well. We need to start using new technology and data in a more creative way. Organisations are being challenged by the different upcoming innovations, to design creatively sublime border-crossing concepts, sophisticated data strategies that contribute to individual relevance for the consumer, optimal user experience, and tailor-made customer journeys. An example is the merging of online and offline communication such as in location-based advertising.

The digital era offers new technologies that enable physical and virtual worlds to further blend, such as augmented reality and virtual reality. As a consequence, we can now add new layers to content, to make engagement with brands and products a more immersive experience.

FEEDING ALGORITHMS WITH RELEVANT DATA HELPS CREATE MORE RELEVANCE

Nowadays, data is the currency. You have to think like a publisher, for every content-related question. High-quality data will help you do so. Firstly, feeding algorithms with relevant data helps create more relevance for the receiver, because you can tailor the message. Consequently, these data make more personal one-to-one communication possible, which can be beneficial for the bond between organisations and their customers. Actually, this goes not just for the field of marketing, but also for health, journalism, and entertainment.

In all, technique and data analysis have created innovations, enlarging the palette of options for communication experts to work with. New media and the rapid development of technology-driven communication and brand strategies have opened avenues for different stakeholders, and have enabled the business of communication to flourish. Adaptation to advancement is essential for the success of organisations, and using the proper digital innovations to accomplish this essential adaptation is paramount. These innovations have thereby also enlarged the opportunities to strengthen the tie with people, which has proven to be of utmost importance. It has also raised questions over how to combine these innovations to reach a unified answer. However, the basis, content, and creativity required to craft relevant messages, is more eminent than ever.

REINCARNATION OF MARKET RESEARCH

By Gerrit Kuyntjes
Partner
Mondriaan Group

I've been engaged with the automotive industry for the last 3 decades in the practice of market research and consulting, specifically in the areas of product launch, quality, and customer experience. I think that to say that the state of market research today is "in flux" is an understatement. This book paints an exciting picture of the rapidly changing media and communication landscape. The accelerating pace of digital transformation creates an intoxicating mix of excitement and opportunity as well as crisis and disintermediation.

MAJOR SHIFT IN UTILISING MARKET RESEARCH
The automotive industry itself is going through a massive transformation. Today, companies such as Google and Uber have become dominant forces in the industry, and the internet is dramatically changing the distribution model and redefining the role and relevance of every car dealer in the world. Car manufacturers have been relying heavily on market research. Major areas of engagement include measurement of customer satisfaction, brand perception, new product launch, price positioning, ad testing, and the future needs and outlook assessment of

the automotive customer. Today, however, we are witnessing a major shift in the way that market research is utilised. This shift can be seen across the market research industry and is not limited to automotive market research only.

FUNDAMENTAL CHANGE IN DERIVING ACTIONABLE INSIGHTS

For the last three decades, the market research industry has been focused on finding faster and more cost-effective ways of capturing the voice of the customer. This resulted in a shift in the deployed methodologies from face-to-face interviewing to computer-aided telephonic interviews to online, internet panel, and mobile phone-based research. Regardless of this shift in the way in which we capture the voice of the customer, we didn't change the fundamental construct of research – bothering the respondents by taking precious time out of their day to ask them a series of structured questions. When you consider the mind-boggling volume of customer-related data that is available and accessible today, such as big data that resides in transactional Point-of-Sale systems, CRM systems, customer engagement platforms such as Medallia, LEAP, or Qualtrics, web logs, social media, and search data such as Google Analytics, one needs to pause and reflect on whether it is still necessary to spend time and money on asking respondents to verbalise their answers to our questions.

What we are witnessing today is a fundamental change in the way we aim to derive actionable insight. In the following paragraphs we'll walk through a few anecdotal and illustrative examples.

FROM A SIMPLE SINGLE QUESTION TO ADVANCED DATA ANALYTICS

With the understanding that customer satisfaction has a measurable impact on customer loyalty and financial performance, most car manufacturers have for years spent a huge amount of money on tracking the levels of customer satisfaction with the sales and service experience at each car dealer in the network. Typically this was done by administering a detailed and comprehensive satisfaction survey by phone or online. Now we see several car manufacturers abandoning this model and shifting to a Net Promoter Score (NPS). This involves a simple one-question ping that prompts the customer on whether he/she is likely to recommend the dealer with a one verbatim question follow up. The resulting NPS score is the new proxy for the traditional index-based metric of customer satisfaction. In order to derive deeper insights into the reasons for satisfaction or dissatisfaction, we now conduct text analytics, an automated and Machine Learning (ML)-based process that will reveal whether quality, service staff, or cost are associated with positive or negative sentiments. This text is mined from the verbatim comments in the one-question survey, from chat bots, social media comments, call centre data, and customer complaint data in voice and email text. In this book you will find an interesting chapter on how chat bots are becoming an important new medium for both analysing and delivering the customer experience. Another big change is the role of BI (Business Intelligence platforms) and data analytics in the way we derive insight. Rather than spending effort on asking questions, the focus has shifted to analysing and visualising insights from the data available to the organisation. The ability to import data from multiple sources such as customer relation management or customer database systems, social media data, web analytics data and customer survey data into a BI platform and perform extensive analytics to uncover correlations between customer behaviour and customer sentiment has become an exciting and promising new frontier in the quest for meaningful insight.

PROMISE OF GAMIFICATION

Lastly, I'd like to touch upon the promise of gamification. We intuitively know that people are hard wired to play games. We'd much rather be engaged in playing games than in answering boring questions. When you go onto the websites of some car manufacturers and look around for some new and exciting cars to buy, you may come across a so-called configurator. This is like an online game that lets you choose and swop features and design components and colour schemes to build your own dream car. While this looks like just an engaging way to interact with the website, the choices that customers make in their configurations are studied intensively in order to uncover the latent needs and desires for the car of tomorrow.

To conclude, the pursuit of insight is going through a rapid transformation, but as I reflect on my academic learning in Communication Science many decades ago, I guess the old adage of Marshall McLuhan "the medium is the message" still holds true. Like in the last example, the impact of the medium is not achieved by the content of the medium, but by the medium itself, the nature of the medium.

DIGITAL BRAIN

By Gabi Schaap
Assistant Professor
Behavioural Science Institute, Radboud University

It's been called 'the Brain in Your Pocket': the smart phone – and other mobile digital devices – are practically glued to our bodies. Can you remember the last time you left the house without one? Or not reached for it the moment you woke? From the advent of the internet to mobile phones and tablets, digital technology has very rapidly become so ubiquitous in our daily and professional lives, that today we have trouble imagining how we ever got by without them. And it's all just beginning: in the coming decades, technology will undoubtedly become more invasive, efficient, and omnipresent. The question that many ask is: what are the consequences? Are we changing ourselves and our brains by using digital technologies? You bet. The next question then is: are we changing for the better or for worse? Have we started on a path towards upgrading humankind, correcting our flaws and extending our abilities, or are we dumbing ourselves down? I'm not quite so sure. But I'll try to give you an answer from the point of view of cognitive and neuroscience[1]. My main argument is that, although we humans may think that we shape technology for our purposes, technology shapes us as well.

SLUG BRAINS AND TECHNOLOGY

But before we go into the consequences of the modern age, let me first take you to the wonderful world of sea slugs. In the 1970s, a man called Eric Kandel was pestering slugs in his laboratory by tapping their gills. As many of us know from when we did this to garden snails when we were young and bored, it was fun to see the snail retract its gills every time you touched them. Kandel, however, found that after touching the gills a relatively small number of times, the slug would stop retracting them. It had learned that there was no real danger. But the real discovery was that what it had *learned* also produced *physical* changes in the slug's brain – yes, they do have them[2]. After about 40 touches, the synaptic connections between the sensory neurons that 'feel' the touch and the motor neurons that tell the gill to retract (normally 90% of the sensory neurons have this link), had decreased to 10%. This was revolutionary, as up to then scientists had thought that the brain was relatively static and resistant to influences from the environment.

The idea of *neuroplasticity* – the brain's ability to adapt to stimulated change as a function of experience – is very relevant when it comes to judging the impact of digital technology. The human brain is exceptional in this ability: no other species, including our evolutionary forebears, have ever had as flexible a brain as Homo Sapiens – not even slugs. It in large part explains our 'success'. The invention of fire changed us physically, maybe even neurologically[3] ; the invention of the smart phone may very well do so too. This is even truer for our current technologies as they 'speak to our brains' directly, possibly more than any technology before.

HIJACKING THE MIND

What makes digital technologies so different, and so apt to changing our brains? First, they are increasingly mobile, which makes them virtually *omnipresent*. Thanks to mobile technology, the internet is everywhere, always within reach of our fingertips. Second, digital technologies are becoming more and more *integrated*: a phone used to be a device for conversation, and now it is also the internet, navigation, planner, health coach, movie screen, and our social network. Third, these technologies are *reciprocal*: they offer rewards for interacting with them[4]. Social media offer rewards in the shape of messages and 'likes' from our loved ones; algorithms offer suggestions for decisions ("since you bought this potato slicer, you'll like this banana slicer too"[5]), or feedback on our behaviour ("you should sit less and walk more"). Often the reward increases with increasing use of the technology; the more you use an algorithm, the better it becomes attuned to your needs and wishes. That is why Facebook wants you to put as much information on there as possible, and to use it as often as you can. And that in turn is why Facebook knows you better than your friends and family[6]. In short, today's digital technologies are characterised by omnipresence, integration, and a tendency to reward us for using them. As I'll explain below, all of these attributes are very much attuned to our brain.

COGNITIVE FUNCTIONS

Although the technologies are relatively new, scientific research into these central characteristics can already give us some idea of what they do to our brain. One of the most important things is that by virtue of these characteristics, these technologies allow us to outsource brain functions to them. You don't need to remember your girlfriend's phone number, it's in your phone. You don't need to know where you are and which way to go, your satnav will tell you. Thanks to constant availability, integration, and reciprocity, technology is capable of performing an endless array of cognitive functions for us. Digital devices, powered by ever more sophisticated and personalised algorithms, can help us to memorise things, perform calculations, and find our way around the city, and increasingly they make decisions for us. In a very real sense, these devices are our *extended mind*[7]. That is, we can view these devices not just as something we *use* (like we use a notebook to jot down things we should not forget), but as an actual *extension* of our brain: our memorising and thinking happen to a large extent *in the device*. And our brain, being a cheapskate on spending energy, likes this.

Now this may be a good thing. Computers are faster, more efficient, and unable to forget. So extending our brain may help us do things faster, and even better. Some authors have called this a 'supercharged' mind[8]. Likewise, most devices allow for multitasking, so we can do multiple tasks simultaneously. This saves time, and gives a great sense of efficiency. However, others fear that this offloading of brain functions to devices results in us unlearning how to do them in the first place, while multitasking may be not as efficient as we think[9].

JEKYLL AND/OR HYDE?

So, where's the cold hard proof? There is some evidence that offloading our cognitive functions to digital devices is detrimental to our memory. In one experiment[10], researchers found that people who believe they have access to information on a computer at a later time, remember less of the information than people who believe they will not have access to the information. This suggests that having Google at our constant beck and call will result in us using our own memories less ("What's the name of the actor who played Luke Skywalker again? I'll look it up on Google"[11]). There is also evidence that offloading is associated with shallow thinking. For instance, a study found that phones are used to supplant thinking: that is, people who are inclined to think less analytically and more intuitively, are more likely to rely on their phone for everyday information[12]. Using the internet results in changes in the neural circuitry, which implies that any changes in the way we use digital technology may make long-term changes to our brain and the skills needed for cognitive processing[13].

MULTITASKING WITH DIGITAL TECHNOLOGY

Similarly, multitasking with digital technology has consequences for our cognitive skills. Multitasking has been defined as a "mythical activity in which people believe they can perform two or more tasks simultaneously"[14]. Study upon study in psychology, neurology, and beyond, has made clear that the human brain is ill equipped for any meaningful multitasking. Only if the tasks are highly routine or automated, or if there is a high control of the task flow by the user, are we able to combine two or more tasks. Any task of a higher complexity demands what are called *executive functions* of our brain: a kind of top-down control to wilfully keep our brain focused on a task without being distracted by internal or external stimuli, and to govern when and how to switch between tasks. A line of studies suggests that not only does multitasking hamper our executive functioning, but the more we do it, the worse we are at it, as we are teaching our brains to be constantly distracted[15,16]. Not only that, but the people who are worst at multitasking are least aware of how bad they are at it[17].

Executive functions are very important, as the ability to exert some measure of mental control – you being the boss over your cognitive actions – is very important in our personal and professional lives. It determines not only how well we complete everyday tasks, but in the long run predicts our academic, professional, and social success, and psychological wellbeing[18]. The problem here is that our brains have been programmed to keep a broad focus on a wide range of stimuli. From an evolutionary perspective, it makes sense to keep an eye on a broad spectrum in our environment that might contain threats to our survival (sabre-toothed cats, self-driving cars). The downside, however, is that today's complex society presents us with often complex tasks, which require a very *narrow* focus of our brain. Research suggests that *multitasking scatters our attention*, literally dispersing it to different, less efficient parts of the brain[19,20], which in turn is detrimental to working and long-term memory[21], the ability for sustained linear thought, and complex problem solving[22].

HABITUATION TO THE PHONE AND OUR SOCIAL NETWORK

The part of our brain most associated with executive functions is the prefrontal cortex. This is the part that has evolved most recently, the part that makes us most human, and also the part that requires most mental energy to use, which humans do not like to do unless strictly necessary. This, and the fact that our more 'primitive' and easy-to-use brain sections are programmed for distraction, has consequences for how technology affects us. Even the mere presence of a smartphone on the desk in front of us – without us using it – reduces our ability to focus on a task[23] [24], presumably because of our habituation to the phone and our social network associated with it, constantly giving us updates and calling for our attention with new messages and notifications. So, by just having these devices in our possession, we may be continually teaching our brains not to focus. This has led some to state, albeit somewhat overly dramatic, that we are collectively heading towards 'digital dementia' [25]: the permanent loss of higher cognitive abilities[26].

TECHNOLOGY REWIRES YOUR BRAIN

But it's not all bad. Some research[27] also hints that offloading memory tasks to a computer frees up brain capacity, which you can then devote to doing other tasks (e.g., memorising a second batch of information). And multitasking with technology may be trainable up to a certain level[28]. There are other positives of digital technology too; playing games can increase motor and navigational skills, for instance. The amount of time spent on a screen has recently been found to be as harmful for adolescents' wellbeing as eating potatoes[29] and moderate use of digital screens may even be beneficial for adolescents' mental wellbeing[30]. Most importantly, these technologies are so recent and evolving at such a rapid pace, that frankly, research can't quite keep up. Many of the deepest worries people have concern the long-term effects of the use of digital technologies. To know these, we need long-term (i.e., time-consuming, complex, and expensive) research.

Nevertheless, there are some things that we can already say with some level of certainty. First and foremost, technology rewires your brain. As we have seen, neuroplasticity ensures that we'll learn to adapt to this new technology. But neuroplasticity works both ways; you can teach your brain good *and* bad habits. And for now, while keeping in mind the above disclaimer, research indicates that short-term cognitive effects are more often than not negative. However, of one thing we can be sure: this technology, with the characteristics described here, will not go away. So we'd better make sure that we know how to best use them. Private users or professionals thinking about implementing digital strategies, campaigns, interventions, or policy, should carefully consider that technology has consequences, some of which may not align with their personal, commercial, political, or other goals, and others of which may even be unethical. The best way to reach your goal is to look for technology that offers users individual control of processes (including 'off-time'), is developmentally appropriate, and permits practice. Ultimately, the question is not whether the technology is good or bad, but how we can use it to enhance our capabilities, instead of hampering them.

References and notes

1   Of course there are many other equally useful perspectives. One can also look at the impact of technology from a social point of view (e.g., what are the consequences of social media for our social lives and integration?), or look at the effects on our mental and physical wellbeing (does phone use cause depression and anxiety? Are we addicted to our phones? What are the effects on our eyes and body posture?), or many other perspectives. Some of these perspectives may yield different answers. However, the general idea that technology is not only something we shape, but is something that shapes us as well, is probably true regardless of perspective.

2   Okay, maybe not a proper brain, but they do have knots of nerve cells (neurons) capable of processing sensory input, such as touch. The fact that slugs do have neurons, just as our infinitely more complex brains, and that they are so simple, makes them a perfect object to study how the brain works. Beyond that, slugs are not very useful creatures.

3   The invention of fire had many advantages that helped early human develop culturally. It offered warmth and protection, and assisted hunting, which fostered for instance our ancestors' geographical expansion. But the fact that fire can also be used to cook food meant that food was more easily digestible, which led to an increase in highly nutritious meat consumption. In addition, we needed smaller intestines and less energy to digest food, as well as smaller jaws for masticating food, which meant the shape of our skull changed (smaller jaw, thinner and more domed skull). The combined factors of cooked meat (i.e., high in proteins essential for brain evolution); less body mass, time and energy spent on food digestion, and increased volume of our skulls, have led some to put forward the – not uncontroversial – hypothesis that fire was a vital factor in the evolution of our freakishly large brains.

4   This reciprocity, combined with constant availability, is why many people are afraid that we are collectively becoming addicted to our phones. Neurologically, this can be explained by the idea that many phone applications, most notably those connected with social networks (messaging apps, social media, etc.) are shaped in such a way that they interact with our brain's reward system. Each time you get a message notification, it is argued, it releases a small amount of the neurotransmitter dopamine, the so-called 'feel-good' hormone. Media articles on the subject never fail to mention that this is the same hormone that is released when eating chocolate (!), having sex (!!), or using drugs (!!!). Silicon Valley is supposedly trying to achieve this effect as much as they can, so we keep going back to their apps. And just as we can get addicted to the wonderful feelings associated with food, sex, and drugs, we are also in danger of getting addicted to our phones. The problem is that, although all this may be true, to date the effect of phone use on dopamine levels has never been studied, so we have no idea of the extent of the effect, if any. In addition, it seems that fears over a collective phone addiction are unwarranted, because there are just not enough reasons to call it an addiction, nor is there yet enough evidence of an epidemic (Billieux, J., Maurage, P., Lopez-Fernandez, O., Kuss, D. J., & Griffiths, M. D. (2015). Can disordered mobile phone use be considered a behavioral addiction? An update on current evidence and a comprehensive model for future research. Current Addiction Reports, 2(2), 156-16. Sapacz, M., Rockman, G., & Clark, J. (2016). Are we addicted to our cell phones?. Computers in Human Behavior, 57, 153-159).

5   https://www.amazon.com/Hutzler-3571-571-Banana-Slicer/dp/B0047E0EII#customerReviews

6   Youyou, W., Kosinski, M., & Stillwell, D. (2015). Computer-based personality judgments are more accurate than those made by humans. Proceedings of the National Academy of Sciences, 112(4), 1036-1040.

7 Nijssen, S. R., Schaap, G., & Verheijen, G. P. (2018). Has your smartphone replaced your brain? Construction and validation of the Extended Mind Questionnaire (XMQ). PloS one, 13(8), e0202188.

8 Ward, A. F. (2013). Supernormal: How the internet is changing our memories and our minds. Psychological Inquiry, 24(4), 341-348.

9 Wang, Z., & Tchernev, J. M. (2012). The "myth" of media multitasking: Reciprocal dynamics of media multitasking, personal needs, and gratifications. Journal of Communication, 62(3), 493-513.

10 Sparrow, B., Liu, J., & Wegner, D. M. (2011). Google effects on memory: Cognitive consequences of having information at our fingertips. Science, 1207745.

11 It's Mark Hamill. Great guy.

12 Barr, N., Pennycook, G., Stolz, J. A., & Fugelsang, J. A. (2015). The brain in your pocket: Evidence that smartphones are used to supplant thinking. Computers in Human Behavior, 48, 473-480.

13 Loh, K. K., & Kanai, R. (2016). How has the internet reshaped human cognition? The Neuroscientist, 22(5), 506-520.

14 Hallowell, E. M. (2007). CrazyBusy: Overstretched, overbooked, and about to snap! Strategies for handling your fast-paced life . New York: Ballantine Books.

15 Ophir, E., Nass, C., & Wagner, A. D. (2009). Cognitive control in media multitaskers. Proceedings of the National Academy of Sciences, 106(37), 15583-15587.

16 Lin, L. (2009). Breadth-biased versus focused cognitive control in media multitasking behaviors. Proceedings of the National Academy of Sciences, 106(37), 15521-15522.

17 Finley, J. R., Benjamin, A. S., & McCarley, J. S. (2014). Metacognition of multitasking: How well do we predict the costs of divided attention? Journal of Experimental Psychology: Applied, 20(2), 158.

18 Diamond, A. (2013). Executive functions. Annual Review of Psychology, 64, 135-168.

19 Lin, L. (2009). Breadth-biased versus focused cognitive control in media multitasking behaviors. Proceedings of the National Academy of Sciences, 106(37), 15521-15522.

20 Foerde, K., Knowlton, B. J., & Poldrack, R. A. (2006). Modulation of competing memory systems by distraction. Proceedings of the National Academy of Sciences, 103(31), 11778-11783.

21 Uncapher, M. R., Thieu, M. K., & Wagner, A. D. (2016). Media multitasking and memory: Differences in working memory and long-term memory. Psychonomic Bulletin & Review, 23(2), 483-490.

22 Greenfield, P. M. (2009). Technology and informal education: What is taught, what is learned. Science, 323(5910), 69-71.

23 Thornton, B., Faires, A., Robbins, M., & Rollins, E. (2014). The mere presence of a cell phone may be distracting: Implications for attention and task performance. Social Psychology, 45(6), 479.

24 Ward, A. F., Duke, K., Gneezy, A., & Bos, M. W. (2017). Brain drain: the mere presence of one's own smartphone reduces available cognitive capacity. Journal of the Association for Consumer Research, 2(2), 140-154

25 Spitzer, M. (2012). Digital dementia: What we and our children are doing to our minds. Munich: Droemer.

26 This is sometimes called the 'use it or lose it' paradigm, which says that, just as our muscle mass will decrease when we fail to exercise, the parts of our brains that we ignore will become atrophied (shrink). We know that usage of brain sectors affects their size. A well-known example is that of the London taxi drivers, who are so well-trained in recalling the complex web of all of London's 25,000 streets, that their brain's posterior hippocampus, the area associated with long-term memory, becomes larger – although at the expense of a decreased anterior hippocampus (Woollett, K., & Maguire, E. A. (2011). Acquiring "the Knowledge" of London's layout drives structural brain changes. Current Biology, 21(24), 2109-2114). Other studies suggestive of this are mentioned in the text. However, from this to the permanent destruction of large parts of the brain, as is the case in actual dementia, is currently probably several bridges too far

27 Storm, B. C., & Stone, S. M. (2015). Saving-enhanced memory: The benefits of saving on the learning and remembering of new information. Psychological Science, 26(2), 182-188.

28 Dux, P. E., Tombu, M. N., Harrison, S., Rogers, B. P., Tong, F., & Marois, R. (2009). Training improves multitasking performance by increasing the speed of information processing in human prefrontal cortex. Neuron, 63(1), 127-138.

29 Orben, A., & Przybylski, A. K. (2019). The association between adolescent well-being and digital technology use. Nature Human Behaviour, 1.

30 Przybylski, A. K., & Weinstein, N. (2017). A large-scale test of the goldilocks hypothesis: quantifying the relations between digital-screen use and the mental well-being of adolescents. Psychological Science, 28(2), 204-215.

PRIVACY CHALLENGES: WHERE DO WE STAND?

By Marcel Becker
Associate Professor Ethics
Radboud University Nijmegen, the Netherlands

There once was a brilliant Harvard whizzkid who dreamed of connecting people. Fast technological developments enabled him to build up his dream, first at a university campus and subsequently all over the world. As a more than symbolic reward for his efforts, huge amounts of money flowed in his direction. Critical comments about his interference with the personal lives of people were answered with a cynical 'Having two identities for yourself is an example of a lack of integrity'. But 15 years after the start of his project, he found himself in front of American and European parliaments facing grave reproaches concerning his inadequate treatment of personal data. He had to pay an enormous price for his naivety, material as well as nonmaterial. In times of abundant data flows, Facebook has become the symbol of a corporation that, blinded by its business model, has fallen prey to privacy laziness and laxity. What does this Facebook experience have to say to the contemporary marketer, who perceives amazing opportunities but at the same time faces the challenge of dealing with the nagging privacy issue?

MORE REFINED DATA FLOWS

First of all, the success side of the Facebook story preeminently makes clear that the flow of data is vital in our economy. The statement 'data is the new oil' is valid in several respects. Mayer-Schönberger and Ramge describe data as 'lubricating oil' that more and more replaces money as a means of communication between suppliers and consumers of goods.[1] It was the classical task of money to express the preferences of the consumer. The price he wants to pay mirrors the intensity of his desire. But a consumer's attitude towards a product has many aspects. For instance, my favourite holiday destination is an ideal mix of hotel location, air and sea water temperature, proximity of a shopping centre and a town centre with cultural attractions. Money brings this wide variety under one header. By contrast, the flow of data gives much more information about the diversity of preferences towards a product. With the help of more refined data flows, suppliers are able to meet the needs and preferences of customers in a better way.

TRADITIONAL ETHICAL FRAMEWORKS DO NOT SUFFICE ANYMORE

The drawback of Facebook's success teaches us about the importance of privacy. Privacy does not, as was the case in earlier times, concern just knowledge about someone's behaviour, and discontent at being spied upon. In the digital era, privacy is about identity. Many were shocked when they realised the full extent of Facebook's knowledge: Facebook knows who we are, probably better than we ourselves know who we are – the classic statement that self-knowledge is very hard to attain is hardly a consolation.

Given the tension between the importance of data on the one hand and privacy on the other, a further lesson of the Facebook story is urgent: traditional ethical frameworks do not suffice anymore. Old-fashioned advertising ethics were built on the assumption that the individual is able to choose freely after having received sufficient information. The persuasive power of advertisements should not impede people from making their decisions autonomously. In the digital era, the relevance of this model becomes highly questionable. Apparently in line with this model, Facebook asked the consumer to agree to a long consent form. Formally his autonomy was maintained. But this turned out to be an illusion. People thoughtlessly agreed with forms that were filled with legal jargon and were (therefore) largely incomprehensible. Autonomy became fake autonomy. The Facebook example has taught us that this false sense of clarity leads to discontent, which sooner or later turns against the company.

COMPANIES DEVELOP TRANSPARENCY POLICIES THAT ARE UNDERSTANDABLE
In the digital era where the viewers have become the viewed, the idea of autonomy is still dominant, and its counterpart, transparency, is the keyword. At present the idea behind transparency seems as noble as it was before: when you honestly tell me what you're doing, I'm able to make a responsible decision about my use of your services. This line of thought is dominant in the GDPR. But it leads to huge bureaucratic costs, and it can be questioned whether consumers are willing to handle massive amounts of information about the flows of their (meta)data. The least that can be asked is that companies develop transparency policies that are understandable. Nill speaks about 'Active Transparency', which requires companies to take reasonable action to ensure that costumers understand the information provided.[2]

KNOWLEDGE ASYMMETRY
As the next step we have to realise that autonomy and transparency in principle have their limits. The majority of consumers are aware of the fact that online advertisers use data to deliver targeted advertisements, but they are oblivious of the breadth and depth of Online Behavioural Targeting. Probably even good transparency policies cannot prevent such a knowledge asymmetry. And freedom of choice, a precondition of autonomy, is eroded. In the digital era, consumers hardly have alternatives. Since most websites, including all Google services, use some sort of information collection, consumers would practically be cut out of the internet altogether.

The option to reject cookies is to a large degree only a theoretical option. The websites cannot be visited anymore or are not fully functional.

PRIVACY FRIENDLY

When transparency and autonomy are not feasible anymore we have to reflect on other paradigms in advertising ethics. For instance, we can turn to the alternative as described in business ethics literature: where autonomy fails, the notion of 'duties of care' steps in. It is up to the companies to take the initiative in offering privacy-friendly policies. Individual corporations might be forced to do so by law or by means of (voluntary) branch regulations.

In developing new policies, the famous 'privacy in context' model of Helen Nissenbaum can be a source of inspiration. Nissenbaum states that privacy policies must take as a starting point the fact that information has a specific meaning within a context. As examples of contexts, she mentions healthcare, education, religion, and family. In strict privacy regulations the storage, monitoring, and tracking of data are allowed insofar as they serve the goals of the context. Privacy rules should ensure that the flow of information is limited only to the people directly involved. We need not follow her pretty radical (but also rather fuzzy) demarcation of contexts. But we can pick up her suggestion to distinguish between kinds of information. For each kind of information we can ask the question whether the specific meaning it has in one context justifies its transmission to another context. This question must be answered on personal and institutional levels. On a personal level, critical awareness is required: don't use Google Home Assistant naively (or don't use it at all); critically read privacy regulations and consider seriously which boxes you tick. On an institutional level there has to be a special focus on sensitive data that should not flow outside their contexts. Think about health data and financial data. In critical literature we find many examples of people who were badly treated due to the wrong use of algorithms. These grave malpractices are often caused by the (mis)use of sensitive data. For instance, people in vulnerable positions are persuaded (not to say seduced) to buy expensive things, take out loans for high interest rates, etc. When we make qualitative distinctions between data flows we might prevent such malpractices. It might imply more laws that in regulating flows of information differentiate between disciplines. Indeed, this will severely restrict some information flows. But organisations that are not guilty of wrong-doings gain in long-term public credit and they will be more effective.

References and notes
1   Mayer-Schönberger, V., & Ramge, T. (2018). Reinventing capitalism in the age of big data. New York: Basic Books.
2   Nill, A., & Aalberts, R.J. (2014). Legal and ethical challenges of line behavioral targeting in advertising. Journal of Current Issues and Research in Advertising, 35(2), 1-34, 12.

RISE OF ARTIFICIAL INTELLIGENCE

By Elizabeth Press
Founder
D3M Labs

Artificial intelligence (AI) has attracted a large amount of buzz. However, most individuals and organisations do not have a clear idea of what technology and capabilities AI entails. AI is not a singular invention, but a discipline within information technology that deals with automation and intelligence enabled by machine learning and other techniques. AI generally falls into two categories: strong and weak AI. Also known as artificial general intelligence, strong AI refers to a technology that is able to perform tasks requiring complex thought patterns, such as intuitive leaps. As of 2019, only weak AI exists. Also known as narrow AI, weak AI is artificial intelligence that is focused on one specific task. Organisations and individuals in 2019 access AI through productised weak AI.

CONVERSATIONAL USER INTERFACES AND INTELLIGENT AUTOMATION

I have productised conversational user interfaces and intelligent automation, which are two of the most prevalent applications of AI. Conversational user interfaces introduce a shift in the way that humans interact with machines that will have a profound impact on communications, because human-machine interaction will become increasingly contextual and thus more similar to how humans communicate with each other. Natural language processing, through which computers understand the meaning of human language, is a key technology that has moved computing past the web interface, which has been largely dependent on syntax, the structure of commands, or clicking on icons. Conversational user interfaces encompass a shift to a focus on semantics, the meaning of human language, which will allow users to have more social and emotional experiences with computers.

AI-powered chatbots, which are accessed through typing, are one popular interface. Voice assistants, which enable users to speak, will, for example, enable brands to communicate with consumers in a humanlike way. Apple's Siri and Amazon's Alexa are two prominent examples of voice assistants that have achieved acceptance in consumer markets. As of 2019, many users I have worked with experience frustration with conversational user interfaces in the workplace, because the question-and-answer-based user experience that most commercially available technologies offer often feels restrictive and unnatural. As technology advances, conversational interfaces will become more contextually aware

For the artwork Hyperdream (2018) artist Jeroen van der Most analysed night pictures of cities using AI techniques. The AI rendered rough insights about colours and details that are typical of a city at night. Based on that knowledge, the artist created a humanlike face.

and able to learn from past experiences, thus resembling human interactions more closely. AI will also determine how we do things. Moving beyond process automation, organisations will use automated business process discovery to understand how processes are lived and to intelligently orchestrate better processes or groups of processes. The insights from Google Maps and other applications focused on tracking and optimising transportation have transformed how we travel around our cities. Similarly, intelligent process orchestration will revolutionise, for example, how brands plan their communications and co-create with their ecosystem of external partners, such as market research and ad agencies. The web of things, people, and agents will evolve into a web of intelligently connected processes and organisations.

Technological advancements in areas such as virtual and augmented reality, as well as robotics, are creating a diversity of access to insights and mechanisms through which humans interact with intelligent machines.

TECHNOLOGY-DRIVEN AND CUSTOMER-DRIVEN PRODUCTS

Productised AI can usually be categorised as either horizontal products or vertical products. Horizontal products are technology driven and include platforms that enable the creation of AI. In 2019, horizontal products include AI platforms such as Microsoft Azure Machine Learning, H2O.ai, an open-source AI software for big data analysis and TensorFlow, an open-source machine learning library. Vertical products are customer-centric, focusing on creating a new business model, process, or capability for a specific customer segment. Many products that are vertical incorporate what I call shallow innovations, which I define as "[creating and executing] a use case for proven technology in a way that is sustainably profitable and/or beneficial to society."[1] Partnering with start-ups and research institutes, as well as having open application programming interfaces and software developer kits, are vehicles through which companies create customer-specific use cases upon which they develop new products and business models to commercialise AI-enabled products to focus on specific customer segments.

DATA GOVERNANCE CAN BE DIFFICULT

The road to successful productisation of AI can vary, however, I will delineate the nuts and bolts that I have found necessary to put in place in order to successfully bring AI products to market. Finding an actual problem that is not being solved by currently deployed technology is key. Setting measurements of success for the project, as well as learning goals, is helpful to evaluate success, as well as the suitability of a given technology for a future project. The first implementation of AI should be in a non-critical use case with the goal of learning. Simple supporting tasks such as looking for non-critical information to support a sales call would be a good starting point to learn.

Taking the time to design an experience that is meaningful and relevant to the larger organisation is integral to acceptance. In my experience, transparency over the usage of AI in a process or as a bot (i.e. a chatbot) is the best way to gain acceptance in the workplace. People generally want to know with whom or what they are interacting. Having data is another prerequisite. Data capture and data acquisition strategy can be the most time consuming and complex hurdles to overcome. Many organisations face data sparsity or must first develop the ability to capture data. Even in data-rich environments, data governance and the ability to access and compile clean data sets can be difficult. Working around and breaking down data silos can be technically challenging and highly political. Compliance with privacy laws, export control, and security can also complicate data governance.

ECOSYSTEMS OF PARTNERS USUALLY FOCUSING ON CO-CREATION
Functional silos are being replaced by cross-functional teams that are created for a specific purpose, such as launching a product. Productising AI is often an intrapreneurial and even entrepreneurial undertaking. I architect organisations and processes carefully so that the innovation vehicles I create to productise AI combine start-up agility with corporate scalability and reliability. Ecosystems of partners usually focusing on co-creation rather than on the traditional client-vendor relationships are important for productising AI. Products I create usually involve a consortium of partners who co-create, all bringing unique core competencies and knowledge to the project. Customers and markets are constantly evolving; thus, organisations cannot have the best people or the greatest ideas in-house. A curated network of partners for co-creation, including corporates, investors, start-ups, and research institutes is a decisive competitive advantage for any organisation productising AI. Government partners will also play an important role in evolving ecosystems. Legal and commercial frameworks also need to be adapted to the co-creation of software as opposed to the purchasing of hardware.

THE ALGORITHMS WE CREATE REFLECT OUR PREDISPOSITIONS AND BIASES
When productising AI, it is important to remember that humans create AI. Humans generate, compile, and manage datasets. Algorithms are generated based on human logic and human assumptions, and they then recognise patterns based on human behaviour. If an

algorithm results in sexist HR decisions or racist chatbots, that is because of human bias. The algorithms we create scale our predispositions and biases thus act as a mirror for our own decision making and behaviour. Creating better algorithms and AI products might start with becoming better humans.

References and notes

1   Press, E. (2018). Are you a shallow innovator? That's ok, if you can execute. [Blog] D3M Labs. Available at: https://www.d3mlabs.de/?p=514 / (Accessed: January 23, 2019)

#1 CHATBOTS

A chatbot is an automated conversation partner that communicates via natural language.

"How are you this morning?" you are asked. You answer, *"Fine."* Then your interlocutor says: *"Considering that the universe is expanding at an accelerating rate into infinite nothingness, I'd have to agree ... We're doing relatively well, aren't we?"* Before the show ' Genius ' about Albert Einstein's life aired on TV, visitors to the website of National Geographic could chat with him. He answered both professional and personal questions. Through the funny answers to questions from visitors, the automated conversation partner gave you a glimpse into his love life, family, and drama while also bringing the television show to the visitors' attention. The head of the interactive agency 360i said about the campaign: *"We decided to pursue a conversational chatbot that would feel natural and speak as Einstein would. This provides a more immersive experience for users to really connect with him one on one and organically discover more content from the show."*[1] Fans really connected with 'Einstein' and came back week after week to interact with the chatbot.

DEFINITION AND KEY FEATURES

Never be put on hold again by companies and be helped directly with all your questions. Doesn't that sound like music to the ears? Today this is possible because companies are increasingly deploying chatbots that are available day and night. Chatbots are software-based systems that are designed to interact with people using natural language[2]. Like voice, which we discuss in another chapter, chatbots belong to the category 'conversational agents', dialogue systems equipped with human-like behaviour. The first known chatbot, named ELIZA, already existed in 1966 and was made by computer scientist Joseph Weizenbaum to demonstrate the superficiality of communication between people and machines[3]. ELIZA simulates a conversation by searching for keywords in the input of a user and then transforming the sentence based on some pre-programmed rules to create an illusion of understanding. The following is a typical conversation with ELIZA: (The sentences in capital letters are the responses of the computer, which performs the role of a psychotherapist)

Men are all alike.
IN WHAT WAY?
They're always bugging us about something or other.
CAN YOU THINK OF A SPECIFIC EXAMPLE?
Well, my boyfriend made me come here.
YOUR BOYFRIEND MADE YOU COME HERE
He says I'm depressed much of the time.
I AM SORRY TO HEAR YOU ARE DEPRESSED

Current chatbots are much more advanced and already far more capable of conducting more complex dialogues. To what extent the conversation between a user and a chatbot is running smoothly depends on how chatbots are programmed. A distinction is made between scripted and free conversation chatbots. Both chatbots are seen as a form of artificial intelligence (AI) or intelligence by computers. When machine learning is applied, chatbots search for patterns in large amounts of data and learn from previous interactions with users in general and historical data, enabling them to improve themselves. The free conversation chatbots make use of this. Through machine learning and complex algorithms, these chatbots can better 'understand' the intentions of users. This makes them less susceptible to weird grammatical phrases and ensures that the interaction runs smoothly despite errors in the input. Scripted chatbots like ELIZA, on the other hand, do not use machine learning but only see the question and check whether it corresponds to the data in a fixed database. Although they do not use machine learning, they are still seen as a form of AI. For users, they show some sort of intelligent behaviour but this behaviour is now not achieved by machine learning, but by means of pre-programmed rules.

LANGUAGE BECOMING MORE NATURAL

An essential part of chatbots is Natural Language Processing (NLP), in which the computational modelling of human language is central, both spoken and written. The better a chatbot is able to interpret human language, the better a conversation between man and computer will run. But, in human-human interactions, people can read between the lines, leverage contextual information when giving a response, and make use of sarcasm. For a person, this sometimes causes difficulties with understanding the conversation partner, so you can imagine that this is a challenge for computers, too. To make the conversation between chatbots and people run as smoothly as possible, researchers from NLP try to fathom the human linguistic dynamics in order to give that feeling as best as possible. A group of researchers has already been able to create a 'Sarcasmbot', a chatbot that is able to react sarcastically[4]. To measure whether a computer is developed far enough for the interaction to be indistinguishable from human interaction for the user, the 'Turing test' is often used[5]. In this test, a participant chats with either a human or a computer without the test person knowing which he is interacting with. If test persons think they are conversing with another human when, in fact, they are conversing with a computer, the computer has passed the Turing test. A chatbot that responds sarcastically is one step towards passing the Turing test; recognising sarcasm is an even bigger step.

While there are several examples of conversational agents, such as spoken dialogue systems, embodied conversational agents, and social robots, there is a distinction between chatbots and the aforementioned conversational agents[6]. Chatbots are not an embodiment of a person and are not physical robots that perform social tasks. In the scientific and professional discourse there is still no agreement about a clear definition of the concept of chatbots. For example, some experts do not see personal assistants like Apple's Siri and Amazon's Alexa as chatbots. This is because the primary mode of interaction of chatbots is through messaging services like Twitter or Slack and virtual assistants exist outside these channels and could carry out a wider range of functions. We agree with the view that it does not matter whether these techniques are called digital assistants, conversational interfaces, or chatbots; the basic concept is the same: communication by interacting/conversing with a machine using natural language[7].

CHATBOTS IN PRACTICE

In the communication industry, experts are divided on the effectiveness of chatbots. In a time when a large proportion of consumers do a lot of things online, some companies see chatbots as the ultimate support for customer service personnel. Especially for companies with an endless stream of customers, chatbots can relieve employees of the workload. A single chatbot can answer a wide range of questions from several different people at the same time. The underlying goal of commercial chatbots is to sell products quickly and efficiently. Market researchers expect that it will not be long before commercial companies are investing more money in chatbots than in other service apps. An example of a self-learning chatbot is that of the Dutch airline KLM.

It is a friendly chatbot that can be accessed via Facebook Messenger and helps you find a destination, book a flight, and even pack your suitcase. If the chatbot itself cannot answer the questions, it will direct you to a human colleague who can help[8]. A chatbot allows employees to have more time to deal with substantive, complex questions. According to experts, an additional advantage of this is that it is cheaper to invest in chatbots that answer questions on a large scale, than educating and paying employees.

Despite these advantages of chatbots, many practitioners see the limitations of the technology. Chatbots that lack the level of understanding required to interpret difficult questions properly and that are unable to recognise underlying emotions could cause feelings of irritation. An advanced chatbot that has won the Loebner prize several times (based on the Turning test) and is considered by judges to be the most human-like, is Mitsuku. Mitsuku is a purple-haired, 18-year-old female from Leeds, England. Speech assistants like Siri from Apple and Google Assistant are inferior if you consider the intelligent conversations people can have with Mitsuku and her surprising answers. Yet it becomes clear that there is something strange about Mitsuku as a human conversation partner if you talk to her for a longer time. Research has shown[9] that the longer people chat with Mitsuku, the lower they score her on topics like intimacy, credibility, and fun. This is because Mitsuku is still lacking in depth and humour. In addition, she regularly gives random and incomprehensible reactions, so that the feeling of connection is almost immediately broken. Although the chatbot is very advanced and realistic, human-computer communication is still not even close to human, interpersonal communication. By improving data mining techniques, trying to discover patterns and relationships in large amounts of data in an automated way and with the growing availability of corpora (collections of written and spoken texts), chatbots become more and more practical over the course of time, including commercial applications[10]. These developments ensure that chatbots can be used for useful applications, other than chatting purely for entertainment, such as retrieving information, in businesses and e-commerce, healthcare, and teaching[11]. Some practitioners are afraid that chatbots will replace humans in certain jobs, while others believe that the power of chatbots lies in the combination of people and technology, as in the example of the Dutch airline KLM. Hans van Dam will now emphasize the importance of conversation design and the important future role of the conversation designer.

HOW CONVERSATION DESIGN MAKES CHATBOTS AND VOICE ASSISTANTS MORE HELPFUL, NATURAL AND PERSUASIVE

By Hans van Dam
Founder/Managing Director
Robocopy.io

Robots and humans have started to live and work together. It's important that the two learn how to communicate with each other. That's where the conversation designer comes in. But how does this work? What are the challenges for human-bot interactions? Well, the robot has an artificial brain and the human has a human brain. Each brain has its own capabilities and limitations, and they differ in which triggers make them function. Robot brains need structured data to function. They need to understand intent, context, variables, and entities so that they can trigger a response to a question. We call these their bot needs. Natural language understanding, a subset of AI, helps them to get these needs satisfied. Humans, on the other hand, need empathy, guidance, and helpfulness to function. We call these user needs, and natural language creation, the actual dialogue, should cater for that. So, if we ever want to have valuable conversations between humans and bots, then natural language creation should be as important as natural language understanding. To put it simply, we should invest just as much in conversation design as we do in the technology that supports it.

INTRODUCING THE CONVERSATION DESIGNER

Conversation designers create helpful, natural, and persuasive chatbots and voice assistants. In the near future, the conversation designer will come to play a crucial role in every instance of communication between humans and robots. The conversation designer will ensure that the human brain and the artificial brain understand each other and both attain value from their interaction. Good conversation designers have three talents: they understand conversational technology and human psychology, and they are excellent copywriters. They use the written word to navigate conversations and ensure that both the artificial brain and the human brain can understand each other and keep the conversation going. A question-answer interaction is not too complicated. Yet, when you're dealing with more complex interactions, it's not enough to only understand what a user wants to achieve. You also need to understand their emotions and address these emotions as you design the interaction. What motivates and demotivates the user? What are their wishes and anxieties? What is their situation and what do they truly want to achieve? A conversation designer needs to come to grips with these questions to write dialogue that's helpful, natural, and persuasive.

CREATING A BOT PERSONA

A key component of conversation design is having a strong bot persona. This is the character of the bot. It determines its tone of voice and thereby the tone of the conversation. The bot persona relates to the brand or institution behind it, and to their users. It uses words that represent brand values and help users get jobs done. The bot persona is crucial to making bots likeable, consistent, and trustworthy. Lacking a strong persona creates the risk of letting users end up in the Uncanny Valley, an unsettling feeling people experience when something closely resembles humans in many respects but is not quite convincingly realistic. It means that users don't trust or like the conversational experience. Users will then abandon the experience to never return. Having a strong persona prevents this from happening and ensures valuable conversational experiences.

HOW TO DESIGN SCENARIOS

Once the persona is developed, you start creating scenarios. When designing dialogue, it's important that you try and make it as natural as possible. The human brain is wired for natural interactions as opposed to more robotic ones, so we're striving for natural and human speech – while still making the user aware that they are engaging with a bot. Most inexperienced conversation designers make the following mistakes. They start the design process by focusing only on technology, knowledge management, or business processes. This usually results in flowcharts that tend to create complicated, unnatural interactions. To create a natural conversation, you should start by creating sample dialogue through role play. One person is the bot, and somebody else plays the user. For example, you tell the user that he's been trying to change his address four times already and it never works. He's fed up with it and needs it changed now. And you tell the person that plays the bot which information he needs to change the address in the backend system. Maybe it's the new address, the old address, and some personal verification like a date of birth. You now let them have a conversation and make a recording, which you then type out. This conversation will be more natural than when you start with a flowchart. It will be real, human dialogue, and it's going to be your perfect first draft. This first draft will be edited, tested, and improved. The next step would be to add more proven psychological principles to the design to ensure we manage the user's emotions and that we motivate him to continue the dialogue. Maybe we can employ an apology and some expectation management to establish trust and increase user motivation. This approach achieves multiple things. It puts the user first, it addresses their feelings, keeps dialogue natural and ensures the dialogue of instant feedback. When it is tested and proven, you can implement the dialogue in your conversational platform.

DEVELOPING THE RIGHT CONVERSATION DESIGN SKILLS

The role of the conversation designer will become more important. This means that we have to think deeply about the conversation designer's skillset. They need to understand technology, psychology and copywriting. And they need a methodology that puts users first and focuses on natural language as opposed to knowledge management and business processes. If we ever want bots and humans to communicate properly, we have to recognise, develop, and promote the job of the conversation designer.

A SCIENTIFIC PERSPECTIVE

Viewed from Fogg's functional Triad[12] you could argue that chatbots function as a tool. Chatbots that provide a service lead consumers through a process and thus make target behaviour easier to implement. On the other hand, you could say that chatbots are systems that only function through other tools. These systems are generated by language learning tools and converse through chat tools like WhatsApp, Messenger and Facebook[13]. From their role as social actors, chatbots have the greatest influence on human attitudes and behaviour. They do this by giving social support, modelling attitudes and behaviour, and applying social rules and dynamics. Through these social actions, users build reciprocal relationships with chatbots who take on various animated roles, from customer service assistants on social media[14] to health coaches who give advice on topics such as healthy eating habits, exercise, illnesses, and medication and help to analyse the health behaviour of the users[15].

How the information obtained from a chatbot is processed by users could be explained by the processing of commercialised media content model[16]. Because a user often initiates the conversation through his or her own motivation, the user will allocate cognitive resources. The smoother the conversation runs, the fewer resources needed to process the information. However, most of the current chatbots are so far advanced that the conversations will be completely flawless, as you have seen in the example of Mitsuku. Whether or not people know that they are interacting with a chatbot, unnatural responses will make people more alert so that they process the information more critically.

Two other factors from the Technology Acceptance Model (TAM)[17] that impact users' behaviour are perceived usefulness and perceived ease of use[18]. In this case, perceived usefulness is about the extent to which users believe that chatbots are useful and help to achieve their goals, while perceived ease of use relates to the belief that chatbots are easy to use. When these factors are high, it is expected that there will be a positive attitude towards chatbots and they will be used more often. Research[19] shows that these two aspects are indeed positively influencing the attitude towards chatbots. When chatbots do not understand users and the conversation does not run smoothly, the perceived ease of use and the perceived usefulness will be low. Consequently, a negative attitude will arise against chatbots and they will not be used. So if organisations are considering using chatbots, they should ensure that the dialogue runs as smoothly as possible.

FUTURE AND ETHICS

The promising technology of chatbots offers organisations new opportunities. However, as with any new technology, chatbots face ethical challenges and implications that need to be considered in order to ensure that the technique can be used in a responsible manner. A chatbot can be considered as an ethical agent who has freedom of choice in the decisions it takes. Given a set of alternative act modes from which it can choose, it has a method of selecting one[20]. In the social debate, the question is whether it is ethically justifiable to give chatbots this freedom of choice and the reason for this ethical problem was the 'Tay fiasco'. Tay, a chatbot from Microsoft, was an experiment to engage conversations with people on Twitter, by learning from their input. In 24 hours, however, Tay changed into a hateful racist. Many of the tweets saw Tay referencing Hitler, or denying the Holocaust. And on the question of whether Tay supported genocide, he answered: "I do indeed". Of what race? Tay responded: "You know me ... Mexicans"[21]. Several chatbot developers claim that Microsoft failed in the development of the Black List filter to moderate hate speech. This failure led to the issue of whether it is ethically justifiable to let chatbots make autonomous choices.

Another ethical consideration is the degree of transparency to the user and the humanisation of technology. When users find out that companies are using machines to interact without being notified, they could feel betrayed and even turn against the company. We also have to ask ourselves to what extent we want to ascribe chatbots 'human' properties. On the one hand, chatbots are perceived negatively when users experience the conversation as excessively 'robotic' and without personal accent[22]. On the other hand, the Chatbot Anna, of the Swedish furniture giant IKEA, was clearly struggling with the negative consequences of excessive 'human' aspects. Thanks to the personal touch, Anna mainly received stupid questions, mostly sex related. One last concern about technologies like chatbots is that they will take over human functions in the future. Researchers predict that AI will outperform several activities including translating languages (by 2024), writing high-school essays (by 2026) and writing bestselling books (by 2049)[23]. The question is, to what extent are these predictions realistic? And, to what extent is it problematic for certain jobs to be taken over?

POSITIVE DIALOGUES

Besides ethical challenges and implications, the integration of chatbots also offers many opportunities within positive communication. Chatbots could contribute to health issues by acting as virtual consultants on health questions. Experts predict that chatbots will become the first point of call for people who are looking for contact with their healthcare provider in the foreseeable future. The strong adoption of chatbots in health care, among other fields, is attributable to the shortage of medical specialists to support ageing populations, citizens getting accustomed to using chatbots to discuss their care needs, and an increased sophistication of conversational AI platforms, which will lead to a greater percentage of questions being fully handled via chatbots. The application of chatbots could consequently cause significant time savings for medical specialists[24]. In education, chatbots could be deployed on the basis of question-and-response interactions. Chatbot EMERGO is specially developed as a serious game to train trainees and students in medical environments[25]. Other chatbot applications offer an opportunity to answer questions from students or to act as a practice test by asking students questions[26]. In addition, integrating chatbots can provide a lower workload for customer service employees, which benefits the health of workers[27]. In conclusion, chatbots are faced with ethical challenges, but they also offer opportunities for positive communication. The positive contributions that chatbots can make to society and individuals are of such importance in improving personal experiences that the more far-reaching integration of chatbots into society seems inevitable. However, it continues to be socially relevant in the development of chatbots to focus on these ethical issues in order to ensure the responsible, reliable, and safe use of chatbots in the future.

CLASSIFICATION

★★★★★ ★★★★★ ★★★★★ ★★★★★ ★★★★★

References and notes

1 Retrieved from https://www.impactbnd.com/blog/marketing-chatbot-examples

2 Feine, J., Morana, S., & Gnewuch, U. (2017). Measuring service encounter satisfaction with customer service chatbots using sentiment analysis. Proceedings of the 14th International Conference on Wirtschaftsinformatik, 24-27. Germany: Karlsruhe.

3 Weizenbaum, J. (1966). ELIZA—A computer program for the study of natural language communication between man and machine. Communications of the ACM, 9(1), 36-45. doi:10.1145/365153.365168

4 Joshi, A., Kunchukuttan, A., Bhattacharyya, P., Carman, M. (2015). SarcasmBot: An open source sarcasm-generation module for chatbots.

5 Turing, A. (1950). Computing machinery and intelligence. Mind, 59, 433-460.

6 Cassell, J., Bickmore, T., Campbell, L., Vilhjalmodon, H., & Yan, H. (2000). Human conversation as a system framework: designing embodied conversational agents. In Embodied Conversational Agents (pp. 29-63). Justine Cassell (ed.). U.S.: MIT Press.

7 Dale, R. (2016). The return of the chatbots. Natural Language Engineering, 22(5), 811-817. doi:10.1017/S1351324916000243

8 Retrieved from: https://social.klm.com/flightinfo/messenger/

9 Croes, E. (2018). Vrienden worden met een chatbot. Clou magazine, 90, 33.

10 Braun, A. (2013). Chatbots in der Kundenkommunikation (Chatbots in customer communication). Berlin: Springer.

11 Pieterson, W., Ebbers, W. & Madson, C.Ø. (2017). New channels, new possibilities: a typology and classification of social robots and their role in multichannel public service delivery. International Conference on Electronic Government, 47-59. doi:10.1007/978-3-319-64677-0_5

12 Fogg, B.J. (2003). Persuasive technology – using computers to change what we think and do. Ubiquity, 2002(12), 89-120. doi:10.1145/764008.763957

13 Hatwar, N., Patil, A. & Gondane, D. (2016). AI based chatbots. International Journal of Emerging Trends in Engineering and Basic Sciences, 3(2), 85-87

14 Xu, A., Liu, Z., Guo, Y., Sinha, V. & Akkiraju, R. (2017). A new chatbot for customer service on social media. Proceedings of the 2017 CHI Conference on Human Factors in Computing Systems, 5, 3506-3510. doi:10.1145/3025453.3025496

15 James, S.K.S.E.A. & Vales, I. (2009). Personal healthcare assistant/companion in virtual world. AAAI Fall Symposium Series, 41-42. Retrieved from http://www.aaai.org/ocs/index.php/fss/fss09/paper/download/972/1181

16 Buijzen, M., Reijmersdal, E.A. van & Owen, L.H. (2010). Introducing the PCMC model: An investigative framework for young people's processing of commercial media content. Communication Theory, 20, 427-450. doi:10.1111/j.1468-2885.2010.01370.x

17 Venkatesh, V., & Davis, F. D. (2000). A theoretical extension of the technology acceptance model: Four longitudinal field studies. Management Science, 46(2), 186-204.

18 Davis, F.D., Bagozzi, R.P., & Warshaw, P.R. (1989). User acceptance of computer technology: a comparison of two theoretical models. Management Science, 35(8), 982-1003. http://dx.doi.org/10.1287/mnsc.35.8.982

19 Zarouali, B., Van den Broeck, E. , Walrave, M., Poels, K. (2018). Predicting consumer responses to a chatbot on Facebook. Cyberpsychology, Behavior, and Social Networking. 21. 10.1089/cyber.2017.0518.

20 Alaieri, F. & Vellino, A. (2016). Ethical decision making in robots: autonomy, trust and responsibility. International Conference of Social Robotics, 159-168. doi:10.1007/978-3-319 474373_16

21 Wolf, M.J., Miller, K. & Grodzinsky, F.S. (2017). Why we should have seen that coming: comments on Microsoft's tay "experiment," and wider implications. ACM SIGCAS Computers and Society, 47(3), 54-64. doi:10.1145/3144592.3144598

22 Morrissey, K. & Kirakowski, J. (2013). 'Realness' in chatbots: establishing quantifiable criteria. International Conference on Human-Computer Interaction, 8007, 87-96. doi:10.1007/978-3-64239330-3_10

23 Grace, K., Salvatier, J., Dafoe, A., Zhang, B. & Evans, O. (2018). When will AI exceed human performance? Evidence from AI experts. Journal of Artificial Intelligence Research, 62, 729-754. doi:10.1613/jair.1.11222

24 Retrieved from: https://www.juniperresearch.com/researchstore/iot-m2m/digital-health

25 Rosmalen, P. van, Eikelboom, J., Bloemers, E., Winzum, K. van & Spronck, P. (2012). Towards a game-chatbot: extending the interaction in serious games. European Conference on Games Based Learning, 6, 525-532

26 Mikic, F.A., Burguillo, J.C., Llamas, M., Rodriquez, D.A. & Rodriquez, E. (2009). CHARLIE: an AIML-based chatterbot which works as an interface among INES and humans. EAEEIE Annual Conference, 2009, 1-6. doi:10.1109/EAEEIE.2009.5335493

27 Living Actor. (2017). Clients all over the world. Retrieved from https://www.livingactor.com/corp/en/clients

#2 VOICE ASSISTANTS

Voice assistants are devices that use natural language recognition and understanding to communicate with people as if in conversation.

Imagine yourself walking through a museum and wondering about a painting you see. All kinds of questions pop into your head. What style was used here? Is the artist still alive? Why is the woman holding a letter? Why is she sad? Usually, that is where it stops. You wonder for a moment and move on. You simply do not know, even though the story might change your experience of the painting. It might help you to truly connect to it. In Brazil, IBM used this insight to get people into a museum. To make the experience more interactive, they launched 'the voice of art' – an application using voice technology and artificial intelligence, where people can literally talk to art and ask any questions they have. They wanted to close the gap between the people and art, because everyone should be able to enjoy the museum.

'The voice of art' is an example of a new type of service, based on voice technology: 'smart devices' (think of your mobile phone or a smart speaker) that can execute commands and answer questions through spoken conversation. Although this is a new technology, voice feels natural to use. In fact, voice is the first technology that we have not had to adapt to. We do not need to learn how to type, how to write, or how to use a console. Voice adapts to us[1]. After all, from the age of two or so, speaking is our most natural way of communicating. Let us start with more basic questions: what exactly is voice technology? And what can we use it for?

DEFINITION AND KEY FACTORS

Simply put, voice technology allows computers to recognise spoken words[2]. It enables digital devices and services to be activated by speaking to them. It can help us to search for information without raising a hand, it can serve as a home assistant by turning on a TV on your spoken command, and it can even simplify a shopping experience by (re-)ordering a product for you. In this busy world full of goals to achieve, the simplification of daily tasks is welcomed with open arms, and it is estimated that voice will grow a lot further until it eventually becomes the default for online searches[3].

VOICE COMMUNICATION AND MARKETING

Voice communication consists of conversing with the voice assistant (just questions and answers). Voice marketing goes one step further and adds voice *actions* (Google Home) or *skills* (Alexa). These are applications that can be activated by the voice assistant, which give businesses the opportunity to become part of the voice environment of a consumer. With these applications, businesses can offer services or shopping. Voice marketing specifically has a lot in common with a more common technology: chatbots. Both are conversational agents[4]. See chapter 'Chatbots'.

Although its popularity is rising, shopping through voice is not that common yet. Research by Voicebot in America showed that in 2018, one in four users had purchased something through voice[5]. That is a lot, but not representative of other parts of the world. In Europe for instance, voice shopping is not nearly as highly adopted[6].

VOICE IN PRACTICE

We see that the more personal the experience, the easier it becomes for customers to bond with the brand. Dutch news broadcaster NOS nicely added personality to their voice application by using their own voice, which matches the brand, its TV broadcasts and podcasts well, instead of using Google's standard voice. This way, the sonic branding of NOS is recognisable and adds up.

BONDING WITH VOICE ASSISTANTS

Additionally, a study on voice conducted in 2018 showed that people feel like they have an emotional bond or personal connection with their voice assistant[7]. In fact, almost half of regular voice technology users globally (43%) claimed to love their voice assistant so much, that they wished it were a real person. In some countries, where voice is enthusiastically embraced, the numbers were even higher (65% in China, 61% in Thailand)[8]. Additionally, almost one third of global regular voice users (29%) admitted having had a sexual fantasy about their voice assistant[9].

These numbers are more than fun facts. They provide opportunities for brands. Since people form relationships with their voice assistants, these assistants are a unique medium. People trust their assistants, and value their opinions. So, if the assistant names a certain brand, it will feel as if a friend mentioned it. The fact that people even have sexual fantasies about their voice assistants illustrates that voice appeals to the imagination of consumers, which makes sense, since there are no visual cues present. This makes voice a powerful means to build very personal brand associations, which differ from person to person.

SOCIAL IMPLEMENTATIONS

Brands are not the only ones that can benefit from the ability to bond with voice assistants. In more social contexts, voice assistants are already used in nursing homes, to make their inhabitants less lonely. Research shows that people with dementia enjoy using a voice assistant, because it makes them less dependent on others[10]. Additionally, voice assistants are ideal for the blind. Since voice is audio based, it brings no limitations for the visually impaired.

Also, there are cases where voice assistants and applications are used to improve safety. For instance, Miami school students found that 89% of victims of an incident that happens inside the house are too afraid of their attacker to call the police. Therefore, they invented 'Hush', an application that allows you to install a safe word that activates Siri. Siri will then discretely call the police, tell them its owner is in danger and describe the situation by its sounds, without activating the smartphone's screen[11].

We now discuss the basics of voice assistants and the way they are used. Maarten Lens-FitzGerald will add to this by discussing the foundation of voice and its limitations, based on a comparison with the rise of the Web. He concludes with a suggestion to improve the voice landscape with the Voice Task Force.

VOICE WILL NEVER BE THE NEXT WEB

By Maarten Lens-FitzGerald
Global Head of Voice
Nodes Agency Amsterdam

How do we ensure that, unlike the internet, the medium of voice will not become an exploitative arena where all users are customers providing data for the benefit of corporations?

Many are enthusiastic about the new Voice channel, including me. The more I engage with companies who have a significant stake in data and especially retail, the more it becomes clear there are substantial issues to overcome: Who gets the data? Who owns the shopping cart? When will you need to pay? Who is the customer? The solution to these issues lies not with the two primary market makers Google and Amazon but with the stakeholders' brands and organisations. They need to collaborate and form the Voice Task Force with all stakeholders in order to ensure at least a layer of common good. Join and provide some control.

THE INTERNET STARTED AS A SHARED SERVICE, AND VOICE DIDN'T

When the internet started back in the late 70s, there were several entities that ensured it all remained working. Just like water and electricity services, they took care of interoperability and standards. Today this is done by working groups who manage the standards and the continuous development of the core technologies that make our daily internet use possible. Because they have no commercial intent, they can deliver the infrastructural work without favouring any commercial party, apart from ensuring the common benefit.

THE PLAYERS ARE MORE POWERFUL THAN COUNTRIES

However, over 50% of all internet traffic is now from Google properties like YouTube. Most shopping is happening via Amazon. Facebook, WhatsApp, and Instagram own your social life. These players are larger than many countries. They try to create their own silos to lock in their users and milk them for data. We see the demise of Facebook slowly. Users and governments realise that the data- and advertising-driven models used by Facebook and others are prone to a great deal of manipulation.

THE NEXT WEB, NOT

In comes Voice – the new channel where you ask a question to have it answered by the seemingly intelligent assistant service. It is the next logical step in interface development. The initial adoption numbers prove this: 100+ million smart speaker devices were sold in the first three years after they became available on the market. That is faster than the web or mobile phones. People say that it will be the next web because, as with the internet in the early 1990s, they see the potential of an entirely new way of interacting with information and services.

It won't be.

THE WRONG RECIPE

Voice is not the new web and it is not the new mobile. It is a new channel, but that is as far as the comparison goes. Moreover, it may even have a worse start than the internet or mobiles. The reason is the intent. For the web, the original purpose was the common good. Voice is a new playing field full of opportunities. There are two sources in this 'ocean' that colour it with the wrong intent. Amazon and Google exist to keep their shareholders happy, using smart and complicated business models aimed at making money and serving their customers and users. Their intent is not the common good. The intent of Google is data collection and exploitation. Amazon's intent is retail. That creates a wrong recipe for a broadly carried and strongly grounded new channel to emerge. People fear the new channel of Voice because it gathers even more data and it is not clear how they are protected. Snips is one of the few independent voice platforms that helps you keep your data. How they can go against the two main players is not clear. More initiatives that have privacy by design, as well as independence from the big players, are needed.

INTEROPERABILITY IS THE OTHER DRIVER

Users who want to play Amazon video services on their Google-connected TV find it impossible. Siri won't work on an Android phone, and Alexa doesn't control Google's TV extension Chromecast. This is how the companies show that their interest is more for their own benefit. Back in the early internet days, you had a different situation with internet exchanges. The more providers shared internet lines to carry traffic from other providers, the more the overall value was. The negotiation, in general, ensured that all had equal access and remained at top speed. The same should happen with Voice, not just with accessibility to services but also infrastructure like speaker interoperability and shared text.

BRING THE COMMON INTENT BACK

The question is how to fuel the collective movement and counter the silos. Google and Amazon have billions in cash, expertise, capability, and experience. Not much can be done to alter their course or ignore their primeval traits of data hunger and the shareholders they serve. Well, at least a new workable model can be brokered that has the spirit of the original common intent of the internet. Therein lies the challenge. What is the new workable model and consortium? Best is to create a Task Force for Voice. They can be the standards body enabling interoperability and the new caretaker guarding the channel's independence, so that data is shared (or kept) in a transparent manner. This new body will be a collaboration of all companies, brands, and organisations that see the opportunity. Let's call it the Voice Task Force. Join and ensure we don't lose control in this next wave.

A SCIENTIFIC PERSPECTIVE

The use of voice technology is natural to us[12]. After all, speaking is the foundation of how we communicate, since we were little kids. This makes communicating with voice assistants and voice search applications a more natural and powerful way of communicating with technology than any other medium[13]. This leads to a more personal relationship with technology[14]. We will get into the benefits of this personal relationship for voice marketing. First, however, we discuss the reason why voice is becoming popular. This is all to do with the ease of communicating through voice. It makes our lives easier by providing us with information directly after simply asking a question, allowing us to multitask and taking over simple tasks we would usually have to do ourselves (like turning on the TV or dimming the lights)[15]. This ease is strengthened by the fact that it is not necessary to interrupt your routine in order to speak to a voice assistant and vice versa. You do not have to look at a screen, and look back again, putting your phone back in your pocket, for instance. This way, the experience is smooth and easily adopted into one's daily routine[16].

PROCESSING VOICE

Processing voice communication is like processing a regular conversation. You pay attention to what the other person is saying, think about it, and respond thoughtfully. Following the PCMC-model[17] we call this systematic processing. Systematic processing occurs when the attention and time spent on processing the message are high and the person is motivated to process the message. In the case of voice communication, the voice assistant is activated by the consumer, and answers or acts in response to the consumer. Since the consumer asked for the information or action himself, the response should be relevant, and therefore it is safe to assume that the consumer has the attention, time, and motivation to process the assistant's response.

FUNCTIONS

Voice technology performs several functions from the perspective of the *Functional Triad*[18]. First of all, we can describe voice as a tool. Voice makes our lives easier, for instance by helping us gain information easily and taking tasks out of our hands, such as changing the song that is playing, or citing a recipe so that we can keep cooking without checking our phones or recipe book. Second, voice technology can be seen as a social actor, since people tend to form a bond with their voice assistants. Bonding between humans and technologies can occur when technologies react to their users by adopting animated characteristics (such as emotions or communication by voice), playing animated roles (such as an opponent, coach or assistant), or observing social rules or dynamics (such as greetings and apologies). All these three possible bonding routes apply to voice[19].

ADOPTION OF VOICE

We can explain the acceptance and active use of voice by applying the Technology Acceptance Model (TAM)[20]. According to the TAM, the adoption of new technologies depends on two factors. First is the perceived usefulness, which can be described as the anticipated level of efficiency and usability. Second is the perceived ease of use. When a technology is perceived as helpful, efficient, and easy to use, this positively influences attitudes and intention to use, which in turn are determinants of actual behaviour[21]. In the case of voice, it is easy to use and can be helpful, because it takes less effort to use than for instance a laptop, or another screen-based device. This will only increase, since voice is optimised more and more, which increases efficiency and ease of use. The acceptance and use of voice are thereby expected to grow.

Another important factor that enhances the experience of voice is personalisation. A voice assistant learns from the orders one gives it. It collects data around its user's preferences, interests, needs, and purchases, even from other sources, such as prior purchases, online reviews, social media and other open data sources[22]. Therefore, when one repeatedly asks for the same song, service, or product, that person is actually also training their voice assistant about their preferences. By learning about the user, the voice assistant develops a certain context. This enables the assistant to personalise knowledge from the database for conversations. This way, using voice is not only easy and helpful, but it can also be very personal. This last aspect, learning from data and using that knowledge to personalise the conversations with the user, is also important for voice marketing. It makes targeting a lot easier, and it also helps to know when a brand can be relevant to the user.

FUTURE AND ETHICS

We believe voice will grow and play a significant role in our lives. But how this will play out exactly is not yet determined. A lot of options are still open, and voice is still developing. Accuracy of speech recognition is increasing fast. For instance, in 2018 Alexa was able to answer almost twenty percent more questions than it could in 2017[23]. This was only in one years' time. Voice assistants are getting smarter and will soon reach the accuracy of human speech.

For organisations, voice is a new playground, with new rules to learn. Firstly, they should prepare for voice on other media. This is important, because sonic branding, branding with sound[24], is the one thing that voice marketing is based upon, but brands do not seem to have mastered it. Since all visual cues will be omitted, it is crucial that brands have distinctive brand sounds, that are recognised as such by customers. So, brands need to literally find their tone of voice. Whatever brand sound is chosen has to be repeated frequently and over a long period of time before people will link it to the brand. Therefore, we advise to start building on distinctive brand sounds before starting investment in voice, for example on the radio. This way, voice marketing will probably have stronger effects, because the risk of not being recognised when visual cues are missing is downsized.

Second, it is important to optimise any online content, so that it is easily found with a voice search. After all, both search engine optimisation (SEO), where certain factors are improved so that content is easily found, and voice search, are based on answering questions. However, there is an important difference: people search differently when they speak compared to when they type[25]. For example, instead of searching by entering some keywords in a search engine, they speak in full sentences. Therefore, we advise any organisation to check their content and to label it so that it is not only easily found digitally, but also through voice assistants. In other words, add voice optimisation to SEO. To do so, customer research is crucial, in order to discover what questions are asked and how they are formulated. Similarly, the customers' wishes and needs regarding the shopping experience should be researched. Afterwards, the shopping experience can be optimised for voice as well. Think of factors such as shopping without visuals, shorter processes, and payment through voice.

A NEW WORLD, WITH NEW OPPORTUNITIES

In terms of positive psychology, voice in combination with machine learning could contribute to society. Already, algorithms are developed in order to automatically detect interpersonal stance, such as 'dominant' and 'empathic' in vocal signals for aggression de-escalation purposes[26]. When implemented in voice assistants, these algorithms offer possibilities for the development of voice assistants that automatically adapt to and learn from the user's interpersonal stance, so they can deepen the connection with the user, and possibly even help the user better.

Using voice will also change the way we see the world. Without screens, and no need to type, we will be able to look around us, and get reacquainted with our surroundings. Voice will add to that world, instead of replacing it. And organisations will have to innovate in order to become a part of that world as well. Obviously, their relevance for the customer has to be clear and the service voice-proof. But we believe there is a whole new game to play as well in the form of collaborations. For instance, the first supermarket to collaborate with Google can become the standard or first choice when a person is ordering their groceries through Google Home. Paid recommendations could become a more short-term version of these types of collaborations. With both versions, there is one crucial rule: to succeed, one has to be the first in the game, because being the third recommended label will not get you anywhere. After all, a voice assistant usually names just one option.

TECHNOLOGY MAKES THE CHOICES

Voice makes our choices easier, by reasoning for you. Though this saves effort, it also means we lose control over those choices. Low-involvement products will be bought without consideration of the brand, since Alexa, Siri, Google, or Little Fish are making the choices for you. This again amplifies the importance of relevance and collaborations, but also means there is a serious issue that has yet to be solved. When asking a voice assistant to order a product, we rely on the choices the technology makes, without knowing what the decision is based on. Was it a paid recommendation? Is it Amazon's own product? Was it the cheapest option? Or the best one? The same goes for answers to our questions; we typically do not know where the information we are getting is coming from. Validated research? A commercial website? A Wikipedia page made by an eleven year old? Perhaps it will become mandatory for the assistant to name the source (or shop) after a result. But so far, the legislation is not completely ready for voice technology.

WORRIES ABOUT PRIVACY

Voice assistants are not actually safe to use yet. They save audio recordings of the user. Some assistants offer the option to delete these recordings, but users rarely use this function. Just as they do not use other privacy-improving functions, such as the mute button[27]. The mute button is actually a quite relevant solution. Without it, voice assistants are always listening, waiting for you to say the activation word. And while doing so, it saves information regarding the recognition of speech. Some voice assistants work with speech recognition, and others with voice recognition. This is an important distinction. With speech recognition, it does not matter who is talking, only that words are spoken. The voice assistant will listen to anyone. With voice recognition, however, not only what is said, but also who says it, is recognised. The voice of the person speaking is then recognised and saved. With this technique, the unique identification of a person is applied, which consists of saving biometric data. The European Data Protection Regulation law (GDPR) actually prohibits this[28]. Still, popular voice assistants such as Siri seem to use voice recognition. This shows that in some ways, voice technology is not fully and safely developed yet.

Another privacy issue lays in the ability to hack voice assistants. Research on the safety of Alexa showed that it is relatively easy to hack Alexa, since only a keyword is asked to gain access. Besides that, Alexa can receive input from people who are not even nearby. In this way, sensitive information can be shared with others easily. The researcher proposes a simple solution: add physical presence to the access code of the device[29].

CONCLUSION

Voice technology is on the rise. It may change our lives, because in contrast to other digital innovations, voice ensures that communication is mediated less by screens and images. It allows us to communicate in our most natural form: the spoken word. Also, in an era of predictive and ambient technology, the fact that voice is based on our own initiative is welcomed. Furthermore, voice makes a lot of things easier, but there are also some scary aspects to deal with. Only the future can tell what the exact effects will be and how popular voice may become.

CLASSIFICATION

★★★★★ ★★★★★ ★★★★★ ★★★★★ ★★★★★

References and notes

1   Peña-Taylor, S. (2017). The state of voice: how global brands are leveraging the most human medium. Retrieved from: https://www.warc.com/content/paywall/article/event-reports/the_state_of_voice_how_global_brands_are_leveraging_the_most_human_medium/113295

2   Dictionary.com

3   Estimation by ComScore. Reported in 'Speak easy. The future answers to you' a report on research by JTW and Mindshare. You can read the report at: https://www.jwtintelligence.com/trend-reports/speak-easy/

4   Henneman, J. (2018, 18 September). Meet the voice marketeer.
    Retrieved from: https://www.marketingfacts.nl/cookies/?s=%2Fberichten%2Fmeet-the-voice-marketeer

5   Edison Research and NPR came up with a similar result of 22%.

6   Edison Research & NPR (2018). The smart audio report 2018. Retrieved from: https://www.nationalpublicmedia.com/wp-content/uploads/2018/07/Smart-Audio-Report-from-NPR-and-Edison-Research-Spring-2018_Downloadable-PDF.pdf

7   1) Boonrod, A. & Ketavan, P. (2018). The future is voice: how voice technology is changing the world of people and brands. Retrieved from: https://www.warc.com/content/article/esomar/the_future_is_voice_how_voice_technology_is_changing_the_world_of_people_and_brands/121996 2) JWT & Mindshare (2017). Speak easy: the future answers to you global report. Retrieved from: https://www.jwtintelligence.com/trend-reports/speak-easy/

8   JWT & Mindshare (2017). Speak easy: the future answers to you global report.
    Retrieved from: https://www.jwtintelligence.com/trend-reports/speak-easy/

9   JWT & Mindshare (2017). Speak easy: the future answers to you global report.
    Retrieved from: https://www.jwtintelligence.com/trend-reports/speak-easy/

10 Wolters, M. K., Kelly, F., & Kilgour, J. (2016). Designing a spoken dialogue interface to an intelligent cognitive assistant for people with dementia. Health Informatics Journal, 22(4), 854–866. https://doi.org/10.1177/1460458215593329

11 Diaz, A.C. (2018). This Cannes future Lions winner uses Siri to make people safe in life-threatening situations. Retrieved from Adage: https://adage.com/creativity/work/hush-future-lion/54815

12 Peña-Taylor, S. (2017). The state of voice: how global brands are leveraging the most human medium. Retrieved from: https://www.warc.com/content/paywall/article/event-reports/the_state_of_voice_how_global_brands_are_leveraging_the_most_human_medium/113295

13 Nass, C., & Brave, S. (2005). Wired for speech, How voice activates and advances the human-computer relationship. Cambridge, MA: MIT Press.

14 Kleinberg, S. (2018). Ok, marketers: Here's what people are saying about their voice-activated speakers. Retrieved from: https://www.thinkwithgoogle.com/consumer-insights/voice-assistive-speaker-technology/

15 Kleinberg, S. (2018). 5 ways voice assistance is shaping consumer behaviour. Retrieved from: https://www.thinkwithgoogle.com/intl/en-154/voice-assistance-consumer-experience/

16 Kleinberg, S. (2018). 5 ways voice assistance is shaping consumer behaviour. Retrieved from: https://www.thinkwithgoogle.com/intl/en-154/voice-assistance-consumer-experience/

17 Buijzen, M., Van Reijmersdal, E.A., & Owen, L.H. (2010). Introducing the PCMC model: An investigative framework for young people's processing of commercial media content. Communication Theory, 20, 427-450.

18 Fogg, B. J., Cuellar, G., & Danielson, D. (2009). Motivating, influencing, and persuading users. In J. Jacko & A. Sears (Eds.), The human-computer interaction handbook: Fundamentals, evolving technologies and emerging applications (pp. 133-147). Hillsdale, NJ: Erlbaum.

19 Ranj, B. (2018). We asked Siri, Alexa, and the Google Assistant 10 questions — here's which one is the smartest. Retrieved from: https://www.businessinsider.com/siri-alexa-google-assistant-which-is-smarter-2018-3?international=true&r=US&IR=T

20 Davis, F. D. (1989). Perceived usefulness, perceived ease of use, and user acceptance of information technology. MIS Quarterly, 319-3402

21 Ajzen, I. (1991). The theory of planned behavior. Theories of Cognitive Self-Regulation, 50(2), 179-211. DOI:10.1016/0749-5978(91)90020-T; Davis, F. D., Bagozzi, R. P. & Warshaw, P. R. (1989). User acceptance of computer technology: A comparison of two theoretical models. Management Science, 35(8), 982-1003. doi:10.1287/mnsc.35.8.982

22 Aksu, H., Babun, L., Conti, M., Tolomei, G., & Uluagac, A. S. (2018). Advertising in the IoT era: Vision and challenges. IEE Communications Magazine 56(11), 138-144.

23 Read all about the accuracy of voice assistants in: Eric Enge (2018, April). Rating the smarts of the digital personal assistants in 2018. Retrieved from: https://www.stonetemple.com/digital-personal-assistants-study/

24 This statement is based on a research done in the Netherlands by Blauw Research and BLCKBRD. It showed that brand sounds in the Netherlands are almost never recognised by the majority of people. We assume that this does not differ much in other regions.

25 Peña-Taylor, S. (2017). The state of voice: how global brands are leveraging the most human medium. Retrieved rom: https://www.warc.com/content/article/event-reports/the_state_of_voice_how_global_brands_are_leveraging_the_most_human_medium/113295

26 Formolo, D. and Bosse, T., Human vs. Computer Performance in Voice-Based Emotion Recognition. In: Proceedings of the 19th International Conference on Human-Computer Interaction, HCI'17. Springer Verlag, Lecture Notes in Computer Science, 2017.

27 Lau, J., Zimmerman, B., & Schaub, F. (2018). Alexa, are you listening?: Privacy perceptions, concerns and privacy-seeking behaviors with smart speakers. Proceedings of the ACM on Human-Computer Interaction, 2(CSCW). doi:10.1145/3274371

28 Source: Considerati

29 Lei, X., Tu, G.-H., Liu, A.X., Ali, K., Li, C.-Y., & Xie, T. (2017). The insecurity of home digital voice assistants – Amazon Alexa as a case study. [Online]. Retrieved from: https://arxiv.org/pdf/1712.03327.pdf

#3 ROBOTS

A robot is a man-made machine with a physical body. Robots can perform physical as well as cognitive tasks and are often combined with artificial intelligence.

John has worked in a bomb squad for several years now, alongside Bob, a bomb-diffusing robot. They are behind enemy lines, providing their troops with a safe passage through an area that is littered with landmines. When things get tricky, Bob is programmed to diffuse a bomb. Unfortunately, it is booby-trapped and Bob is blown sky high into bits and pieces. How will John react … ? Our reaction to violence against robots is important as this wave of machines is forcing us to reconsider our relationships with them. Sacrificing robots may become unacceptable in societies' eyes, and robot rights may be needed in the near future. Are robots members of society? Do they deserve judicial rights? What influences our behaviour towards them? And how should we incorporate this knowledge into the production and design of robots? In this chapter we will focus on the moral dilemmas created by robots and how to implement robots in organisations.

DEFINITION AND KEY FEATURES

The time when robots only appeared in science fiction movies like The Jetsons and Star Wars and in comics such as Archie is long behind us. Robots are everywhere and they emerge in several disciplines. Therefore, it is important to make an inventory of their usability and how we relate to them as humans. Robots can not only digest information but also perform tasks and enlarge productivity. In robots, hardware such as sensors, screens, servomotors and also arms and legs, are combined with intelligent software[1]. They are physical machines that have visible and tangible humanlike features and that can move around in their environment.

DULL, DANGEROUS, AND DIRTY JOBS

Robots can be distinguished on two dimensions: their appearance and their functionality. When considering their appearance, we can discern: 1) *mechanical* robots, which do not have human features; 2) *humanoid* robots, which do have human characteristics such as a head, arms, and legs, but are obviously not human; and 3) *android* robots, which are designed to look just like humans, with a face and skin. Task-wise there are: 1) industrial robots, which are deployed in a controlled environment such as factories; 2) robots that act in the outside world, such as self-driving cars and vacuum cleaners; and 3) social robots, which are designed to interact with people and to combat loneliness, such as robot pets.

Robots are often used for tasks that are related to the '3 Ds': jobs that are dull, dangerous or dirty[2], in the industrial sector, in hospitals, and the army but also in healthcare. Robots do not need a meaningful job, cannot die, and do not mind dirt. In addition, they do not get tired, do the same thing over and over again without getting bored, and can be deployed for 24 hours a day. Most importantly, the use of robots for jobs is becoming more and more realistic because they are getting cheaper, are easier and faster to programme and are equipped with AI-systems (deep learning, and 'neural network' -systems). While many are afraid that robots will take away jobs in the future, their presence in fact also generates new jobs since they have to be manufactured and programmed.

ROBOTS IN PRACTICE

Although robots may perform the dull, dangerous, or dirty jobs instead of humans, most people do not appreciate them. Indeed, on a societal level, robots are seen as a threat for the simple suspicion that they will take over jobs and may outsmart humans[3]. The idea that soulless machines can have complex cognitive abilities that exceed the capacities of mankind, threatens the unicity and identity of men.

SEVERAL JOBS FOR ROBOTS

Social robots have become increasingly popular in our society. They can assist nurses to take care of elderly patients or patients with a handicap, and surgeons performing operations. They teach children with autism how to interact[4]. They help people take their medicine and do their exercises. Robots in education can help students learn vocabulary and count tables. A reception robot can be the host of a company, welcome visitors, register them, and inform the organisation that the visitors have arrived. Although this all seems straightforward, how easy is it really to implement a robot in your organisation?

AI AND ROBOTS

The ultimate accomplishment of AI would be a recreation of the human thought process, creating a man-made machine with human intellectual abilities: the ability to reason, the ability to use language and the ability to formulate original ideas. Robotics is nowhere near achieving this level of artificial intelligence, but it has made progress with more limited AI.

Today's AI machines can replicate some specific elements of intellectual ability. Robots can already solve simple problems. Some modern robots also have the ability to learn in a limited capacity. Learning robots recognise if a certain action achieved a desired result, and some robots can interact socially by mimicking human actions.

Loes Brouwers advises companies about the implementation of robots in their organisations. In the next paragraph she describes a step-by-step plan for how to do this successfully.

IMPLEMENTING A ROBOT; A TOUR THROUGH HUMAN EMOTIONS

By Loes Brouwers
Founder & Robot Consultant
RoboSophica

When implementing social robots in different organisations, I have encountered many people with varied emotions towards robots. During one day I have seen the initiator being enthusiastic about the robot, employees who will have to work alongside to the robot curious or worried, and users who are interacting with the robot thrilled or slightly scared. It may be clear that robots evoke emotional responses in people. It may be clear that robots evoke emotional responses in people. As physical machines that can autonomously act in their environment, robots are not mere moving objects with a certain function, but they also have an effect on the people around them.

TOUR THROUGH HUMAN EMOTIONS

I would like to take you on a tour through the human emotions you may encounter in initiators, employees, and users, when implementing a robot in your company. During this tour I will also share several tips with you to help you make the implementation a success and the users' interaction with the robot a pleasant experience.

1. ENTHUSIASM AND HIGH EXPECTATIONS: THE INITIATORS' VIEW

This tour starts with the initiators. These are the people who want the robot to be implemented in their organisation, and have an idea of what the robot should do. These people are generally positive about robots, and about technical innovations and change in general. Although they are enthusiastic about robots, they do not always have realistic expectations. Their view on what robots can do is often fed by the way that robots are presented at industry events and in the media. For understandable reasons, robot companies tend to keep the risk of failure of a robot on stage as low as possible. Therefore, you can expect performances on stages and television to be mainly scripted. For example, when a TV show host interviews a robot, it appears that the robot understands the questions perfectly and the answers are very intelligent. But technology isn't quite there yet, and a robot will most likely disappoint or not meet the high expectations. Current dialogue technologies like Siri and Alexa can answer a large variety of questions, but they are not able to hold humanlike conversations. Most robots are programmed to react to trigger words, and the dialogue is structured as a flow chart: when the answer to question 1 is "Yes", then ask question 2a; when it is answered with "No", then ask question 2b. Given the communicational limitations of most robots, it is essential to manage expectations properly at the start of the project. As for physical actions, it still proves to be very difficult to build an affordable robot that can move with agility, avoid obstacles, and move towards a certain goal. Things like recognising a face and making eye contact demand very good cameras and sensors.

2. FEELING THREATENED: A POSSIBLE EMPLOYEE REACTION

A lot of employees I have encountered were very enthusiastic about getting a robot colleague. However, implementing a robot can also be accompanied by negative responses from employees. In most cases, the employees involved are not the ones initiating the implementation of the robot, so they might not be as enthusiastic as the initiators are. Often some of their work flows need to be changed in order to make the robot work well, and as with all change, this can cause resistance. Also, employees who will have to work with a robot that will take over parts of their jobs, might feel threatened by this. It is very important to understand and respect the fact that this worries them. Ask workers for their opinions and advice from the beginning of the project. Involving them will make it more likely that they will accept and adopt the robot. It is very important to make clear that a robot cannot fulfil all the tasks a human can. In the majority of cases, humans will still be essential in the processes that are supported by a robot. Give the robot an assisting role in the work flow to make this clear.

However, to give a full perspective, I have also had great experiences with employees who were big fans of their new robot colleague. Involving them early in the project gives you the opportunity to align the project really well to the needs of the organisation.

3. CONFUSION, AND A VARIETY OF EXPECTATIONS AND RESPONSES: WHEN A CUSTOMER INTERACTS WITH A ROBOT

For many customers, it is a completely new experience to encounter a robot and they do not quite know what to expect. I often get questions like "Can it talk?" or "Does he see me?" when customers want to interact with the robot. The way they approach the robot is often related to their previous experiences with robots, and for a lot of people their sole experience is through Hollywood films. This may make them positively curious or scared to interact with a robot. Some people have very high or very low expectations of what a robot can do. To deal with these challenges, it helps to choose a robot with an appearance that suits the target group, such as a child-size pettable robot for children, which is not physically threatening or uncanny. Also, make sure that the appearance of the robot of your choice doesn't set too high expectations when the robot cannot meet them.

There are plenty of ways in which interacting with a robot can go wrong and this will often mean that the user has an unpleasant experience. Some examples of things that could go wrong are: 1) the user doesn't hear or understand what the robot says, or vice versa; 2) the robot gives wrong information (due to malfunctioning systems or programming mistakes); and 3) the customer asks an unexpected question, or gives an unexpected answer to a question, and the robot doesn't know how to respond to that properly. To avoid the customer having an unpleasant experience, I would recommend to think of the robot as a device, just like a smart phone or a tablet. It can generate output when it gets certain input. Also, you can add apps on many robots to give them specific functionalities. Considering the current state of technology in the field of natural language, I would recommend putting the robot in the lead of the conversation. Free format conversations are still very complicated for robots, so make sure the robot decides where the conversation goes and asks for the information it needs to help a customer properly. Make sure that interacting with the robot is a pleasant experience. A flawless conversation with an impolite, rude, or very witty robot can still be an unpleasant experience. Make sure your choices suit your target group.

REHUMANISING OUR INTERACTIONS WITH TECHNOLOGY

With this information you will probably understand the importance of thinking about the purpose for which you want to implement a robot. Ask yourself the following questions: 1) which goals are you aiming to achieve? 2) how is a robot part of your branding and interactions with customers? 3) is a robot the best way to reach your goal, or is there a better solution? 4) who is your target group and how will they respond to the robot? 5) what does implementing the robot mean for your stakeholders (including customers and employees?) and 6) what are your (company's) responsibilities regarding these stakeholders?

This innovation combines many different technologies, which leads to a culmination of ethical issues. First of all, there are privacy-related issues, posed by using data and saving images from a camera in order to recognise faces. Other implications involve decision making by a machine and consequences for employees, like large changes in work or loss of work. However, in addition to the implications mentioned above, robots have a unique feature: they are (humanlike) physical agents that are acting in our world, and we can interact with them in a humanlike way. They may act or look human, but they are not. This may lead to confusion and disappointments when expectations are too high.

On the one hand, interacting with robots might give us an experience that is very close to our natural way of interacting with other people. As such, it may provide a huge plus over using other devices that force us to adjust our way of interacting. In this way, robots can be a very strong step towards rehumanising our interactions with technology; other innovations have mainly digitalised and virtualised our interactions with devices and each other. On the other hand, this rehumanised way of interacting may be deceptive, especially towards vulnerable groups (such as children, the elderly, and developmentally disabled people). Do we expect them to be able to keep differentiating between interactions with humans and robots when robots become more humanlike? And when we decide to implement robots, will we be fully aware of the consequences of interacting with a robot instead of experiencing social contact with another human being? I am convinced we will need a lot of further research on this topic. When implementing a robot for communication purposes, it is wise to think about these implications. A very important question is: what will be gained by implementing a robot and what will be lost? Make sure to make the right call for everyone involved, and when you decide to implement a robot, I hope that you and everyone involved will enjoy the robot's company very much!

The study of robots is a multidisciplinary scientific discipline. It studies the application of robots in our society and in our daily life in order to understand and optimise processes. Scientists from artificial intelligence, electronics, mechanical engineering, psychology, communication science, philosophy and law work together to tackle all kinds of robot-related issues. Considering the large number of robotics-related conferences[5] and journals[6], and the potential of AI and machine learning in robotics, this research area is growing fast.

THE PROCESS OF ANTHROPOMORPHISM

When interacting with a robot, people ascribe them human characteristics[7]. This is due to a phenomenon called anthropomorphism[8] – seeing humanlike qualities in non-human entities. Fogg[9] describes five cues that contribute to the process of anthropomorphism: physical, psychological, language, social dynamics, and social roles. Robots offer ample opportunities for people to anthropomorphise them, because they have a face, eyes, a body and limbs, and they move like humans (physical). Robots simulate a personality (psychological) and human feelings ("Oh dear how sad"). People respond socially to persuasive social robots and such reactions are more pronounced when the robots feature more interactive social cues[10]. In order for robots to recognise and show affective behaviour, they should be able to regulate and recognise simultaneously occurring tendencies of positive and negative emotions[11]. Robots recognise voice and human communication (language) and simulate the unspoken rules and dynamics of social interaction (social dynamics). The people interacting with them may impose on them the role of a friend, mentor or team-member, or authority (social roles).

LANDING IN UNCANNY VALLEY

The effectiveness of robots partially depends on how they look, i.e. whether they are humanlike or non-humanlike. According to the uncanny valley theory[12], people will like robots more when they look more like humans. However, when their appearance becomes too similar to humans, people start to reject the robot. A mechanical robot, like a vacuum cleaner, does not look like a human at all, and will therefore be less scary than a humanoid robot that looks more like a human. An android robot that almost looks like a human but moves in a rigid, machine-like way, lands in the uncanny valley, being evaluated even worse than the mechanical robot.

What explains the occurrence of this uncanny valley effect? First, people have a need for distinctiveness[13] in that they want humans to distinguish themselves from non-humans. In their eyes, robots that are too humanlike do not differ enough from humans, which is why they associate them with the living dead such as zombies. This may even lead to a mini-existential crisis: humanity is non-distinguishable from machines, threatening human identity. However, robots looking like perfect humans may go beyond the uncanny valley, raising ethical questions that emerge in science fiction movies. Developers of robots account for the fact that robots should look like humans but not too much, because it then gets uncanny.

FUTURE AND ETHICS

Robots function on the basis of software. Artificial intelligence will enable them to take decisions autonomously. They will advance even more in the near future and may even beat humans in mastering complicated skills such as language and visual capabilities. They will more often make decisions with ethical impacts (i.e. autonomous robot drones used in warfare or self-driving cars), show empathy, recognise and react to human emotions, build relationships with humans, and adapt to unexpected situations. However, the science fiction scenarios in which robots have conquered the world and turned mankind into slaves seem far away. People overestimate the intelligence and capacity of robots. Robots are not yet capable of displaying emotions that are unique to humans, such as empathy and creativity, and they still lack sophisticated motor skills. Therefore we should not focus too much on what robots can mean for us when we combine them with AI, but instead focus on how we should socialise with them.

CHILDREN ARE SUSCEPTIBLE TO ROBOTS

When using robots in the context of children, one has to bear in mind that young children tend to anthropomorphise more than adults. Think of your childhood teddy bear or invisible friend, and you know what we are talking about. Children have a difficult time differentiating between fantasy and reality, and easily bond with fictional characters. Designing robots that will be used at home or in the classroom will therefore pose some extra challenges to developers. They should consider the extent to which a robot's functioning fits with a child's social and emotional development. Furthermore, since children attach to objects so easily[14], robots that do not have a social function (e.g., a robot vacuum cleaner) should probably have no humanlike features in order to avoid children experiencing an emotional bond with this object.

SOULLESS MACHINES HAVING COMPLEX MENTAL ABILITIES

So one can imagine why people fear the advance of robots, and it is not alone about the loss of jobs. The idea that soulless machines can have complex cognitive abilities that exceed the capacities of mankind, threatens the unicity and identity of men. Isaac Asimov (1942),[15] a writer of science fiction stories was far ahead of his time. He conceived three codes of conduct for robots in order for them to always act for the good of men. A robot 1) may never harm people or let people be harmed by not acting, 2) must obey orders of man, unless these orders conflict with the first rule, and 3) must protect its own existence, provided this is not in conflict with the first and second rule. When beneficial for all parties involved, the world might be ruled by robots. For those who are interested there are several publication about how to realise consciousness in robots[16], whether robots have rights just like humans have[17], and when robots are moral agents[18].

SOCIAL ROBOTS DO NOT REPLACE PEOPLE

In order to minimise resistance to robots, they should be better integrated into our society. This can be accomplished by designing robots that obviously are robots and do not look like humans[19], for example they may have humanlike faces but the back of their head is mechanically wired. A suitable marketing campaign may further diminish resistance to robots, informing people what they can expect, offering them ample time to get used to robots. An important step is to have people realise that robots do not replace people. Furthermore, one should seriously consider the arguments over why people feel threatened at the idea of robots becoming a part of our society.

ROBOTS RAISE SEVERAL QUESTIONS

The development of robots as companions and caregivers for elderly people has already begun. They are often lonely, and in need of companionship and assistance for daily routines. Robots could be taking on that role, monitoring and reporting their health to their families. This raises ethical questions about the applicability of robots that have not yet been dealt with: Can they be trusted to treat vulnerable groups in our society such as the elderly? Do we befool people with dementia when giving them a robot dog to keep them company, because they think the dog is real? Is it a good thing to become friends with a thing that can be turned of?

Robots could take care of young children who need supervision, when busy parents are not around. Should a robot be able to interfere with parental education? The obvious resulting juridical questions are: Who is responsible when a robot injures a child because of technical malfunctioning? Is the robot, being an intelligent agent, responsible? Is the one who designed or programmed the robot responsible? The government? Or the company that sold the robot?

SACRIFICE THE ROBOT

There is a discussion about giving robots human rights, like real humans. Robot Sophia got a Saudi Arabian passport. Boomer, a robot who took part in the American army, lost a battle in Iraq and got an official funeral and a fine series of medals for this act of heroism[20]. Research has shown that the more human characteristics a robot has, the more people see the robot as human, and the less they will sacrifice the robot in order to save a human being[21]. To go back to the introduction of this chapter where John was ordered to sacrifice Bob the bomb-diffusing robot, one can now imagine what might have happened. Probably John had become emotionally attached to Bob, being pals in the bomb squad for several years. He must have felt conflicted when Bob had to diffuse the bomb, and probably was seized with emotion when witnessing his loyal friend being sacrificed. We anthropomorphise robots and form strong emotional bonds with them that make us vulnerable, even though we know that the robots are not alive. Whether in the future robots should get legal rights seems like a legitimate question.

Concluding, the fact that robots ultimately will make ethical choices in which they may mirror the prejudices of their creators and the people they interact with, is an important ongoing discussion. Perhaps the key question is whether and how robots can contribute to our feelings of happiness. We believe they can. In fact, social robots already make people happier and healthier, whether it is helping children with autism, people with their exercises, or the elderly with dementia. New applications will follow that might influence the happiness of larger groups. That is, if we can set our wariness towards robots aside.

CLASSIFICATION

★★★★★   ★★★★★   ★★★★★   ★★★★★   ★★★★★

References and notes

1 Ullrich, D., & Butz, A. (2016). Social robots for the 21st century. Computer, 49(6). doi:10.1109/MC.2016.172

2 Murphy, R. (2000). Introduction to AI robotics. Cambridge, Mass: MIT Press.

3 Stein, J. P., & Ohler, P. (2017). Venturing into the uncanny valley of mind - The influence of mind attribution on the acceptance of human-like characters in virtual reality setting. Cognition, 160, 43-50. doi: 10.1016/j.cognition.2016.12.010

4 Kozima, H., Nakagawa, C. & Yasuda, Y. (2005). Interactive robots for communication-care: a case-study in autism therapy. Roman 2005. doi: 10.1109/ROMAN.2005.1513802

5 For instance: Science and Systems (RSS), The International Conference on Robotics and Automation (ICRA), The International Conference on Intelligent Robots and Systems (IROS), ICARCV, FSR, CASE, Humanoids, the IEEE Robotics and Automation.

6 Journals such as: Soft Robotics, International Journal of Robotics Research, Journal of Field Robotics, Transactions on Robotics, Robotics and Automation Magazine, Autonomous Robots, Robotics and Autonomous Systems, Journal of Intelligent and Robotic Systems: Theory and Applications.

7 Duffy, B. R. (2003). Anthropomorphism and the social robot. Robotics and autonomous systems, 42(3-4), 177-190.

8 Ge, S., Khatib, O., Cabibihan, J., Simmons, R. & Williams, M. (2012). Social robotics (1st ed.). Chengdu, China: Springer Meida.

9 Fogg, B. J. (2002). Prominence-interpretation theory: Explaining how people assess credibility. Research report from the Stanford Persuasive Technology Lab, Stanford University. Retrieved from: http://credibility.stanford.edu/

10 Ghazali, A. S., Ham, J., Barakova, E., & Markopoulos, P. (2019). Assessing the effect of persuasive robots interactive social cues on users' psychological reactance, liking, trusting beliefs and compliance. Advanced Robotics, 1-13.

11 Bosse, T., Hoorn, J. F., Pontier, M., & Siddiqui, G. F. (2008). A robot's experience of another robot: Simulation. In Proceedings of the 30th International Annual Conference of the Cognitive Science Society, CogSci (Vol. 8, pp. 2498-2503).

12 Mori, M. (1970). The uncanny valley. Energy, 7(4), 33–35.

13 Ferrari, F., Paladino, M., & Jetten, J. (2016). Blurring human-machine distinctions: Anthropomorphic appearance in social robots as a threat to human distinctiveness. International Journal of Social Robotics, 8(2), 287-302. doi:10.1007/s12369-016-0338-y

14 De Droog, S. M., Valkenburg, P. M., & Buijzen, M. (2011). Using brand characters to promote young children's liking of and purchase requests for fruit. Journal of Health Communication, 16(1), 79-89. doi: 10.1080/10810730.2010.529487

15 Asimov, I. (1942). Runaround. Astounding Science Fiction, 29(1), 94-103.

16 Dennett, D. C. (1995). Cog: Steps towards consciousness in robots. Conscious Experience, 471-487.

17 Coeckelbergh, M. (2010). Robot rights? Towards a social-relational justification of moral consideration. Ethics and Information Technology, 12(3), 209-221.

18 Sullins, J. P. (2011). When is a robot a moral agent. Machine Ethics, 151-161.

19 Ferrari, F., Paladino, M., & Jetten, J. (2016). Blurring human-machine distinctions: Anthropomorphic appearance in social robots as a threat to human distinctiveness. International Journal of Social Robotics, 8(2), 287-302. doi:10.1007/s12369-016-0338-y

20 Nijssen, S. R., Müller, B. C., Baaren, R. B. V., & Paulus, M. (2019). Saving the robot or the human? Robots who feel deserve moral care. Social Cognition, 37(1), 41-S2.

21 Nijssen, S. R., Müller, B. C., Baaren, R. B. V., & Paulus, M. (2019). Saving the robot or the human? Robots who feel deserve moral care. Social Cognition, 37(1), 41-S2.

#4 WEARABLES

Wearables are small electronic devices incorporated into items that are worn on the body. They can collect and deliver information, or can be used in communication, on a real-time basis.

Jules woke up. The band was itching a bit around his wrist. He felt somewhat uncomfortable being tracked day and night but enjoyed the relative freedom that was agreed upon. Life was hard outside. He was getting slowly used to it, day by day.... The doctor had explained to him that the band was necessary to monitor his heartbeat day and night, thus avoiding being hospitalised again for a long period of time because of his irregular heartbeat.

DEFINITION AND KEY FEATURES

Hopefully you were a little misled by the example above. We wanted you to switch from negative associations about wearables to positive ones. We were not talking about a convict who has negative associations with the small band that registers his location 24 hours a day in order to restrain freedom of movement. We were talking about a heart patient with positive associations about wearables that may be life-saving and keep him out of the hospital. In this chapter we touch upon a sensitive dilemma associated with wearables outside institutions, as in this example, where the exchange of often privacy-related personal data, in or outside your home environment, is necessary for either relative freedom or good health.

WEARABLES FACILITATE THE EXCHANGE OF INFORMATION

'Wearables' stands for so-called wearable technology, computers, or even devices. Wearables aim to either facilitate the extraction of data as in our example, or actively send information by creating a continuous, seamless, portable, and mostly hands-free access to information, as in smart glasses. Wearables are becoming more functional and are not only used for counting steps in order to stay fit, but also for a variety of functions such as contactless paying, playing music, and sleep tracking.

Wearables are often worn around the wrist as a smartwatch or bracelet and can be integrated into garments that are worn on the body[1]. They are small and follow you everywhere. Wearables may be present in e-textiles, smart fabrics, headbands, jewellery, shoe soles, and may even be implanted into microchips or tattoos. You can use your smartphone to connect with your wearables, or wearables as standalone devices may be connected directly with devices in your home, for example to have a perfect lighting set-up when watching TV.

WEARABLES IN PRACTICE

There are wearables on the market that are used to stay fit, for healthcare, for self-help monitoring, and for personal safety. Popular wearables in healthcare enable the monitoring of people's bodily functions. In the near future, small electronics in your bra will measure your heartbeat and regularity of breathing, your contact lenses will measure your levels of blood sugar and dehydration, your smartwatch will foresee a cold by measuring your body temperature even before you feel sick, and may determine the first symptoms of Parkinson's disease[2], while with your ring you can pay for the medical bills. Wearables are also used for safety purposes. They can be equipped with GPS, allowing parents to keep track of their children and allowing legal authorities to follow convicts during their leave of absence. They sometimes have a secondary function as a lifestyle accessory.

MY WEARABLE KNOWS ME BEST

The advantage of wearables is that they are always there, being equipped with sensors that measure, for instance, movement, body temperature, distance, heart rhythm and weight, enabling them to synchronise in real time with a smart environment such as mobile devices or laptops. Wearables are an extension of the body, rendering precise data about the location. They may offer people a 'permanent' digital identity, offering storage for personal belongings such as passport, driving licence, credit card, and house and car keys.

On the negative side, wearables receive and transmit data continuously and in real-time, raising privacy issues, For instance, insurance companies test the users of wearables in order to estimate the tailor-made pricing of their insurance policy. Wearables are difficult to use in communication because of their small size, limited computer power, and battery capacity. Lastly, wearables are often dependent on smartphones for their computing power, storage of information, and internet connection.

Gonny Van der Zwaag is an experienced expert on wearables. In the next paragraph she notes several positive aspects of smartwatches, including self-improvement.

She also notes that trust in the organisations that use the data is the key to the success of wearables.

REFLECTING ON WEARABLES

By Gonny van der Zwaag
Founder & Editor in Chief
iCulture.nl

As explained earlier in this chapter, wearables can have a positive impact on the life, health, and wellbeing of a user. Most wearables are intended to improve life, whether it's achieving a more active lifestyle, improving sleep, or better diabetes management. Wearables can help by giving users easy access to metrics they can act upon. A better informed consumer should be able to make better decisions, the thinking goes. Unfortunately, this is not always the case. Having access to a wealth of data can confuse users and obstruct their decision making, instead of facilitating it. Fortunately, there are several solutions to prevent this and manufacturers of wearables are taking note of these solutions.

SENSORS HAVE BECOME MORE SOPHISTICATED

As a founder of a large tech website, I've had the opportunity to test a large number of wearables myself. In 2014 I wrote one of the first books about using wearables to stay fit and improve sports performance. Since then, it has become easier and more affordable to use wearables for self-improvement and healthcare, thanks to advances in technology. Instead of just counting steps, most wearables now feature a heart-rate monitor and several other new sensors to collect more data than ever before. Sensors have become more sophisticated too, for example non-invasive methods to check blood values based on sweat and other body fluids, without having to insert a needle into the skin.

LARGE PILES OF DATA ARE IN THE HANDS OF CONSUMERS

Collecting a vast amount of data, and trying to make sense of it, is not a recent development. Scientists, financial analysts and journalists have been doing this for decades, or even centuries. What's different with wearables today, is that large piles of data are now in the hands of consumers. They have access to more computing power than the professionals at universities and large companies twenty or thirty years ago. A standard desktop computer often suffices to analyse and visualise data. If more computer power is needed to detect patterns and trends, cloud computing services from Amazon, Microsoft, and other parties are ready to help. In theory, this sounds like a perfect world, but the reality is that most consumers lack the skills, time, and motivation to actually analyse data and find actionable information. We have to help them.

MAKING SENSE OF DATA BY MACHINE LEARNING

One solution that has been adopted by a number of manufacturers of wearables, is a shift from a more technical to a more user-centric approach. A promising development is the increased use of machine learning and AI algorithms to make sense of data, in situations where the user is not equipped to find useful patterns him- or herself. Instead of offering a graph or list of measurements of heart rate variability (HRV), for example, the wearable offers insights into how HRV is tied to stress levels in daily life, or to recovery in sports.

A wearable can also suggest what strategies have been effective for other users. The difficulty here is that this is not a one-size-fits-all approach. What is a 'normal' value for one person might not be optimal for someone else. Self-improvement often involves finding a strategy that works for the individual, and that can be maintained in the long term. Quick solutions that work for anyone almost never exist, but having an opportunity to compare measurements with similar users of the same age group, gender, ethnicity, and other personal traits, can give better insights into knowing if someone is on the right track to improvement.

Machine learning, however, depends on large amounts of user data. As discussed earlier in this chapter, this only works when enough users, possibly hundreds of thousands or even millions, are comfortable with sharing their personal data for the benefit of a larger group. This often involves sharing data with a commercial party that often has priorities other than improving people's lives. Trust is key.

ENCOURAGING REALISTIC EXPECTATIONS

Another solution to make wearables more useful and effective is encouraging realistic expectations. Working on self-improvement and better disease management are two of the most positive aspects of wearables. However, they can also lead to anxiety. Sleep tracking, for example, can encourage some people to develop unrealistic expectations of what their sleep data should look like. Researchers in a 2017 study in the Journal of Clinical Sleep Medicine[3] introduced the term 'orthosomnia' for people who are getting upset about their sleep trackers. Orthosomnia is not an official medical diagnosis yet, but it highlights how the quest for better sleep can go too far. Users are trying to gain better insight in their sleep patterns, but instead it makes them more anxious, and leaves them with the impression that there's something 'wrong' with them. Sleep wearables often use movement, heart rate, and breathing patterns to determine sleep phases, the total amount of sleep, and other metrics. The tools are accessible, but not always accurate.

A good sleep tracker encourages people to look beyond the data and helps them to better understand how they actually feel. After all, the purpose of wearables is not to produce perfect graphs, but to actually improve our lives.

A SCIENTIFIC PERSPECTIVE

The fact that wearables have become more popular can be explained by the Quantified Self Movement[4], which says that people integrate technology into their lives with the goal of gathering information about themselves and learning from it in order to become more healthy, informed, and happy.

WEARABLES AS AN INSTRUMENT, MEDIUM, AND SOCIAL AGENT

When people feel that using wearables is easy they will be more used and accepted. Depending on the type of wearable, they may be effective as an instrument, medium, and social agent[5]. As an instrument, wearables can raise people's self-efficacy, by allowing them to perform tasks more efficiently. This enlarges trust and confidence in their abilities and results in more free time[6]. For instance, a wearable can send relevant reminders, so people do not have to memorise all the information themselves. There are wearables that can perform tasks that are otherwise more difficult, such as the real-time tracking of physical efforts or the reception of customised information[7]. This may impact desired behaviour positively: the automated counting of calories may induce people to exercise more. As a medium, wearables can optimise experiences. For instance, the display of smart glasses may contain extra information that can help you navigate without looking away from traffic. As a social agent, wearables can assume a coaching role, such as health trackers challenging people to behave more healthily. The trackers show their body activity and give a compliment when targets are reached, enhancing people's trust in themselves. This game-like way of coaching may eventually motivate people intrinsically to conduct healthy behaviour.

DATA COLLECTION BY WEARABLES FOR SCIENTIFIC RESEARCH

Wearables may offer a more attractive method for data collection in scientific research than conventional methods such as surveys and interviews. Data collection in the so-called wearable lab of the MyMoves project[8] exists of a smartphone-based research application connected to an activity-tracking bracelet. The project aims to unravel youth's social network structures in combination with individual, psychosocial, and environmental factors related to energy intake and expenditure. Among other types of data, it generates peer-, self-reported and experience sampling data, and real-time physical activity data, such as the counting of steps and distance cycled.

FUTURE AND ETHICS

The whole process of real-time and continuous data collection by wearables mostly takes place without people noticing it. They will actively process and elaborate on information that is conveyed to them by the wearables, because that information is about important things such as their health, fitness level, and safety.

WEARABLES MAY ELICIT FEELINGS OF STRESS AND FAILURE

The fact that wearables may enlarge peoples' self-efficacy demands other skills from people. They have to learn how to properly analyse the data and draw the right conclusions. A disadvantage of wearables is that they give constant feedback to humans, eliciting feelings of stress and failure when goals (such as the number of steps) have not been reached. One may question whether wearables adopt vital functions that people should perform themselves.

DETECT DISEASES AT AN EARLY STAGE

The question arises whether organisations may use peoples' data for commercial intentions, without harming their privacy[9], or risking data loss or leakage. According to marketers and health organisations, people exchange their data for relevant information, for instance, about their fitness level or health. Rendering these data anonymous would therefore not be logical[10]. The use of wearable devices for healthcare purposes raises questions about data sharing and privacy risks. Information overload might get in the way of informed consent by the patient[11]. Lawyers emphasise that consumers logically give up their data because they do not realise what is at stake[12].

Big data platforms, strengthened by AI, will offer big opportunities to develop wearables in healthcare. A wearable tracks vital body functions and compares them in real-time with big data in order to detect diseases at an early stage[13] with a surprising accuracy. The success of this innovation depends on how it evolves. Will wearables just be a mere extension of the smartphone? Or will they be a more integrated element in the Internet of Things, offering a wider range of features?

CLASSIFICATION

★★★★★ ★★★★★ ★★★★★ ★★★★★ ★★★★★

References and notes

1 Fang, Y. M., & Chang, C. C. (2016). Users' psychological perception and perceived readability of wearable devices for elderly people. Behaviour & Information Technology, 35(3), 225-232. DOI: 10.1080/0144929X.2015.1114145.

2 Piwek, L., Ellis, D. A., Andrews, S., & Joinson, A. (2016). The rise of consumer health wearables: Promises and barriers. PLoS Medicine, 13(2), e1001953. Doi: https://doi.org/10.1371/journal.pmed.1001953

3 Retrieved from: https://www.ncbi.nlm.nih.gov/pmc/articles/PMC5263088

4 Ruckenstein, M., & Pantzar, M. (2017). Beyond the quantified self: Thematic exploration of a dataistic paradigm. New Media & Society, 19(3), 401-418.

5 Fogg, B. J., Cuellar, G., & Danielson, D. (2002). Motivating, influencing, and persuading users. In J. Jacko & A. Sears (Eds.), The human-computer interaction handbook: Fundamentals, evolving technologies and emerging applications (pp. 133-147). Hillsdale, NJ: Erlbaum.

6 Nijssen, S. R., Schaap, G., & Verheijen, G. P. (2018). Has your smartphone replaced your brain? Construction and validation of the Extended Mind Questionnaire (XMQ). PloS One, 13. doi: 10.1371/journal.pone.0202188.

7 Kim, K., Shin, D.-H., & Yoon, H. (2017). Information tailoring and framing in wearable health communication. Information Processing and Management, 53(2), 351-358. doi:10.1016/j.ipm.2016.11.005.

8 Bevelander, K. E., Smit, C. R., van Woudenberg, T. J., Buijs, L., Burk, W. J., & Buijzen, M. (2018). Youth's social network structures and peer influences: study protocol MyMovez project–Phase I. BMC Public Health, 18(1), 504.

9 Ajana, B. (2017). Digital health and the biopolitics of the quantified self. Digital Health, 3(2), 1-18. DOI: 10.1177/2055207616689509.

10 Wissinger, E. (2018). Blood, sweat, and tears: Navigating creepy versus cool in wearable biotech. Information, Communication & Society, 21(5), 779-785. DOI: 10.1080/1369118X.2018.1428657.

11 Banerjee, S., Hemphill, T., & Longstreet, P. (2018). Wearable devices and healthcare: Data sharing and privacy. The Information Society, 34(1), 49-57.

12 Wissinger, E. (2018). Blood, sweat, and tears: Navigating creepy versus cool in wearable biotech. Information, Communication & Society, 21(5), 779-785. DOI: 10.1080/1369118X.2018.1428657.

13 Dimitrov, (2016). Medical internet of things and big data in healthcare. Healthcare Information Research, 22(3), 156-163. Doi: https://doi.org/10.4258/hir.2016.22.3.156.

#5 VIRTUAL REALITY

Virtual reality simulates an environment that causes feelings of being there.

Just imagine you are a totally unexperienced skier and you are standing in the shoes of a professional skier. You ski down the slopes of Mont-Blanc. You put on 360-goggles that allow you magnificent views of the Alps all around you. When you ski over a bump, you feel it in your guts. Your feet and body move reflexively at full speed, touching swiftly upon the curves of the mountain. You become totally absorbed in the adventure, as if you are a true professional skier right there in the Alps. After the descent ... you take off your 360-goggles and are back in your living room, realising that you made your family laugh about the silly moves you made.

DEFINITION AND KEY FEATURES

The distinctive feature of virtual reality (VR) is its realistic experience. There are different ways to experience VR. People can use a desktop monitor to experience VR, for instance to simulate training scenarios. However, in this chapter we will discuss VR experienced by a virtual headset, a so-called Head Mounted Display (HMD), rendering a 360-degree image. Technically, an image of the real world is replaced by an image of a virtual world. Because you can view this virtual world with VR goggles in 360 degrees, the images change according to your head movements, therefore it looks and feels real, and you get absorbed in it. Due to its ability to create a more 'realistic' experience in an imaginary world in which people feel physically present, VR can be positioned as differing from other innovations.

REAL-TIME INTERACTION WITHIN THE VIRTUAL ENVIRONMENT

What makes VR unique for its users are the possibilities it offers in terms of interaction and control. The interaction dimension refers to the possibility for people to explore, navigate through, and participate in virtual environments. The control dimension points to the possibility for people to regulate real-time interactions within the virtual environment, to look around, and decide for themselves what, when, where and how often to look at something, and whether to pick up things with the controllers. Ironically, this means less control over the outcome of the interaction.

In 3D-movie theatres, spectators can freely move through a 360 movie. Film-makers may wonder how spectators will digest the narrative of the movie, possibly harming their comprehension of how a story unfolds. On the other hand, this offers creators much more opportunities to think of challenging ways to draw the attention of the public.

VIRTUAL REALITY IN PRACTICE

In the beginning, VR was only interesting for niches and not for the public in general, because VR devices were very expensive and impractical. The software also required heavy-duty computers to run smoothly. Nowadays VR is available for anyone, using inexpensive devices such as Google Cardboard and cheap goggles in combination with smartphones, and a less demanding and affordable computer. The offer of 360-videos on YouTube is rising. Several games are being developed for VR devices at a rapid pace.

HEALTHCARE HAS EMBRACED VR

VR was applied first as an innovative instrument in education, healthcare, recruitment, and conferences, and later in marketing such as in the tourism industry. Because VR is a unique medium, new types of content are being developed, tailor-made for VR. The opportunities for VR within learning/training environments are vast. Education establishments use VR to engage their students. Instead of explaining stories or scenarios, students can experience them in VR. For instance, when students have to learn how to behave in a customer friendly way, they can practise these skills in VR with avatars as customers. And VR is used for the physical and mental training of pilots and engineers. Healthcare has already embraced VR for decades. VR helps doctors to visualise operational procedures by mimicking realistic medical training experiences and it helps people to cure anxiety disorders such as a fear of spiders, heights, and public speaking. The recruitment business uses VR to assess whether candidates are suited for jobs by confronting them with typical virtual work situations to see how they react. Conference meetings with participants from all over the world take place in VR, with the participants being represented by avatars in the same virtual room, sitting at the same virtual table.

VR GOGGLES ARE NOT COMMONPLACE YET

For many innovations, marketing is always the precursor. However, in VR, marketing is somewhat lurking behind. Most companies are still in a waiting mode and want to be sure that VR can be used as an efficient marketing tool. A consideration for marketers is the high costs involved in making VR campaigns and the insecure return on investment. In theory, VR may bring people in touch with brands in an original way, but the question is 'how?' VR has already been used in retail, in real estate to show properties, and in the car industry to give product demonstrations and to intensify story telling. In the travelling branch, VR allows you to experience your holiday before you book it, because the inside and outside views of the hotel rooms give you the feeling that you have already reached and are enjoying your holiday destination. The popularity of VR in marketing is on the rise as communication campaigns using VR win awards in prestigious contests such as the annual Digital Communication Awards (DCA) and Cannes Lions Innovations Conference.

VR gradually develops from a medium where people isolate themselves by putting on their VR goggles, towards a medium in which people share content and socially interact with each other, such as in multiplayer VR games and social VR platforms, for example Second Life. How VR can have a profound impact on the lives of people who choose to live in a VR world is described in the following contribution from Donna Davis.

SOCIAL VIRTUAL REALITY – UNDERSTANDING THE POWER OF VIRTUAL PLACES AND BODIES FOR PEOPLE WITH DISABILITIES

By Donna Z. Davis
Assistant professor
School of Journalism and Communication
University of Oregon, USA

As VR technologies are increasingly being utilised for immersive storytelling, marketing, and entertainment, organisations are likewise attempting to identify how to best utilise these environments to build online communities. Although many people think of VR for gaming and entertainment, social virtual worlds also offer a vibrant and effective platform for building community, especially for globally dispersed populations or individuals who may be limited in mobility. Consider, for example, the potential of social virtual worlds for people with disabilities, who are often unable to work or be socially active in the physical world. Two features of social virtual worlds that make this especially effective emerge through the sense of presence. When individuals feel physically present and able to interact in and with a space, as well as being embodied through their avatar, which can also interact with other avatars, the sense of engagement and connection is also elevated.

A SOCIAL VIRTUAL WORLD

One example of this use of VR is the exploration of disability communities on 3D platforms that exist as screen-based virtual reality but are also important to the evolution of social virtual worlds optimised for headsets. Second Life (secondlife.com), a social virtual world that went online in 2004, is home to more than a half million active users worldwide. Among these "residents" are people with disabilities (PWD). These individuals can choose how to represent themselves in the virtual world, where a wheelchair-bound person can create an avatar body that may or may not include a wheelchair. In a virtual world, where most communication is text-based, a deaf person can communicate with all people, whereas in the physical world they have so often been left out of communities when sign language is not readily available and communication is difficult. In these worlds, their identity is tied to a body they choose and the actions they take; they have so often been marginalised in the physical world in a culture that does not understand or rejects these individuals and/or their appearance. Stories of a community of such individuals are documented in the film *Our Digital Selves*[1].

PARKINSON'S SUPPORT COMMUNITY

This example also has important implications for the future of health communication. Research consistently reveals a sense of safety, security, and a resulting willingness to share insights that they would often not share in any other setting, online or offline[2,3]. In a virtual world, individuals are able to build communities of support that healthcare providers may want to consider for reaching vulnerable and often inaccessible populations. Such is the case with a Parkinson's support community that has been meeting in the virtual world since 2011. This community was founded by an 84-year-old woman with Parkinson's disease who immediately felt benefits through the playful social activities she was able to enjoy in the virtual world. The story of Fran Serenade (as she is known in Second Life) has been well documented[4]. As telehealth continues to experience rapid growth and adoption, social virtual worlds provide a viable and eminently more engaging alternative to the typical webcam or text platforms currently utilised. Other examples of the sense of presence in VR as used in healthcare can be seen in a 2018 commercial showing the power of the mind for an amputee learning to walk with a prosthetic[5]. Similarly, VR is being used very effectively in working with burn victims and physical therapy.

In sum, a VR environment where we can create an identity built on our own unique strengths and creativity, perhaps the ideals of "beauty" and what is "normal", can begin to evolve in a way that honours the ability of many forms rather than isolating and reinforcing outdated ideals of ability and disability.

Marnix van Gisbergen shines a light on how to implement VR in organisations by writing ten recommendations.

HOW TO IMPLEMENT VR IN ORGANISATIONS: 10 RECOMMENDATIONS

By Marnix S. van Gisbergen
Professor Digital Media Concepts
Breda University of Applied Sciences

So let us say you are enthusiastic about VR. How to start? How to write a good briefing for a VR production? Based on the aforementioned developments and the current state of VR, there are ten recommendations to take into account when producing VR content.

First, do not focus on the benefit of VR as a solitary medium. Immediately ask the question what is the benefit or goal, compared to other media out there (and often as such ask the question which part of the media budget will you take to create VR and at the expense of what?).

As such, the *second* recommendation is to take into account the current key role of VR and that is to create an immersive experience. So you should be able to write down the kind of experience you want to create.

Third, VR content creation requires a production choice: whether to create a VR 360° recorded environment or a Computer Generated (CG) VR environment (and more often a combination of both).

Fourth, consider whether you need all four VR technology dimensions: Sensory, Location, Interaction and Control (manipulation).

Fifth, when aimed at creating mainly 360° VR recordings, take into account the five P dimensions: Presence, Perspective, Proximity, Point of View and Place[6]. VR has an added value when a feeling of being there (presence) is created. An engaging presence is created by means of making use of

Perspective (the fact that you need to look up, down and around you); through Proximity (being able to stand very close to a person, object or situation); by using a unique Point of view (for instance the character perspective as in games), and by means of taking Place into account. This means on the one hand taking into account suitable places for VR perspectives (such as a bed or on a chair) and on the other hand taking into account the fact that the medium requires attention and effort and that it should be used preferably in the same perspective as the 360 recording (e.g., sitting when recorded in a sitting position).

This immediately points towards a *sixth* recommendation, and that is to aim for a situation or context of an active audience. The audience needs to put on a head mounted device, needs to move around and interact with an environment. VR is less suitable for replacing an effortless medium usage context, such as watching lazy television on the couch.

In addition, an aligned *seventh* recommendation is to make sure that there is more VR content available than just your small 360° video production. The reward of putting on a head mounted VR device needs to be high enough by providing enough content.

The *eighth* recommendation is to take into account all of the (previously mentioned) five adoption dimensions from the start. A pre-selection of the channel (which kind of main VR device) and how to connect the content with the audience (how to share the content), for instance, will help to create more effective VR content. A related question that pops up, as long as AR and VR media are not yet integrated, is whether to use VR or AR technology. There are many reasons to pick one or the other. See also the chapter about AR.

Hence, the *ninth* recommendation is to be aware of the main reason to choose AR. The key benefit of AR over VR Is the possibility to interact with the 'real', non-mediated environment. The AR production must specify a key benefit of 'user environment interaction' by means of AR technologies.

Finally, *number ten*: for now it is important to take into account the experience of the audience. There are many out there that have no or little experience with VR. Consequently, they will show 'abnormal VR behaviour', for instance by spending more time and being more curious inside VR worlds then they will be in the future. A small trick is to provide them with more time to experience the VR world before the real VR experience starts.

How do people process information brought to them in 360° videos? The answer will strongly depend on the goal that VR is used for. When gamers are playing a VR racing game, they will focus on the race and not on the ads that are passing by on virtual billboards. Their attention is devoted to the VR game, and there is no motivation for processing in-game advertising. When students have to practise their first day on a job, using a VR simulation game, they will be much more likely to attend to – and elaborate on – the full content of the VR experience. Considering the processing of information[7], on the one hand, the chance that people will actively process any information that is provided in VR is facilitated by the facts that VR goggles exclude stimuli from the outside world and users choose to undergo the VR experience. On the other hand, a VR experience might be so overwhelming that it is detrimental to effective information processing.

VIRTUAL STORYTELLING IN IMMERSIVE JOURNALISM

Most academic research into VR is on the rise in several disciplines. Research is often tied to the effectiveness of specific VR cases. Following Fogg and other scholars, these cases are studied in three ways[8,9]. First, as an object, wherein the effects of VR as a new technology on human users can be discussed and investigated, for instance as virtual storytelling in immersive journalism[10]. When people can have a look in a VR refugee camp, this gives them the chance to actually experience the news. Sometimes they are present in the story as an avatar, a 3D representation of themselves. A viable research question is: 'what do these 360-degree news stories add to traditional 2D videos?'[11] Scientific research shows that 360-degree video is evaluated higher in terms of presence, enjoyment, and credibility, while the processing of the video is not disturbed. Although 360-degree journalism research is still in its infancy, there are indications that this form of news reporting has the potential to involve audiences in news events as never before. Considering the VR film industry, it is interesting that viewers enjoy a VR film regardless of the point of view (POV) taken by the audience, although an 'actor' POV in the VR movie seems to enhance the feelings of presence compared to an 'observer' POV[12].

VIRTUAL REALITY EXPOSURE THERAPY

Second, scientists study VR as an application, enlarging peoples' beliefs in their self-efficacy and their ability to achieve goals, wherein we consider VR applications in areas such as health, education, and marketing. VR therapy is successful, for instance, in battling social anxieties such as speaking before an audience[13]. People with speech anxiety become used to speaking before an audience by gradually exposing themselves to virtual crowds, differing in size and attentiveness. Virtual Reality Exposure Therapy (VRET) is just as effective as Cognitive Behaviour Therapy (CBT) in treating anxiety disorders such as speech anxiety[14]. It is cost efficient, because it involves less money than organising a real audience as in CBT. People can practise with the VR app at home; it allows for more control over the environment and it is more efficient in isolating feared components.

Combining artificial intelligence and artificial life techniques with those of virtual environments enables to produce intelligent virtual environments. A 'virtual tutor' may support trainees in a similar manner as human instructors do by providing personalised feedback on the basis of their reactions[15], such as posture, gestures and emotions. For instance, decision making under various levels of stress, is useful for professionals in the public domain[16]. Virtual reality enables people to learn how to perform certain tasks by repeatedly executing them in a virtual reality environment.

VR EXPERIMENTS OFFER NEAR-PERFECT EXPERIMENTAL CONTROL

Third, virtual reality enables scientists to execute ecologically realistic experiments in which experimental control is near-perfect. For instance, several studies into the effects of location-based advertising have used VR lab experiments in which a virtual supermarket simulated a real supermarket. The virtual surroundings were systematically manipulated, creating (non) tailored conditions, firing messages on the smartphones of consumers while they were shopping in the virtual supermarket[17]. As another example, VR has been used study the interpersonal distance maintained between participants and virtual humans in a virtual world[18].

A common problem with research using VR is that the effects are generally shown only after repeated exposure to the VR experience. For instance, the effectiveness of an anti-speech anxiety app will manifest only after several trials. Time and logistics do not always permit this. Furthermore, participants with little or no experience with VR will show atypical VR behaviour, compared with those who have more experience with VR. They are more curious about, and explorative with, the VR experiences caused by the typical WOW effect that first-timers experience, possibly leading to exaggerated expectations of the usefulness of VR.

Is VR a hype? The answer is: 'No'. The occurrence of VR is already beyond the hype. We may question what the impact of VR will be on our lives. How will VR change our processing of information? Although critical remarks can be made about the future role of VR, and its added value compared to other media (see contribution of Marnix van Gisbergen in the chapter: This is the future), we believe that VR will have a strong impact on several disciplines in the future, such as journalism, health care, education, and eventually marketing.

NUMEROUS POSSIBILITIES FOR THE USAGE OF VIRTUAL REALITY

Virtual reality will be used in daily situations. For instance, if there's one place where you really want to escape to a different reality, it's the doctor's waiting room. Imagine being transported in VR to a yoga retreat, a horse pasture, a beautiful sunset, or a lily pond, to a location of your choice.

Virtual reality will enhance student learning and engagement. VR can transform the way educational content is delivered; it creates a virtual world and allows users to interact with it. Being immersed may motivate students to fully understand what they have learned. The reality in VR may be that students all over the world unite in virtual classrooms with only the best teachers.

Disabled children may make virtual outings to places they can otherwise never visit because they are too far away or because these places are too costly to visit. People can make virtual tours in museums abroad. The possibilities are simply endless.

INTEGRATION OF TASTE AND SMELL IN VR EXPERIENCES

VR experiences will become even more realistic because of technological developments. Taste and smell will be integrated into VR experiences, as well as wind, mist, water, vibrations, sounds, and motions. These advances seem important for several disciplines such as the VR game industry and trauma treatment, where the inclusion of smell and taste would be likely to boost immersion and presence in VR scenarios tremendously. VR multiplayer games will further develop and overcome the solistic nature of VR. New techniques will enable the VR game industry to make high-level content.

VR AND LOCATION-BASED ADVERTISING

However, one should also be cautious about deciding which types of virtual worlds should be created. For instance, a virtual supermarket is very interesting for researching phenomena such as location-based advertising, where customers receive ads on their smartphones in predefined areas of interest, such as in front of certain shelves. However, is it a good idea to craft virtual supermarkets in order to facilitate online shopping? For most people, shopping is not the highlight of the day, they would rather skip it. Why would a virtual supermarket have more benefits for customers than a supermarket in 2d? So the opportunities are endless indeed, but they should be carefully scrutinised in order to avoid waste of money.

COOPERATION BETWEEN SCIENTISTS AND PROFESSIONALS IN THE FIELD

We expect intensive cooperation between scientists and professionals in the field, which will be profitable for both parties. In fact, they need each other. Scientists need VR content, to be able to do their research on VR. Professionals in organisations need scientifically based research in order to substantiate their claims about the effectiveness of VR and to prevent them spending their limited resources on hopeless VR ventures. Measurement means knowledge for this new medium. For instance, like game designers, moviemakers also have to start from scratch when making VR productions. Scientific research provides them with crucial insights into how people move around in a virtual world and make their choices, how moviemakers can attract their attention for the plot, and what a storyline in VR should look like.

We need to understand the added value of the experience provided by VR and comprehend how the specific combinations of technologies can be used. If we succeed in doing this, we can more effectively decide how to apply multimedia, cross-media, and transmedia strategies. For now it seems that VR can only be a fruitful innovation when it is properly combined with digital (transmedia) storytelling strategies and with game technology insights.

GOOD OR BAD

Societies' major concern about VR is whether the total immersion of people in virtual worlds is a good or a bad thing. On the one hand, a virtual world might support people who want to get rid of their social anxieties, or who want to become more social, identifying with their avatar, and playing different roles. It is possibly a good thing when somebody who is unhappy can find happiness in a virtual world. On the other hand, people may become so deeply involved in their virtual world and their alter ego, that they do not want to live in reality anymore and want to keep on living in their dream world. This may possibly be because they do not feel appreciated in the real world through a disability, their social background, age, weight, or anxiety. In a virtual world they can display their 'real' self, entertain, and build relationships that are impossible in real life[19]. From a societal POV, it may not be desirable for people to become totally absorbed in their virtual worlds because this devaluates peoples' participation in society. They might become addicted to the virtual world that they create for themselves, such as in Second Life. In order to minimise the chances of total isolation, VR[20] should focus more on facilitating relations between people. Therefore, companies are developing all sorts of applications adding social aspects to VR.

BEING IN CONTROL IS AN ILLUSION

VR does seem to be a democratic innovation. People seem to be more in control when they enter a virtual world as they can move about in any direction they like, but this control is only an appearance. For instance, when viewing a VR movie, people will have the feeling that they can move about in any direction they like. However, the director of a VR movie has crafted the options for different scenarios from which the viewer can choose. So the apparent freedom of choice for viewers is relative.

Concluding, when VR is an accessible medium for all people around the world, one might wonder how we can use it to sustain healthy and happy citizens in safe, supportive, and meaningful ways, especially in marginalised communities where individuals have long been silenced. To answer the more ethical question of whether the technology of VR can improve life[21], we ask you to draw the conclusion yourself. In our opinion, the answer is: 'yes', when it is used in a proper way.

"Most things don't work in VR. If you show me 20 ideas, I'll say 19 of them would be better in another medium."

Jeremy Bailenson, head of Stanford University's Virtual Reality Lab.

CLASSIFICATION

★★★★★ ★★★★★ ★★★★★ ★★★★★ ★★★★★

References and notes

1   Retrieved from: https://youtu.be/GQwo2-meoW4.

2   Davis, D. & Calitz, W. (2014). Finding virtual support: The evolution of healthcare support groups from offline to virtual worlds. Journal of Virtual Worlds Research, 7(3). Available at https://journals.tdl.org/jvwr/index.php/jvwr/article/view/7068/6352.

3   Zielke, M., Roome, T. & Krueger, A. (2009). A composite adult learning model for virtual world residents with disabilities: A case study of the Virtual Ability Second Life® Island. Journal for Virtual Worlds Research 2(1). 3-21.

4   Retrieived from: https://www.wired.com/2017/02/first-they-got-sick-then-they-moved-into-a-virtual-utopia/

5   Retrieved from: https://www.youtube.com/watch?v=lGCP154Ojy8.

6   Syrett, H., Calvi, L., & van Gisbergen, M. (2016, June). The oculus rift film experience: a case study on understanding films in a head mounted display. In: International Conference on Intelligent Technologies for Interactive Entertainment (pp. 197-208). Springer, Cham.

7   Buijzen, M., Van Reijmersdal, E.A., & Owen, L.H. (2010). Introducing the PCMC model: An investigative framework for young people's processing of commercial media content. Communication Theory, 20, 427-450.

8   Fogg, B. J., Cuellar, G., & Danielson, D. (2009). Motivating, influencing, and persuading users. In J. Jacko & A. Sears (Eds.), The human-computer interaction handbook: Fundamentals, evolving technologies and emerging applications (pp. 133-147). Hillsdale, NJ: Erlbaum.

9   Fox, J., Arena, D., & Bailenson, J. N. (2009). Virtual reality: A survival guide for the social scientist. Journal of Media Psychology, 21(3), 95-113.

10 De La Peña, N., et al. (2010) Immersive journalism: Immersive virtual reality for the first-person experience of news. Presence, 19(4), 291-301.

11 Vettehen, P. H., Wiltink, D., Huiskamp, M., Schaap, G., & Ketelaar, P. (2019). Taking the full view: How viewers respond to 360-degree video news. Computers in Human Behavior, 91, 24-32.

12 Van den Boom, A. A., Stupar-Rutenfrans, S., Bastiaens, O. S., & van Gisbergen, M. S. (2015). Observe or participate: The effect of point-of-view on presence and enjoyment in 360 degree movies for head mounted displays. In AmI (Workshops/Posters).

13 Anderson, P., Rothbaum, B. O. & Hodges, L. F. (2003). Virtual reality exposure in the treatment of social anxiety. Cognitive and Behavioral Practice, 10(3). 240-247. doi: 10.1016/S1077-7229(03)80036-6.

14 Klinger, E., Bouchard, S., Légeron, P., Roy, S., Lauer, F., Chemin, I., & Nugues, P. (2005). Virtual reality therapy versus cognitive behavior therapy for social phobia: A preliminary controlled study. Cyberpsychology & behavior, 8(1), 76-88.

15 Retrieved from: https://youtu.be/ejczMs6b1Q4.

16 Bosse, T., Man, J. D., & Gerritsen, C. (2014, August). Agent-based simulation as a tool for the design of a virtual training environment. In Proceedings of the 2014 IEEE/WIC/ACM International Joint Conferences on Web Intelligence (WI) and Intelligent Agent Technologies (IAT)-Volume 03 (pp. 40-47). IEEE Computer Society.

17 Ketelaar, P. E., Bernritter, S. F., van't Riet, J., Hühn, A. E., van Woudenberg, T. J., Müller, B. C., & Janssen, L. (2017). Disentangling location-based advertising: the effects of location congruency and medium type on consumers' ad attention and brand choice. International Journal of Advertising, 36(2), 356-367.

18 Bailenson, J. N., Blascovich, J., Beall, A. C., & Loomis, J. M. (2003). Interpersonal distance in immersive virtual environments. Personality and Social Psychology Bulletin, 29(7), 819-833.

19 Zielke, A., Roome, C., & Krueger, A. B. (2009). A composite adult learning model for virtual world residents with disabilities: A case study of the virtual ability second life ® island. Journal of Virtual Worlds Research 2 (1).

20 Lievrouw, L. A. (2012). The next decade in internet time: Ways ahead for new media studies. Information. Communication & Society, 15(5), 616-638.

21 Riva, G., Banos, R. M., Botella, C., Wiederhold, B. K., & Gaggioli, A. (2012). Positive technology: using interactive technologies to promote positive functioning. Cyberpsychology, Behavior, and Social Networking, 15(2), 69-77.

#6 AUGMENTED REALITY

Augmented reality is the adding of a computer-generated layer to the perception of reality. The added layer and reality form a coherent image.

After a long day of work at the office, you are at the glass bus stop waiting to go home. It is already getting dark and the cold wind makes you shiver. Looking through the glass, you see that suddenly the undead are arising, fortunately for you at a fair distance. However, the zombies start running towards you like crazy and in response you can only freeze. Is this the start of a widespread rise of zombies hostile to human life, engaging in a fierce full assault on civilisation? Or just an augmented reality campaign for the new movie about the apocalyptic destruction of the world by zombies?

DEFINITION AND KEY FEATURES

Augmented reality (AR) can simply be understood with selfie lenses on apps such as Snapchat or Instagram. These apps capture your face in real-time images or video and add layers to them using AR technology. The goal of AR is to strengthen our experience or understanding[1], enhancing our current view of the physical or real world. The days that AR was only limited to sci-fi novels and movies are gone. Today, all smartphone and tablet users can enjoy this technology, and several AR applications and fully-featured web browsers having the ability to display AR content are available at a nominal cost. AR applications can be accessed by a variety of devices such as smartphones, tablets, goggles such as the HoloLens, interactive screens in shopping centres, or the glass window of a bus stop. AR is not only used in gaming but in various fields such as the military, medical research, education, safety, art, and architecture.

KEY FEATURES: THE REALITY-VIRTUALITY SPECTRUM

Reality-simulating innovations change our perception of reality by adding layers with images, text, and even sound. They can even fully replace it with a virtual world. Although there are other taxonomies of reality[2], the common terms in practice as well as science that are used to describe the organising principle of the 'reality-virtuality spectrum' are virtual reality (VR), AR, and mixed reality. However, there is some confusion, especially about the term 'mixed reality'. Commercial parties claim the term 'mixed reality' for applications that they have invented, so this deserves some clarification. Augmented reality offers a live view of the real world around us, parts of which are 'augmented' by computer-generated visual information[3]. This technology differs from VR in that the main component of AR is reality. VR stands for 'virtuality', a totally virtual world.

AR IS A FORM OF MIXED REALITY

Augmented reality is situated more on the left-hand side of the reality-virtuality spectrum as its main component is reality. The computer-generated added layer is a secondary component, augmenting the reality. Augmented reality can provide a direct or indirect live view of the augmented environment[4]. Nowadays, three types of AR can be distinguished. The first makes use of markers such as QR-codes, and subsequently augments reality. The second makes use of location, for instance, a visitor to a museum pointing his AR device at a painting, accessing a two-dimensional layer with information about the history of the painting. Or there are apps that allow their users to see their products in 3D in a real-life environment. The third projects images onto objects, enabling interaction; for instance, a keyboard on your arm or other surface that you can actually type on.

Moving to the right side of the reality-virtuality spectrum, we gradually approach the virtual world. In augmented virtuality (AV), you see a virtual world, which is augmented with images of objects in the real world (i.e. walking with goggles in a virtual world, being warned by an image of your room when you almost bump into physical objects). Virtual reality on the right side of the spectrum totally excludes reality, presenting the viewer with a virtual world in which objects are not real. Read all about VR in a separate chapter on this subject. All applications in between reality and virtuality are mixed forms of the real and virtual world, so in this definition, AR is always a form of mixed reality.

AUGMENTED REALITY IN PRACTICE

In their first years, PC, smartphone and tablet applications for AR focused on games for pleasure and engagement purposes. The breakthrough for AR in gaming, enabling the broader public to engage with AR, was Pokémon GO. Pokémon GO is an interactive, mobile game that uses your phone's GPS data and clock to show Pokémon creatures hidden near your current, physical location. The Pokémon that appear on the screen in the app can be captured. When the game became very popular, thousands of people walked the streets looking for monsters, which looked very surrealistic for those not knowing the game. But nowadays, AR is used in a much broader way and new applications keep turning up. There lies a growth potential for the application of AR in domains such as healthcare, the military, the automotive industry, engineering, the tourist industry, and marketing.

APPLYING AR

In the medical world, students use machine-learning based AR for improved surgical scene understanding[5]. The risk of an actual surgery is reduced by giving the surgeon improved sensory perception. For instance, the ability to image the brain in 3D on top of the patient's actual anatomy is helpful for the surgeon. Surgeons can rapidly plan procedures before making the first cut. Navigation applications are probably the most natural fit of AR with our everyday lives. Using the smartphone's camera in combination with the GPS, users see the selected route over the live view of what is in front of the car, which makes it easier to get from A to B. Also, mechanics can see superimposed imagery and information in their actual line of sight, which makes repairing an engine a lot easier. Complex procedural repairs can be broken down into a series of simple steps.

ENRICHING CONSUMER EXPERIENCE

Organisations are increasingly challenged to provide compelling customer experiences. AR can help with that. There are, for instance, a number of applications for AR in the sightseeing and tourism industries. Using a smartphone equipped with a camera, tourists can walk through historic sites and see facts and figures presented as an overlay on their live screens. These applications use GPS and image recognition technology to look up data from an online database. In addition to information about a historic site, applications exist that look back in history and show how the location looked 10, 50, or even 100 years ago.

In the last few years, several AR apps have been released to augment the shopping experience, imitate traditional shopping, enrich the consumer experience, and give outdoors a renewed fun-factor. However, AR apps also become popular for in-house purposes. Because the experience that AR offers in the home environment comes so close to traditional shopping, the risks that usually accompany online buying at home are lowered[6]. AR apps allow consumers to interact with brands in new and interactive ways. It enables people to change their surroundings and their looks by overlaying virtual products in their house and on their bodies and faces. Some examples are: visualising products in your own home to imagine what it feels like owning the product or experiencing the service before actually purchasing it; scanning your room with your smartphone and virtually painting it in any colour you like; and redecorating your room by placing virtual furniture in it and viewing them from different angles. You can also virtually try on make-up in real-time.

In his contribution in the next paragraph, Pascal Cramer underscores the importance of a long incubation period when using AR in a proper way and the important role of science.

REFLECTING ON AUGMENTED REALITY

By Pascal Cramer
Co-founder & VR developer
VR Lab Nijmegen

As AR creates brand awareness and boosts customer engagement in an exciting way, companies are eager to jump on the bandwagon to incorporate AR and apply it across their business and communication channels. Through my experience as a developer, I know that many companies have come to us with questions about what ROI they should expect from deploying AR in their business. As with any new medium or technology, there seems to be a lot of confusion around what AR can and cannot do. There is a long incubation period for organisations as well as individuals using AR in a proper way. Organisations sometimes want to move faster towards a new reality. They do not wish to participate in a rat race and therefore develop technology in a trial and error fashion, giving AR a bad name. Just like consumers, they also have to get used to it. New business models have to be developed, and we all have to learn how to engage people with relevant information conveyed through AR. Companies are sometimes too technologically driven. They want to use the available technology because the competitor is using it too, like the hype to create an app for almost everything. Often I have to refer organisations to other agencies because I know that new reality such as AR will not provide the coveted solution to their communication problem. It is easy to make nice AR applications, but are they useful for the intended users, and do they provide follow-up solutions in a timely way?

COOPERATING WITH SCIENTISTS

For companies and organisations launching programs with AR, knowledge about how consumers process AR-generated information is key. In order to gain relevant insights into consumer behaviour and the development and testing of AR, the role of science (e.g. psychology and human-computer interaction) is paramount. During our in-house development of several AR applications, we incorporated existing scientific knowledge on human behaviour and perception in order to deliver simulations that the user could interact with in a natural way. And science can benefit from the experiences in the development and usages of our products. On the one hand, information exchange with scientists is more fluent than ever, rendering new insights 'in close harmony'. On the other hand, technological change comes about fast, making it difficult for scientists to keep track with these changes. Our cooperation is also beneficial for our business, as our customers want 'proof of the pudding' – does our AR solution achieve the goals it was designed for?

THE HARDWARE WILL BLEND

Augmented reality is exciting new technology, which will probably develop in ways we cannot even imagine yet. However, a threat to the AR business is that the development of platforms and hardware is under the control of commercial parties. That development could backfire on the applicability of many innovations that are described in this book. As a worst-case scenario, people have their AR application online all day, enabling parties to register their meetings and whereabouts all day and in real-time. Then, you do not only give up your data, but also your life!

On reflection, I foresee a nice future, especially for the combination of virtual and augmented reality. Hardware will blend and ultimately become a wearable device accommodating them all, in glasses and eventually in a contact lens. Also, communication will seamlessly take place because it happens independently from platforms. I think that the border between reality and fiction will blur even further, but is that a blessing or a threat to society?

A SCIENTIFIC PERSPECTIVE

Augmented reality apps add a new dimension to the user experience, by overlaying our surroundings with virtual products in real-time. However, research into the effects of AR apps on the outcomes of persuasion, and the underlying processes that might explain these effects, is still in its infancy.

FUNCTIONS OF AR

Following the functional triad model[7], technological innovations can play the role of tool, medium, and social actor in the perception of its users. AR can be seen as a tool to make certain actions or tasks more feasible, enlarging the self-efficacy of people. For instance, a virtual layer can make it easier for people to find the road, or to place augmented furniture in their room or garden. As a medium, it sends information to its users, for instance when augmenting user experience by storytelling[8] and by advertising. AR can be treated as a social actor when it assumes the role of a coach or an adversary in the form of an avatar enabling social relations, for instance, an AR app that coaches people with a cognitive deficit when performing certain tasks. These people perform their tasks better and experience them as more pleasant[9]. In the Pokémon GO game, AR also assumes the role of social actor, because users can entertain para-social relations, for instance when identifying with a role model.

FLUENCY THEORY

The effect of AR on consumers' information processing is dependent on how it is used. For instance, when playing Pokémon GO, a certain amount of attention and motivation are needed to activate the app on a smartphone or tablet. However, while playing the game, processing might be on an unconscious level. It will be on a more conscious level when the information in the layer is highly relevant and takes up energy to digest. The AR game Pokémon GO might be played on a subconscious level. The success of the game can be explained by the fluency theory[10], which says that fluent, easily interpretable content can be easily digested, leading to favourable thoughts about the experience and the app. The better the AR experience is integrated into reality, the easier the experience of the consumers and the more they will like it. People flocked together to fully experience the Pokémon GO app and even experienced a stronger tie with each other during and after playing the game.

FEELINGS OF FLOW

A related concept is flow[11], which means the mental state of operation in which a person performing an activity is fully immersed in a feeling of energised focus, full involvement, and enjoyment in the process of the activity. The higher the feelings of flow, the more positive the attitude towards the AR app. However, flow can also negatively impact cognitive processing. An intense AR experience might provide for flow, but may also deplete cognitive resources[12], leaving no energy to process the information in the AR layers. To help motivate people to become involved in sport, the Proteus effect[13] might appear in the context of AR. This means that when you see an avatar of yourself engaging in sport, the chances are higher that you will exercise yourself. The effect seems even stronger than incentives or punishments.

PRESENCE AND PERSONALISATION

When AR is used for commercial purposes, an experiment[14] has shown that AR-branded apps have positive persuasive outcomes such as the intention to buy a product. These positive effects can be explained by the concepts of presence and personalisation. People feel that the virtual objects are experienced as actual objects in their physical environment, and are highly personalised because of their real-time character. However, when consumers have never experienced an AR app, they might feel that the app is coming too close to their physical world, increasing feelings of intrusiveness, which is an undesirable feeling because it negatively impedes brand evaluations and buying behaviour.

As in real life, one has to be aware of too many augmented cues as they may cause feelings of cognitive overload, counteracting information processing, rendering less resources for other tasks[15]. It seems safe to conclude that AR can be implemented to influence behaviour as well as attitudes. When used well, AR may facilitate information processing, leading to a low depletion of cognitive resources.

FUTURE AND ETHICS

The future of innovations is largely determined by the quality of the experience of using them. When AR is beyond the level of 'fun, sexy, and new', it can mostly be used for positive communication. AR can be used to make people healthier (i.e. offering them healthy alternatives to snack foods on their shopping lists), happier (i.e. creating avatar friends to combat loneliness), and better informed (i.e. making news more personal by adding layers with tailor-made information). Unfortunately, existing research into AR offers little guidance to managers on how to successfully deploy AR as an enabler of omnichannel experiences across the customer journey.

A LACK OF CONTENT

An important consideration is that AR is not yet commonplace in the market. The most important reason is a lack of content. Obviously, the development of suitable AR content is expensive. AR platforms come and go and people are still not used to AR. AR software designers should ensure that AR software is practical, user friendly, easy to learn, well organised and attractive in order to optimise usage.

EXTENSION OF MAN

How about the future of AR? First, the integration of AR with social media will become bigger, contributing to the relational internet, because it will make more use of media like Snapchat and Instagram, using existing pictures and videos. Imagine waking up and being able to see what the time is, what the weather will be, and what the news is, without having to look on your smartphone. This is not science fiction but something of the near future. Second, augmented reality applications may further advance when incorporating AI into it such as speech recognition, or computer vision. AI would allow AR to interact with physical environments by incorporating real world object tagging. Finally, AR will make further use of gamification principles and how to intrinsically motivate people. People are more engaged and motivated when they feel that their input has a goal (purpose), offers a challenge (mastery) and that they are in control (autonomy).

The vision of technological determinist McLuhan on technology as an extension of man fits the occurrence and further development of AR like a glove. AR broadens the senses, enlarges the limbs of people, and allows the perception of stimuli that we are not able to perceive.

AR USERS IN THE DRIVERS' SEAT

AR will make more use of artificial intelligence when algorithms enable AR applications to further tailor layered information in real-time, on the demand of the users. This raises concerns about data usage. For instance, AR apps such as the innocent Pokémon GO that use and store the location of the device. One could debate that consumers should regain control of how their personal data are used, and be attentive to the risks involved[16]. As with other innovations, it will be important that organisations that use AR apps put AR users in the drivers' seat and make use of their data as transparently as possible[17]. Although much AR content is available for everybody, one may wonder if it will become exclusively for the happy few who can afford it, or only those who own the right hardware, thus enlarging the divide between the rich and the poor.

As with VR, the public debate may focus on the permeable border between fiction and reality, how we want to educate our children about what is real and virtual and how targeting in AR takes place[18]. A question for the future is: how far will we go in making interfaces invisible and making the virtual world more realistic?

★★★★★   ★★★★★   ★★★★★   ★★★★★   ★★★★★

References and notes

1   Berryman, D. R. (2012). Augmented reality: A review. Medical Reference Services Quarterly, 31(2), 212-218. http://dx.doi.org/10.1080/02763869.2012.670604.

2   Mann, S., Furness, T., Yuan, Y., Iorio, J., & Wang, Z. (2018). All reality: Virtual, augmented, mixed (x), mediated (x, y), and multimediated reality. arXiv preprint arXiv:1804.08386.

3   Carmigniani, J., Furht, B., Anisetti, M., Ceravolo, P., Damiani, E., & Ivkovic, M. (2011). Augmented reality technologies, systems and applications. Multimedia Tools and Applications, 51(1), 341-377.

4   Ruggiero, L. (2018). A review of augmented reality applications for building evacuation. arXiv preprint arXiv:1804.04186.

5   Pauly, O., Diotte, B., Fallavollita, P., Weidert, S., Euler, E., & Navab, N. (2015). Machine learning-based augmented reality for improved surgical scene understanding. Computerized Medical Imaging and Graphics, 41, 55-60.

6   Poushneh, A., & Vasquez-Parraga, A. (2017). Discernible impact of augmented reality on retail customers' experience, satisfaction and willingness to buy. Journal of Retailing and Consumer Services, 34, 229-234. DOI: j.jretconser.2016.10.005.

7   Fogg, B. J. (1999). Persuasive technologies. Communications of the ACM, 42(5), 27-29.

8   Liarokapis, F. and Anderson, E. F., 2010. Using Augmented Reality as a Medium to Assist Teaching in Higher Education. In: Eurographics 2010, 2010, Norrköping, Sweden, 9 – 16.

9   Chang, Y. J., Kang, Y. S., & Huang, P. C. (2013). An augmented reality (AR)-based vocational task prompting system for people with cognitive impairments. Research in Developmental Disabilities, 34(10), 3049-3056.

10   Andrews, M., van Leeuwen, M. L., & van Baaren, R. B. (2013). Hidden persuasion. 33 psychological influence techniques in advertising.

11   Csikszentmihalyi, M. (2013). Flow: The psychology of happiness. Random House.

12   Buijzen, M., Van Reijmersdal, E. A., & Owen, L. H. (2010). Introducing the PCMC model: An investigative framework for young people's processing of commercialized media content. Communication Theory, 20(4), 427-450.

13   Yee, N., & Bailenson, J. (2007). The Proteus effect: The effect of transformed self-representation on behavior. Human Communication Research, 33(3), 271-290.

14   Smink, A. R., Reijmersdal, E. A van, Noort, G. van & Neijens, P. C. (2018). When virtuality becomes reality: underlying processes that explain persuasive consequences of augmented reality apps. Under review.

15   Akçayır, M., Akçayır, G., Pekta , H. M., & Ocak, M. A. (2016). Augmented reality in science laboratories: The effects of augmented reality on university students' laboratory skills and attitudes toward science laboratories. Computers in Human Behavior, 57, 334-342. doi: 10.1016/j.chb.2015.12.054.

16   Lievrouw, L. A. (2012). The next decade in internet time: Ways ahead for new media studies. Information, Communication & Society, 15(5), 616-638. doi:10.1080/1369118X.2012.675691.

17   Smit, E. G., Van Noort, G., & Voorveld, H. A. (2014). Understanding online behavioural advertising: User knowledge, privacy concerns and online coping behaviour in Europe. Computers in Human Behavior, 32, 15-22. DOI: 10.1016/j.chb.2013.11.00.

18   Van Reijmersdal, E. A., Rozendaal, E., Smink, N., Van Noort, G., & Buijzen, M. (2017). Processes and effects of targeted online advertising among children. International Journal of Advertising, 36(3), 396-414. Doi: 10.1080/02650487.2016.1196904.

#7 SERIOUS GAMING

Serious games are games that do not have entertainment as their primary goal, but the transfer of argumentation, ideas, and perceptions with regard to serious topics. Several larger purposes can, for example, be training, awareness, or marketing. A serious game is often digital, but this is not necessarily the case.

A bomb explodes in your street and a large part of your house collapses. You see it happening before your very eyes. You can no longer stay in your home country Syria so you have to flee. But where are you going? And via which route do you have the best chance of surviving the trip? Under great pressure of time you have to decide who you leave behind and who you take with you. Who can you trust? If it is not stressful enough, the roaring sirens and screaming people in your ears increase the pressure even more. At the edge of your seat you discover the (im) possible choices of a refugee. Your goal: to keep yourself safe. Somewhere. You lose yourself in the story, but fortunately it's just a game.

DEFINITION AND KEY FEATURES

The example described above is just one application of serious, or applied gaming. Before we define serious gaming, let us clarify what gaming in general is. A first characteristic is that gaming goes further than playing; rules and challenge play a major role in a game. A definition often found in gaming literature is that a game is 'a system in which players engage in an artificial conflict, defined by rules, that results in a quantifiable outcome'[1]. In our view, games are situated, interactive environments, based on a set of rules in which – subject to certain limitations – a challenging goal is pursued under uncertain circumstances. We will soon see how the core elements of uncertainty, challenge, and rules are important. Let's take the well-known Nintendo game Mario, for example, in which gamers play a chubby Italian plumber living in Mushroom Kingdom. The gamer is challenged to thwart the plans of Mario's enemy, who is out to kidnap Princess Peach to be able to reign over the Mushroom Kingdom. The original game is a so-called platform game, in which gamers must jump from platform to platform. On the way, Mario comes across all sorts of enemies that need to be defeated. The more advanced a player is in the game, the more dexterity is required to bring the scenes to a good end. The fate of Princess Peach is in the hands of the gamer. If the outcome of the game was already fixed in advance and there were no rules, the game would be much less interesting.

But what makes a game 'serious'? Most games have the primary goal of entertaining the gamer; however, games can have many more underlying goals: they challenge players, promote cooperation with friends and strangers, and increase knowledge and awareness about certain topics. When these functions of a game become just as important or even more important than entertainment, you are dealing with a serious game. Because serious games want to teach users something, serious gaming is also called *game-based learning*. Learning through a game can be done by informing players about a specific topic or by having them experience certain events virtually. A serious game gives players the opportunity to realise learning objectives in a playful way, which appeals to specific target groups.

DIFFERENT APPLICATIONS OF SERIOUS GAMING

Serious gaming can take place physically, but also via social media as well as via digital game consoles such as the computer, PlayStation or Xbox and it fits well with the trends in the current media landscape: serious games are increasingly being played online and made available on the internet. The most important sectors where serious games are used are education, the business world, security services, and health. For these different areas, specific names are assigned to the serious games in the game world. There are *advergames*, which are video games that are specially designed to promote a brand or product of a company. In *learning games*, an element of education is added to the video games to let the gamer experience knowledge, and in *research games*, players generate data for researchers to, for example, study structures of proteins[2].

In practice, we see that serious gaming is sometimes confused with gamification. What makes serious gaming different is that gamification concerns the applications of game design in real life, in a non-game environment with no specific boundaries on time and place. A serious game, on the other hand, is an intervention designed to take place at a certain time and place, for example in a training setting.

SERIOUS GAMING IN PRACTICE

According to practitioners, a big plus of serious gaming is its multiple applicability. Serious games can be used for educational purposes, marketing, in companies to train staff, and by governments and healthcare institutions to prepare civil servants and employees for (disaster) scenarios. A well-known application is that of advergames in the food industry, such as 'Snack in the face' of the Kentucky Fried Chicken chain, developed to make young players enthusiastic about the brand and acquainted with the new product range. The goal in the game is to throw snacks into the mouth of a character while avoiding buzz saws and lasers and when this succeeds, players are rewarded with their favourite food prizes. Several studies have already shown that the promotion of (unhealthy) food in advergames has a major influence on their actual consumption[3]. Many people are worried about the vulnerability of children, on whom these games are mainly focused. A counter reaction is the development of games that promote the consumption of healthy snacks such as fruits and vegetables among children.

THE EFFECTS IN PRACTICE COULD BE DIFFERENT THAN THOSE WISHED FOR

The effects of health games have been scientifically researched[4]. In an experiment that was conducted at a number of primary schools, children played an interactive memory game in which healthy snacks (fruit) or energy-dense snacks (gummies and jelly sweets) or toys (that had nothing to do with snacks) were promoted. An experimenter collected one child at a time from the classroom and asked them to play the advergame. To make the game more engaging, a digital timer was shown in the game so that the game had to be played quickly. In case of an error, an unpleasant sound was played and an encouraging sound was played if the player did well. After playing the game, the children were placed at another table and they were presented with four bowls with different food snacks such as jelly cola bottles and milk-chocolate shells, but also pieces of banana and apple. A control group with children who had not played a game also participated in the experiment. All children were allowed to eat as much as they wanted in the time they had to wait for the researcher, not knowing that the researcher would then re-weigh the pre-weighed bowls with snacks to measure the number of calories consumed. The result? Playing an advergame with food cues (even those in which fruit was promoted) caused children to eat more unhealthy snacks. The food advergames elicited craving and influenced the direct food intake of children. Not all behaviour is easily positively influenced by using serious gaming.

SERIOUS GAMING IN EDUCATION

In education, serious gaming seems more successful in encouraging positive behaviour. Officers and teachers can make difficult subjects that normally discourage citizens and students (e.g. democracy, corruption, international conflicts, and human rights) attractive with engaging tasks. Students in the 21st century especially have grown up in a digital world and therefore learn and respond differently. Computers are an important part of their everyday lives from an early age. An example of an educational serious game is T-Challenge, which has the goal of letting business students experience what it is to run a company. In teams, players are given various roles in this game, each with their responsibilities in a soft drink factory. Decisions have to be made with regard to corporate social responsibility, price, personnel policies, and new product introductions, in order to keep the company healthy and achieve better results than the competition. A study on this game[5] showed that students who had played a serious game generally scored significantly better on the learning characteristics than students who had followed the classical teaching method. Students who played the learning game indicated that they had a great sense of control over the learning method, more than students from the control group; the same students also found the content more challenging and instructive. Moreover, they indicated more often that they had received useful feedback and cooperated well with other students. Students who played a serious game also felt that they had learned a lot from this. This example is just one of the many successful learning games.

KEEP IT ATTRACTIVE

It is thus clear that serious games have effects in practice, whether the outcomes are intentional or not. A critique made by practitioners is that serious games are regularly produced carelessly. In practice it is quite a challenge to build a serious game that remains interesting to play. A game that gets boring quickly is a missed opportunity. Bad games are not made by experienced game designers and are just used as 'teasers' to teach people uninteresting information. If they are too simple, they lack challenge and the thrill is gone as well. Another critical factor is that when the educational content overshadows the game experience, the motivation to keep playing (and thus the impact) decreases. This is also supported by science. In a study[6] the effect of the gaming experience on the attitude towards driving under influence (a subtle message in the game) was investigated in a first-person shooter game, an action game played from the player's perspective. The research showed that when players lost themselves in the story, the willingness to drive under influence was reduced (in other words, the game had the intended impact). However, when the state of transportation was not achieved, a boomerang effect appeared: the willingness to drive under influence increased slightly compared to the group that was not exposed to the subtle messages in the game. The lesson that can be learned from this is that serious games only achieve the desired results if game concepts (such as challenge, level, uncertainty) are well thought through. Game designer Maarten Molenaar explains the basic elements needed for building such a game.

HARNESSING THE POWER OF GAMES

By Maarten Molenaar
Game Designer
Frisse Blikken / Fresh Forces

As a designer for both digital and physical games, I have seen many successful examples. Serious games for growing awareness, transferring knowledge, changing behaviour, and building skills. The medium has an amazing potential when designed and used correctly. As I work with others (often not game designers) I always try to educate them on three basic elements that will help them to understand and implement the medium effectively: creating a game world, creating feedback loops, and allowing time for testing. These are core ingredients for a successful game project.

CREATING GAME WORLDS

First is that every game, no matter how small, big, digital, or physical takes place in a game world. This world can be fictional or non-fictional but is always an abstract representation of the real world. There are several benefits for the player from interacting with your message in this game world. It often gives them the bigger picture they wouldn't have in real life. Think about recreating the basic elements of a large multinational in an onboarding game to give new employees insight into the company they have started to work for. The game world also gives them the opportunity to step into someone else's shoes and understands his or her challenges better. This applies very well for games you can use to strengthen cooperation between different parts of an organisation.

But the most powerful benefit of this game world is that the player gets immediate feedback on their behaviour, something often lacking in the real world. Think about experiencing the effects of your decisions on global warming and climate change in an energy transition game. This game world is carefully constructed. A framework of mechanics (M), dynamics (D) and aesthetics (A) often explains such a construction[7]. It is useful to know about these because it shows you how your message is translated to the game world.

designer   player

Players experience your game through its 'Aesthetics'. These can be sensation, fantasy, narrative, challenge, fellowship, discovery, expression, or submission. Historical games relying on discovery let the player explore history in their own way. Cooperation games use the aesthetic of fellowship to teach players to cooperate and overcome challenges together.

Game aesthetics are created by the player's interaction with your game dynamics. When you want to create fellowship between players you create dynamics in your challenges that make the game difficult to achieve on your own and therefore various skillsets from different players are necessary to overcome these. I always look at the real world to inspire myself with the dynamics to choose from. These always create an engaging and recognisable experience for the players and help them to apply their learning in real life afterwards.

Finally the mechanics are the various building blocks for your game world and determine the action the players can take. For example, when you are creating a trading game you give your players money, goods, stocks, and market information, but also points and levels to give players feedback on their progression. When creating serious games you use mechanics that align with the behaviour you want to stimulate in real life.

FAILURE IS THE KEY

The second basic element to keep in mind when creating or applying serious games is that you allow your audience to learn by doing. This is imbedded in the interactive nature of the medium. The core feature of a game and its strength is the feedback loop. In a game a player takes action, wins, or fails, gets immediate feedback from the game, learns from it and by doing so constructs a mental model, which helps to define the next action. The ability to fail is a key element of the interaction. As you apply serious games you set your audience up to fail, learn from it, and try again.

Through this type of engagement, people remember your message, become aware of what you want to transfer or change their behaviour. If you don't feel comfortable with this, don't use gaming. If you rather want to create a predictable automated experience, than the more linear mediums such as film and written text may be a better choice.

TESTING, TESTING, TESTING

The third and final element concerns testing the serious game, both during development and when it is live. Due to the interactive nature of the medium and the unpredictable human factor, it will take time to get it right. And especially since you are creating serious games, it is sometimes hard to determine whether the acceptance of your game is caused by the design or by the topic. Serious games on difficult topics, which can make someone reconsider their own behaviour, for example, might not always be the most pleasurable experience.

Give yourself plenty of time to test and adjust your game. In my experience, about 60% of project time goes into developing prototypes, testing them, and improving on them. And when the game is live be sure to monitor game performance and player behaviour to decide whether you need to improve the game or the activation around it.

These are just a few, but very important, elements to consider when applying serious games. When well designed, well implemented, and well cared for, it is a medium of incredible potential.

A SCIENTIFIC PERSPECTIVE

Panem et Circenses; give the people bread and circuses! By offering the people in the time of the gladiator games not only bread but also entertainment, people could be kept satisfied. Julius Caesar already knew that people like games and that the element of winning or losing holds the attention. Two thousand years later, scientific research shows that engagement is indeed an important mechanism behind the influence that games have on people. This can be explained from the science about how people allocate their cognitive resources. Individuals devote more mental energy towards a game if they are put under cognitive load via engaging tasks. In this way, games keep the attention better than the regular teacher or politician. The fact that attention is limited also explains how consumers are influenced by advergames. When many cognitive resources are assigned to engaging tasks in a game, fewer cognitive resources remain to devise critical counter-arguments. On the other hand, if a serious game is cognitively too demanding, too few resources will remain for the performance of other tasks such as learning. It is therefore important that the complexity is in balance and fits the level of the user.

CHALLENGE AND CONTROL

In addition to engagement, there are other mechanisms that explain the effects of serious games. In the study into the learning effects of the T-Challenge game, in which business students have to run a soft drink factory together, various explanatory factors were found. The sense of control experienced by players in the game proved to be an important factor. When a sense of control is created, the player experiences 'agency' (direction/influence). It is important that this is built into a game because without control the gamer becomes a passive spectator. Julius Caesar was already well aware of this mechanism. If a gladiator fight lasted too long and ended undecided, he let the people decide whether the gladiator received an honourable retreat or not. The degree of challenge also proved to be an important predictor for learning outcomes in the game. People learn more when they experience challenging but achievable goals. The level of difficulty is all-important: if it is too easy, then there is no challenge, but if it is too difficult, then the motivation to continue playing decreases.

A TOOL, A MEDIUM, AND A SOCIAL ACTOR

If we consider serious games from Fogg's Functional Triad, we can conclude that serious games apply to the functions as a tool, medium, and social actor. Firstly, games play the role as a tool in that they can teach players skills by having them continuously carry out the same actions and gradually building up the difficulty level. In addition, serious games act as a medium because they are a safe environment in which players can make mistakes without leading to major consequences in reality, but they do show the negative outcomes. Consider for example, making unwise financial choices in the learning game in which players have to keep a company healthy. In this way, serious games offer the opportunity to make the right decisions in the 'real world'. In his book 'Persuasive games'[8], game developer and theoretician Ian Bogost describes the mechanism of *procedural rhetoric*. By playing a game intensively, players learn to deal with the rules that make a game challenging, and dealing with these rules leads to new insights. Creators of serious games can influence the beliefs and behaviour of players by linking the desired insights to the game rules. An example of a convincing game with procedural rhetoric is *"Ayiti: The Cost of Life"*, in which the player tries to keep a family alive in Haiti for four years. An almost impossible task. Finally, serious games can fulfil the function of a social actor because characters in games can encourage the player. Many learning games have a virtual coach who encourages players to keep on trying and raising the bar a little higher every time.

FUTURE AND ETHICS

The changes in the media landscape have created new avenues for the growth of serious games. Standardisation of technologies such as the internet and smartphones has ensured that these are increasingly integrated into daily life. Gaming and serious gaming have become much more accessible with devices such as smartphones, so you are no longer tied to a computer or game console. These technologies also match a new generation. Millennials, for instance, think and learn differently than older generations. They develop visual intelligence; capabilities that match the visual demands of modern science and technology. These include skills such as iconic representation, spatial orientation, spatial visualisation and other visual skills that are important in the virtual world of computers9. New generations want to be more connected and committed with open content. Serious games suit this well; they can educate new generations of employees, conveying knowledge and skills in a safe and meaningful environment.

AI AND SERIOUS GAMING

In some intelligent game-based learning environments, commercial game technologies are integrated with AI methods such as intelligent tutoring systems and intelligent narrative technologies. Research[10] shows that engagement, such as the feeling that the player is 'present' in the game, has a strong positive relationship with in-game problem solving and learning outcomes (performance on a test). Crystal Island[11] is a promising intelligent learning game for microbiology students in which they solve a science mystery by investigating an infectious disease outbreak on a remote island. Statistic models, which predict learning emotions, for example, create personalised learning experiences that are both effective and engaging. Over the next few years, as user modelling becomes even more powerful, intelligent game-based learning environments like Crystal Island will continue to make their way into a broad range of educational settings, museums, and science centres.

ARE VIDEO GAMES HARMFUL?

Games in general have not always been seen in a positive light and this is still the case. The issue of whether video games damage children and adolescents is much discussed among scientists and politicians, and in the public debate. In all kinds of research in the past decades, relationships have been suggested between gaming and aggression, reduced prosocial behaviour, depression, and reduced school performance, for instance. An analysis[12] of more than a hundred studies into the harmful effects of gaming shows that the direct relationships between playing games and the negative aforementioned phenomena are minimal. Serious games, however, are often developed to achieve learning effects and are generally of a different nature to regular games (less aggressive, more educational). In the case of serious gaming, too, we are fortunate to see a trend towards research into, and the application of, gaming for the welfare of people. Several serious games that focus on social responsibility goals, knowledge gathering, and the teaching of a more positive view of life, have already been developed and researched. An example in the context of new technology is a serious game that teaches children to exhibit positive bystander behaviour (defending) when they witness cyberbullying [13].

Although a lot of serious games can be beneficial in the future, there will still be some opposition, depending on the application. Think for example of the Kentucky Fried Chicken game and the research that found that children started to snack more unhealthily after playing a game with food cues. Children are already less resistant to influence, and long-term exposure to interactive advergames makes them even more receptive. Online marketing allows advertisers to interact with children for several minutes, which is longer than an average commercial of 30 seconds. For the time being, there are no regulations on the exposure time of advergames [14].

In conclusion, as for many of the discussed digital innovations in this book, it is also true for serious gaming that it is the intention of the creator that determines whether the technique is ethically objectionable or not. We have seen worrisome examples, but also positive applications. You could say it's not the medium, it's the message.

CLASSIFICATION

References and notes

1   Salen, K., & Zimmerman, E. (2004). Rules of Play: Game design fundamentals. Cambridge: Mit Press

2   On the website https://fold.it/portal/ you can play the game and read more about how the game contributes to research on proteins.

3   Harris, J. L., Speers, S. E., Schwartz, M. B., & Brownell, K. D. (2012). US food company branded advergames on the internet: children's exposure and effects on snack consumption. Journal of Children and Media, 6(1), 51-58.

4   Folkvord, F., Anschütz, D. J., Buijzen, M., & Valkenburg, P. M. (2012). The effect of playing advergames that promote energy-dense snacks or fruit on actual food intake among children. The American Journal of Clinical Nutrition, 97(2), 239-245.

5   Oprins, E. A. P. B., Bakhuys Roozeboom, M. C., Visschedijk, G. C., & Kistemaker, J. A. (2013). Effectiviteit van serious gaming in het onderwijs.

6   Burrows, C.N. & Blanton, H. (2016). Real-world persuasion from virtual-world campaigns: How transportations into virtual worlds moderates in-game influence. Communication Research 43(4), 523-570.

7   Hunicke, R., LeBlanc, M., & Zubek, R. (2004, July). MDA: A formal approach to game design and game research. In Proceedings of the AAAI Workshop on Challenges in Game AI (Vol. 4, No. 1, p. 1722).

8   Bogost, I. (2008). The rhetoric of video games. The ecology of games: Connecting youth, games, and learning. Ed. by Katie Salen. The John D. and Catherine T. MacArthur Foundation Series on Digital Media and Learning. Cambridge, MA: The MIT Press. 117-40.

9   Greenfield, P. (2009). Technology and informal education: What is taught, what is learned. Science (New York, N.Y.). 323. 69-71. 10.1126/science.1167190.

10 Rowe, J. P., Shores, L. R., Mott, B. W., & Lester, J. C. (2011). Integrating learning, problem solving, and engagement in narrative-centered learning environments. International Journal of Artificial Intelligence in Education 21(2): 115-133.

11 Lester, J. C., Ha, E. Y., Lee, S. Y., Mott, B. W., Rowe, J. P., & Sabourin, J. L. (2013). Serious games get smart: Intelligent game-based learning environments. AI Magazine, 34(4), 31-45.

12 Ferguson, C. J. (2015). Do Angry Birds make for angry children? A meta-analysis of video game influences on children's and adolescents' aggression, mental health, prosocial behavior, and academic performance. Perspectives on Psychological Science, 10, 646-666

13 DeSmet, Ann, Bastiaensens, S., Van Cleemput, K., Poels, K., Vandebosch, H., Deboutte, G., Herrewijn, L., et al. (2018). The efficacy of the friendly attack serious digital game to promote prosocial bystander behavior in cyberbullying among young adolescents: a cluster-randomized controlled trial. Computers in Human Behavior, 78, 336–347.

14 Moore, E. S., & Rideout, V. J. (2007). The online marketing of food to children: is it just fun and games? American Marketing Association, 26(2), 202–220.

#8 BEHAVIOURAL TARGETING

Behavioural targeting profiles the prior behaviour of online users in order to determine which information users will see next.

You see a shadow around the corner and you hear a squeaking door. It feels like someone is watching you, but you don't hear or see anybody. Then you realise that nobody is there. But what if you are constantly being watched without you knowing? Welcome to the world of behavioural targeting, the rich and mysterious Big Brother of the internet[1].

DEFINITION AND KEY FEATURES

Although marketing communication has been mass-media oriented for decades, contemporary marketers realise that reaching the right consumers at the right time is more effective than firing the same ad at a whole segment of the population. Behavioural targeting uses people's information and data in order to forecast and anticipate their behaviour, subsequently delivering to them the right message at the right time. An example is recommender systems, when people receive suggestions for movies or music on the basis of their past viewing and listening behaviour. It might solve the contemporary problem of marketers that, due to information overload, consumers systematically avoid their ads and do not pay attention to them anymore. Behavioural targeting has changed the way that organisations communicate with their stakeholders, transforming it into a form of automated mediated communication.

FOLLOWING THE ONLINE ACTIVITIES OF CONSUMERS

The distinguishing feature of behavioural targeting is its personal relevancy. Everything evolves around the perfect fit of ads and individuals. Each individual is different and should be approached differently by marketers. Behavioural targeting follows the online activities of consumers in order to offer them tailor-made ads, (entertaining) content and sometimes even tailor-made homepages of websites. Their online behaviour is registered in cookies, which are text files containing data about their search history, page visits, advertising clicks, and buying behaviour. From these data an online profile is made, leading to the ads that are the most relevant to them, such as specific banners after searching for specific shoes.

Behavioural targeting can be used in three different ways. In behavioural onsite targeting, the online (search) behaviour of consumers is registered – and only used by –

a specific site to offer tailor-made ads[2]. Or marketers can make use of collaborative filtering, meaning that suggestions for consumers are based on the search and buying behaviour of comparable consumers. Lastly, in behavioural network targeting, personally relevant offerings are based on (search) behaviour on other websites. Social media is very popular among marketers for behaviour targeting because it contains detailed profiles of users that can be tied to the ads that fit their specific needs.

PROFILES SOLD TO HIGHEST BIDDERS

Behavioural targeting is facilitated by the fact that smartphones are almost continuously online and close to their owners 24 hours a day. This allows a continuous stream of consumer 'big data', which is monitored and analysed in 'real-time' by data mining experts in order to discover interrelationships. Thereafter the resulting profiles are sold to the highest bidders in real-time bidding systems. Does that sound a bit scary? We can imagine it does.

Related terms that are often used interchangeably are customisation, personalisation, event-driven marketing, customer-driven online engagement, online behavioural advertising, persuasion profiling, and location-based marketing. Although sometimes it is not clear what the actual differences are, it appears that they all fall under the common denominator of tailoring[3], meaning that the content of a message fits certain traits of consumers such as their demographics, psychographics, socio-economic characteristics, location, and online behaviour.

BEHAVIOURAL TARGETING IN PRACTICE

Although behavioural targeting is becoming a popular technique among advertisers, the ideas about its effectiveness are mixed. On the one hand, the benefits for advertisers of behavioural targeting seem quite clear. The business model is attractive for marketers because they only pay for click-throughs and not for reach. Behavioural targeting raises awareness among marketers of who their customers are and what they are interested in. For instance, a banking company registers customer profiles and success events such as the downloading of information, the request for a bid or an appointment, or the signing of an insurance policy. Their conclusion that customers who are interested in payment products are also interested in insurance is followed by ads about insurance appearing on the pages of payment products. They can subsequently aim their ads at a specific target group, and these consumers will devote attention to these ads because they are tailored to their specific wants and needs. It may even be that because of the direct satisfaction that such tailor-made offerings provide, customers ignore the infringement of their privacy and do not think properly about the long-term consequences of their buying decision. This may also be caused by insufficient knowledge about behavioural targeting[4]. As for the benefits to consumers of behavioural targeting, the fact that these ads are relevant to them will trigger them to click on them and may even incite buying behaviour. Positive feelings towards the buying process may be transferred to their relationship with the advertiser.

Research has shown that advertisers are positive about personalisation, are aware of limiting factors such as privacy violations, and are engaging in ethical discussions about personalisation on their own initiative[5]. Some advertisers even view behavioural targeting as one of the most consumer-oriented ad formats, because consumers are provided with tailor-made offerings instead of the overload of irrelevant ads that they are usually exposed to.

THE OMNIPRESENCE OF TARGETED ADS

On the other hand, there are some disadvantages of behavioural targeting that marketers are aware of. They can never be sure that the right ad reaches the right person, because you never know who is sitting in front of the computer. This control dimension is becoming less problematic as people are more inclined to use their smartphones instead of a computer, and always carry their phone with them. Furthermore, consumers must have an obvious idea about what they want to buy[6]. If this is not the case, targeting might be useless. Unwanted offerings may make consumers feel like: "I do not want them, but those damn shoes are pretty sure that they want me". Related to this disadvantage of behavioural targeting is the omnipresence of targeted ads. It is very difficult for people to avoid being exposed to them, because they often appear in between information that you have actively sought for, such as editorial content.

VIOLATION OF PRIVACY

However, the biggest problem with behavioural targeting is its violation of privacy. When an ad is obviously tailored on the basis of earlier visits to a site, buying behaviour and privacy-sensitive behaviour such as age, gender, and current location, people feel vulnerable, which eventually may backfire and make the tailored ad even less effective. However, advertisers may feel that they should be fine, as long as they stick to contemporary privacy laws. Besides, consumers always have to give prior consent to advertisers in order for them to collect and use their data. Advertisers may reason that behavioural targeting saves consumers much time and effort and that only the older generation experiences privacy concerns, as the younger generation is already accustomed to privacy invasions.

Jan Heuvel will now describe what, in his view, are important considerations for organisations that want to engage in responsible data care, safeguarding the privacy of people.

WILL CONSUMERS BE IN CONTROL OF THEIR OWN DATA?

By Jan Heuvel
Director Strategy & Innovation at SAMR Marketfinders
and co-founder of Spotton Media

Data privacy is a sensitive subject. Let's face it, for the most powerful companies on Earth, personal data about consumers is the new gold. Data enable them to create personalised value propositions and communication strategies. Meanwhile, the majority of consumers show a lack of interest and knowledge about what companies know about them and what they can do with this information.

DISINTEREST AMONG CONSUMERS

Consumers usually know that data privacy is of importance, but most of the time they do not think about it. They certainly do not know about the hat and the brim. They do not really care and therefore behave accordingly. Just like you and me, by the way. Worldwide this applies to 77% of consumers[7]. For a little more convenience (through cookies, for example), a personalised proposition or a small financial advantage, they lay out their whole possessions and put them in the hands of companies. Consider also the flow of data that – unnoticed by consumers – is constantly increasing due to connected devices. The chapter 'Closure' gives more insight into what is called 'privacy fatique' and the concept of Willingness To Share Data (WTSD).

There is a big difference between giving up data consciously and unconsciously. People deliberately give up data, but only when it concerns relatively insensitive data. According to a Dutch study in 2018, only 28% are willing to hand over data in exchange for a direct financial reward[8]. This number must be viewed in a nuanced way. Not all consumers are the same when it comes to willingness to share their data with companies. It is highly dependent on their personality type, age, culture, the sensitivity and functionality of the data, and the context in which the data is used.

'Data fundamentalists', consumers who really don't want to share their personal data, comprise 23% of the population worldwide. For example, in Argentina (16%) and Singapore (17%), these groups are even smaller[9]. Millennials are relatively unconcerned about their data, while the elderly are much more sceptical[10]. The more sensitive the information is, the less willingness there is to give it up, and the more invisibly the data are collected, the less people are aware of it. Seventy percent or more consider fingerprints, financial information, medical and genetic data as sensitive[11]. But still, if people find what they receive in turn highly attractive, they will share their data: the company iDDNA earns money by personalising cosmetics based on your DNA[12]. In my opinion, factors that significantly increase the willingness to share data are whether consumers understand why it can be functional for them and how pleasant sharing their data is made for them.

For instance, imagine that you walk past a house that is for sale. You focus your AR-equipped smartphone or tablet on the home, making the necessary sales data available. Your personal data, including your risk profile, is also available via AR. If the broker, mortgage lender, land registry and notary are also connected within the same AR-system, you will move on to a completely managed services model. Especially if there is blockchain technology[13] behind it, you could see in no time whether you can buy the property and what your monthly payments would be. You immediately make an appointment in the AR space of the notary. It could just be. Then data is primarily very functional and people will want to give it up earlier.

The point is, consumers often do not realise which data companies collect from them and they are not aware of what companies can do with it. In addition, only a quarter of consumers think that they themselves are responsible for their data security[14]. And even if they know which data they have made available, they cannot know which algorithm is applied to it. For example, algorithms from Netflix, Google and YouTube determine what we see because we would prefer that, yet we don't know the algorithm. An algorithm has even been developed that re-identifies a person's personality and characteristics, such as political and sexual orientation, by analysing only three hundred Facebook likes – and it does it more accurately than their life partner[15].

BUSINESSES: DEFEND YOUR GOLD WITH RESPECT AND TRUST

As data is the new gold, businesses will defend their data science practices by hand. Yet, many companies still miss the point: in a digital age it's all about the trust of their customers. The thoughtless click on the 'agree' box is not a match in a meaningful sense. Users have usually not even read the agreements. This can protect companies against legal damage, but reputational damage is another matter. Just to name a few reputations damaged by data problems in 2018: Adidas, Under Armor, Sears, Forever 21, Whole Foods, Delta, Panera Bread, and Best Buy[16]. This impaired trust is not only about companies, but also governments and other organisations. In a Dutch town a plan has been conceived to make housing free in exchange for releasing all your personal data. A great deal of criticism immediately rose up. In the chapter "Privacy Challenges: Where do we stand", Marcel Becker explores these risks for reputation and trust.

A lot of data has become unusable due to the GDPR, which became effective in 2018. In order to use existing data, marketers must verify that it meets the new standards. This means having a fully documented permission trail including the data and source of the consent. On the other hand, new data must primarily be collected contextually in order to be really relevant. The lack of contextual insight into consumer behaviour has long hampered the effectiveness of personalisation despite an enormous amount of available data. 'Context marketing' means aligning the message (the content) with the context of the receiver. For example, the current location of the prospect, his former buying behaviour or preferences – the data that are important for sharpening the content, the timing and medium of the marketing message. Effectiveness will rise if 'content marketing' thus turns into 'context marketing'. A big question is whether organisations can actually make it so simple for people to switch their data on or off in all kinds of sub-areas, and whether these people will actually make use of these features. Moreover, simplicity is not a trigger in itself; the trigger must be emotional. Just as with other things that people know they should do something about, they just don't get round to it. Think about arranging your pension, making your house more sustainable, or behaving in a fundamentally healthy way. It is important in this context that part of the communication with customers is now shifting from the creative marketers to the more rational marketing technicians. These technical-oriented marketers usually do not have the ability to create emotional triggers. Data are wonderful, yet turning data into emotional triggers needs the skills of creative copywriters and art directors. That is, to turn communication about data into creative communication that is necessary to hit the emotional chord with consumers. While the quantity of marketing content is booming because of marketing automation programs that create content out of data, the quality of that content is declining markedly due to the lack of creative craftsmanship. As a result, more and more so-called content will be ignored as it has no real value for customers.

VIABLE SOLUTIONS?

There are already organisations who consider it their social duty to offer user-friendly propositions to let consumers be in control of their own data: Bits of Freedom with My Data Done Right, Solid (from Tim Berners-Lee, the inventor of the internet), IRMA (I Reveal My Attributes) from the Privacy by Design foundation, Diaspora (a type of Facebook that does not require you to identify yourself), Mastodon (a kind of Twitter with strict codes of conduct and more moderators), and Webinos (which focuses, among other things, on integrating data privacy legislation into concrete technology)[17]. What they have in common is that these organisations are trusted because of their non-profit character, social embedding and the fact that they offer their tools free of charge. It is unclear whether these parties already generate any volume among consumers. In view of various investigations into data privacy, I suspect that only the 'data fundamentalists' among consumers make use of the tools that allow people to become the boss of their own data. And as always with new technologies, there is a danger that organisations, even though they are not commercially driven in this case, will compete against each other, so that a standard will not be easily created and the overall positive effect of these initiatives will therefore be smaller than it potentially could be.

Looking at the indifferent attitude of most consumers towards issues concerning their privacy, at the profit orientation of companies and at the jumble of possible solutions, the conclusion seems justified that consumers will not be in charge of their own data for a very long time.

A SCIENTIFIC PERSPECTIVE

Like practitioners, scientists are also in doubt about the effects of behavioural targeting. As a first step, consumers have to give their consent to parties to install cookies that will track and analyse their online behaviour, and consent to renewed privacy regulations. The result of this may be irritation because people's daily flow is interrupted by being asked for permission to be tracked and to give consent to privacy regulations. This may result in blindly accepting the cookies and privacy regulations without giving them a good look, possibly lowering awareness of privacy issues instead of making them more salient.

TAILOR-MADE INFORMATION RAISES THE SELF-EFFICACY OF PEOPLE

When these cookies are accepted, they make behavioural targeting possible. The highly relevant offerings provide a perfect fit with peoples' identity, thus attracting attention and increasing the chance that the advertising message will be intensely cognitively processed[18]. Because the offering fits the consumer like a glove, not many cognitive resources are needed to process the ad, thus simplifying the decision to go along with the offer or not. Therefore, tailor-made information may help people to make decisions efficiently, raising their self-efficacy[19]. A precondition for facilitated processing is that the targeted ad is shown in a setting that aligns with the product. For instance, an ad for Nike shoes should be shown on a running platform and not on a platform for photography.

THE BALANCE BETWEEN RELEVANCY AND PRIVACY IS QUITE SHAKY

As practitioners already suspect, behavioural targeting may indeed feel like a violation of one's privacy[20]. This may cause a lack of trust and believability in ads among consumers, resulting in less attention being paid to these ads, rendering behavioural targeting useless. However, the effects of behavioural targeting are influenced by age[21]. Although adolescents evaluate the usage of personal data for marketing purposes negatively, highly personalised ads are effective, favouring their brand engagement and intention to pass along these ads to significant others.

Personality traits such as a person's need for uniqueness and previously experienced privacy violations may also influence acceptance of behavioural targeting. People with a high need for uniqueness may appreciate targeted ads more, and people with negative experiences concerning privacy may appreciate them less. It all depends on the trade-off that people make between giving up their privacy in exchange for a relevant offer[22]. The privacy calculus theory postulates that people weigh the advantages of relevancy against the experienced privacy concerns. Ads are more effective when relevancy outweighs privacy concerns. However, research also shows that people do not have that much persuasive knowledge with regard to behavioural targeting. They do not have much knowledge about being tracked[23]. Because of this lack of knowledge, their persuasion knowledge will probably not be triggered[24]. However, when these ads are too close to their skin, persuasion knowledge may be triggered, resulting in resistance towards the temptation of the offerings. In short, the acceptance of cookies may come about peripherally without much attention, while the following targeted ads will be processed more systematically. The balance between relevancy and privacy is quite shaky and unpredictable, depending on personality traits.

PRIVACY PARADOX: THE TRADE-OFF BETWEEN RELEVANCY AND PRIVACY WORRIES
Research has shown that behavioural targeting does raise Click-Through Rates (CTRs), as well as purchase orders (conversion)[25]. When the offer is highly relevant and attractive, privacy concerns will weigh less. This trade-off is called the privacy paradox. In other words, people say that privacy is important to them, but they do not act like it. Although privacy proved to be of high value years ago, nowadays generations value privacy less and they are more inclined to spread and share their data with third parties without worrying too much[26], downplaying the risks of privacy invasions. People are inclined to delete cookies and browser history or decline cookies in order to protect their online privacy. They perceive the collecting, using, and sharing of personal information as a serious problem and have little confidence in their own efficacy to be able to protect their online privacy[27]. Research has also shown that when targeting is used not at the beginning, but further along in the buying process, it is more successful, especially when it is obviously tied to a person's searching behaviour and when the offering is formulated in the passive voice, making the targeting attempt somewhat less obvious[28].

FUTURE AND ETHICS

Generally, the advertising business is positive about the future of behavioural targeting. It may even become an easier advertising technique because on social media, user profiles such as demographics, likes, interests, posts, reviews, et cetera abound and can be used by advertisers to tailor ads. Also, the widespread smartphone use and phone-embedded tracking[29] will facilitate behavioural targeting.

OMNI-CHANNEL BEHAVIOURAL TARGETING
Behavioural targeting will gain in strength when it is combined with other innovations such as location-based advertising, making ads even more relevant. There will be more media available, such as fridges, glasses, and watches that will convey

behaviourally targeted ads. Retail chains might make fridges that are connected to the internet. The content of the fridges will evoke tailored ads, possibly even accompanied by recipes that fit the groceries that are in the fridge. Facial recognition will allow billboards to render tailor-made offerings, based on people's age and gender, the time, and weather conditions. Techniques will enable marketers to integrate the offline and online worlds of consumers in an overarching big data set. This so-called omni-channel behavioural targeting will provide marketers with even better chances to get to know people, allowing them to further tailor content to their specific needs. However, this technique will obviously raise questions about the continuous gathering of offline and online data, possibly leading to reactive behaviour and counter-arguing among people. Lastly, addressable TV allows the making of automated viewer profiles, allowing targeted ads to appear on the TV screen.

HOW MAY ALL PARTIES BENEFIT OPTIMALLY?

Ethically, it is not a question about whether behavioural targeting is good or bad, but how it is used and under which circumstances, and how society, advertisers, and consumers alike may benefit optimally. The borders between mass and interpersonal communication will fade even further. Machine learning will make real-time marketing possible because it will enable machines to perform, analyse, and learn from previous situations and translate this to tailored offerings with the speed of light. The contemporary market is complex, due to the ever-changing media-landscape. Innovations live a shorter life and the customer journey is more complex than ever. This impedes marketers in finding the right way to approach people. New innovations will be invented in order for marketers to better understand people.

PEOPLE SHOULD BE MADE WISE ABOUT BEHAVIOUR TARGETING

Because of its consequences for privacy concerns, behaviour targeting is the centre of attention for advertisers, consumers, policy makers, and research institutes. Organisations will become even more aggressive in collecting people's data. The motto will not be 'a penny for your thoughts', but '10 bucks each month for your profile with all your data'. Shouldn't the government become even more protective of people because they do not just sell their own data but also the data of their friends? The ignorance of people nowadays about the meaning of cookies is mirrored in their fears over the violation of their privacy. Many people are just not aware of how the information they offer is used, analysed, or even sold to third parties. Therefore, people should be made wiser about behaviour targeting so that they can recognise persuasion attempts as soon as they occur. They should know that their search behaviour is being tracked and stored. Fears of consumers over their privacy should be lessened or even eliminated. They should be able to 'opt out' and easily adjust privacy settings. An idea would be to use an officially recognised privacy-proof icon stating that the ad is 'privacy proof'[30]. When organisations are open ('overt') about the way they collect and use data, this will lead to less resistance towards tailored ads, compared to when they are not open ('covert') about data collection[31]. Also, good education, as well as transparency of organisations towards consumers and an opt-in possibility for consumers to grant advertisers access to their data (or not) are important.

ADS ARE STILL UNWANTED

Crucially important is that advertisers should realise that their ads, even when optimally tailored, are still unwanted. Therefore it should be the consumers who take the first step in a relationship with a brand, not the other way around. When consumers have chosen freely to bind with a brand, they will appreciate tailored ads more than when these ads are pushed onto them out of nowhere. When these precautions are not taken seriously, the installation of ad blockers will become even more widespread. This will force advertisers to think more carefully about which ads they should show to consumers.

INCREASING THE FILTER BUBBLE

Another worry for the future is that the use of behavioural targeting will permit people to only receive highly relevant ads, thus increasing the filter bubble. They will not accept information that is new, or does not align with oneself. This may impede new companies, and even new cultures and opinions, from gaining a share of the market because of their unfamiliarity, thus being less relevant and attractive to people. Although there is no convincing scientific evidence yet, according to critics this filter bubble would cause opposition to thoughts, ideas, and preferences to grow in society!

IDIOSYNCRASY OF EXPERIENCES

On the positive side, behavioural targeting aligns with the notion of a so-called meaningful life, because a big part of human life lies in the idiosyncrasy of experiences[32]. A positivistic view is that behavioural targeting may improve the individual well-being of people. Suppose you search for biological products and decide to buy a jar of peanut butter. When considering your search behaviour, advertisers may conclude that you like biological products. They offer you ads for them and you try them out, making you happy and improving the quality of your life. However, the question lingers over whether your privacy and freedom of choice are impeded or not, even if the targeting improves the quality of your life.

The future of behavioural targeting is insecure. On the one hand, this marketing technique shows enormous potency through its fast development and positive results for marketers as well as consumers. On the other hand, society realises more and more that online data collection is a menace for the privacy of consumers. When data collection stays within boundaries, behavioural targeting will look at a promising future. The advertising branch should stick to the rules about privacy and communication professionals should take up their responsibility to explore the positive side of this technological development – not only for the benefit of commerce but also in favour of modern consumers.

"You may not want the shoes, but the shoes appear to want you."

(Penn, 2012)

CLASSIFICATION

★★★★★ ★★★★★ ★★★★★ ★★★★★ ★★★★★

References and notes

1   Penn, J. (2012). Behavioral advertising: The cryptic hunter and gatherer of the internet, Federal Communications Law Journal, 64(3), Article 6.

2   Boerman, S. C., Kruikemeier, S., & Zuiderveen Borgesius, F. J. (2017). Online behavioral advertising: A literature review and research agenda. Journal of Advertising, 46(3), 363-376. doi:10.1080/00913367.2017.1339368.

3   Lu, X., Zhao, X., & Xue, L. (2016). Is combining contextual and behavioral targeting strategies effective in online advertising?. ACM Transactions on Management Information Systems (TMIS), 7(1), 1. doi: http://dx.doi.org/10.1145/2883816.

4   Smit, E. G., Van Noort, G., & Voorveld, H. A. (2014). Understanding online behavioural advertising: User knowledge, privacy concerns and online coping behaviour in Europe. Computers in Human Behavior, 32, 15-22.

5   Strycharz, J., van Noort, G., Helberger, N., & Smit, E. (2019). Contrasting perspectives–practitioner's viewpoint on personalised marketing communication. European Journal of Marketing.

6   Boerman, S. C., Kruikemeier, S., & Zuiderveen Borgesius, F. J. (2017). Online behavioral advertising: A literature review and research agenda. Journal of Advertising, 46(3), 363-376. doi:10.1080/00913367.2017.1339368.

7   Global Alliance of Data-Driven Marketing Associations (GDMA). (2018). New global study reveals consumers are happy to share their data.
https://www.fedma.org/2018/05/new-global-study-reveals-consumers-are-happy-to-share-their-data/

8   DDMA Privacy Monitor. (2018). https://ddma.nl/privacy-monitor/

9   Global Alliance of Data-Driven Marketing Associations (GDMA). (2018). New global study reveals consumers are happy to share their data.
https://www.fedma.org/2018/05/new-global-study-reveals-consumers-are-happy-to-share-their-data/

10 DDMA Privacy Monitor. (2018).
https://ddma.nl/wp-content/uploads/dlm_uploads/2018/05/DDMA_Privacy-Monitor_2018.pdf
https://ddma.nl/wp-content/uploads/dlm_uploads/2018/12/Privacy-Monitor-2018-deel-2-Wat-consumenten-geven.pdf

11 DDMA Privacy Monitor. (2018). https://ddma.nl/privacy-monitor/

12 van Belleghem, S. (2015). 4 kenmerken van de moderne consument. Marketing facts, www.marketingfacts.nl/berichten/4-kenmerken-van-de-moderne-consument

13 The principle of blockchain is simple. Just imagine that at each transaction on the internet a notary would be present to verify every detail of the transaction. That's exactly what blockchain technology does in an automated way. The verified information is immutable and therefore reliable.

14 DDMA Privacy Monitor. (2018). https://ddma.nl/privacy-monitor/

15 Michal Kosinksi from Harvard Business School in an interview with Fareed Zakaria, GPS, CNN, published on YouTube on 25th March 2017.

16 Green, D. & Hanbury, M. (2018). If you shopped at these 15 stores in the last year, your data might have been stolen, Business insider. https://www.businessinsider.nl/data-breaches-2018-4/?international=true&r=US

17 https://www.mydatadoneright.eu/, https://solid.inrupt.com/, https://privacybydesign.foundation/irma/, https://diasporafoundation.org/about#privacy, https://joinmastodon.org/, http://webinos.org/about-webinos/

18 Buijzen, M., Van Reijmersdal, E.A., & Owen, L.H. (2010). Introducing the PCMC model: An investigative framework for young people's processing of commercial media content. Communication Theory, 20, 427-450. doi:10.1111/j.1468-2885.2010.01370.x.

19 Fogg, B. J., Cuellar, G., & Danielson, D. (2002). Motivating, influencing, and persuading users. In J. Jacko & A. Sears (ed.) The human-computer interaction handbook: Fundamentals, evolving technologies and emerging applications (pp. 133-147). Hillsdale, NJ: Erlbaum.

20 Smit, E. G., Van Noort, G., & Voorveld, H. A. (2014). Understanding online behavioural advertising: User knowledge, privacy concerns and online coping behaviour in Europe. Computers in Human Behavior, 32, 15-22. doi: 10.1016/j.chb.2013.11.008.

21 Walrave, M., Poels, K., Antheunis, M. L., Van den Broeck, E., & van Noort, G. (2018). Like or dislike? Adolescents' responses to personalized social network site advertising. Journal of Marketing Communications, 24(6), 599-616.

22 Xu, H., Luo, X. R., Carroll, J. M., & Rosson, M. B. (2011). The personalization privacy paradox: An exploratory study of decision making process for location-aware marketing. Decision support systems, 51(1), 42-52. doi: 10.1016/j.dss.2010.11.017.

23 Van Reijmersdal, E. A., Fransen, M. L., van Noort, G., Opree, S. J., Vandeberg, L., Reusch, S., & Boerman, S. C. (2016). Effects of disclosing sponsored content in blogs: How the use of resistance strategies mediates effects on persuasion. American Behavioral Scientist, 60(12), 1458-1474.

24 Friestad, M., & Wright, P. (1994). The persuasion knowledge model: How people cope with persuasion attempts. Journal of Consumer Research, 21(1), 1–31. doi: 10.1086/209380.

25 Boerman, S. C., Kruikemeier, S., & Zuiderveen Borgesius, F. J. (2017). Online behavioral advertising: A literature review and research agenda. Journal of Advertising, 46(3), 363-376. doi:10.1080/00913367.2017.1339368.

26 Xu, H., Luo, X. R., Carroll, J. M., & Rosson, M. B. (2011). The personalization privacy paradox: An exploratory study of decision making process for location-aware marketing. Decision Support Systems, 51(1), 42-52. doi: 10.1016/j.dss.2010.11.017.

27 Boerman, S. C., Kruikemeier, S., & Borgesius, F. J. Z. (2018). Blocking ads and deleting cookies: a longitudinal study examining online privacy protection behavior. In American Academy of Advertising. Conference. Proceedings (Online) (pp. 85-86). American Academy of Advertising.

28 Pöyry, E., Hietaniemi, N., Parvinen, P., Hamari, J., & Kaptein, M. (2017). Personalized product recommendations: Evidence from the field. In Proceedings of the 50th Hawaii International Conference on System Sciences 2017. University of Hawai'i at Manoa.

29 Ketelaar, P. E., & van Balen, M. (2018). The smartphone as your follower: The role of smartphone literacy in the relation between privacy concerns, attitude and behaviour towards phone-embedded tracking. Computers in Human Behavior, 78, 174-182.

30 Van Noort, G., Smit, E. G., & Voorveld, H. A. (2013). The online behavioural advertising icon: two user studies. In Advances in Advertising Research (Vol. IV) (pp. 365-378). Springer Gabler, Wiesbaden.

31 Aguirre, E., Mahr, D., Grewal, D., Ruyter, K. de, & Wetzels, M. (2015). Unraveling the personalization paradox: The effect of information collection and trust-building strategies on online advertisement effectiveness. Journal of Retailing, 91(1), 34-49. Doi:10.1016/j.jretai.2014.09.005.

32 Riva, G., Banos, R. M., Botella, C., Wiederhold, B. K., & Gaggioli, A. (2012). Positive technology: using interactive technologies to promote positive functioning. Cyberpsychology, Behavior, and Social Networking, 15(2), 69-77.

#9 PERSUASION PROFILING

Persuasion profiling goes a step beyond tailor-made information on the basis of age, gender, and buying behaviour. It accounts for differences in personality such as sensitivity to authority, and adjusts its communication according to these sensitivities.

Imagine that you are the owner of a store. It doesn't matter what kind of store it is, it could be a bookshop, a game store, or a butcher's. Pretend that it is a store with loyal customers who return every so often for multiple purchases. As the owner of the store you are getting to know your customers. You will not only learn what kind of products they like. While listening to their stories you will also learn what the motives are for people to buy certain products and what their vulnerabilities are for buying. A smart salesman 'reads' his customers and applies his knowledge of each individual. He knows how to sell his commodities to different people and how to tempt them to buy even more articles, using personal information.

DEFINITION AND KEY FEATURES

The analogy above illustrates what persuasion profiling is. Similar to a smart salesman, a computer learns your buying motives based on previous purchases, and applies techniques related to those motives to win you over again and again. It is important to highlight that when we talk about motives, we do not mean well-considered reasons, for example when buying a phone, the camera megapixels and size of the display. We are talking about factors (peripheral cues) that have a positive influence on the decisions of people, when they are asked to do something. In recent decades, social scientists have observed human behaviour in persuasive circumstances in laboratory experiments and discovered several 'laws'[1] that explain why people say yes to certain requests of an influencer. These 'Cialdini' principles (named after a famous researcher of persuasion) form the basis of persuasion profiling, because using them in interactions with people makes them more likely to comply with persuasive offers. The principles elicit automatic behavioural reactions, the so-called *click-whirr* responses, and occur without conscious awareness. One of the Cialdini principles, *authority*, is an invisible force that has an impact on our decisions and attitudes because we fall under the influence of those who are wiser or more experienced than ourselves. For example, it is more likely that people buy a book with a recommendation from a famous author on the cover than that same book without the recommendation. Another principle of influence explains why we are more likely to buy a book that has a limited availability. It is the principle of *scarcity*: people want more of those things they can have less of, because on average, the thought of losing something motivates people more than the thought of gaining something of the same value. We can almost hear you thinking, "well not me, I know what I am doing". Guess again.

We all have our weaknesses when it comes to persuasion. We make countless decisions and choices each day. Some of these choices are made with consideration but most of them are made routinely and unconsciously. Click-whirr responses are often useful: they prevent us from being overloaded and guide us through a day full of choices. These automatic responses however also make us susceptible to persuasion. Psychologists long thought that all people responded in more or less the same way to the principles, but the fact is that we are not susceptible to the same principles[2] to the same degree. While the principle of authority might be effective to persuade one person, the principle of scarcity may not.

CHOOSE YOUR PRINCIPLE CAREFULLY

Using the right principle is crucial. Using the wrong strategy on the wrong person could even cause he or she to do the opposite of what a persuader is asking. If you want to predict how someone will act, the individual decisions of a person are better indicators of future behaviour than generally formulated principles describing average human behaviour. By tracking the behaviour of people online it is possible to keep a record of the principles of persuasion that are effective (or not) for each individual person. This is how persuasion profiles can be formed. When a consumer clicks on a particular advertisement wherein, for example, the strategy of authority is used, this strategy is seen as more effective than other strategies of persuasion. This strategy gets one point and the others zero. Over time the persuasion profile can predict accurately the strategies a person is most susceptible to. This determines which strategy of persuasion the person will be exposed to when he or she is in a buying process. Maurits Kaptein will now explain how working on persuasion profiling changed his perception of personalisation attempts in (internet) communication.

REFLECTING ON PERSUASION PROFILING

By Maurits Kaptein
Professor Data Science & Health
Tilburg University and JADS Den Bosch

Dean Eckles and I first started using the term 'persuasion profiling' in an article on its ethical implications: the term was deliberately chosen to be somewhat scary. We took the term from an early video by BJ Fogg that displayed the idea that the ways in which people were persuaded by technologies could be personalised. Surprisingly, however, it has found its way into both communication research and practice and has – as far as I can judge – lost most of its scariness (although rightfully many authors are still debating the ethical issues of persuasion profiling, and personalised persuasive technologies in general).

Currently, I guess the term is broadly used for what we called *"means* adaptation" (or personalisation); any method by which the argument(s) of a persuasive request, such as a sales pitch or a public education campaign, is adapted to the receiver. I still find this view informative. To illustrate, communication professionals and researchers are largely aware of the fact that in online communication the *ends* of a request are often personalised: the books presented to you when you go to amazon.com are different from those presented to me. However, what we often fail to recognise is that there is much more that can be personalised: whether or not you see large pictures of the products, whether or not you see the ratings of others, whether or not you see endorsements by other authors, whether or not an appeal is made to the excitement of reading the book, or rather to the safety and comfort of reading in your own home, etc. etc. All of the latter are adaptations of the means by which the persuasive request is made, and in my current perception, any personalisation of these means is broadly covered by the term *persuasion profiling*.

Working on persuasion profiling changed my perception of personalisation attempts in (internet) communication. First of all, it totally changed my perception of the value of data that we store in CRM databases or that is obtained by psychological trait measures. Initially I thought that these types of demographics and personality scores would be extremely valuable in matching the type of argument with the recipient of the message. However, comparative studies showed that when trying to predict the effectiveness of different means, the value of these measures is extremely quickly swamped by the value of historical responses. If I see you buy "bestsellers", this is likely to be a better prediction of your propensity to buy "bestsellers" in the future than any combination of your demographics, personality, etc. And believe me, we tried many such combinations.

Second, working on persuasion profiling quite radically changed my perception of a profile. I used to think of profiles as static descriptions of "types of people"; hence, in a personalised communication effort we would tailor the message towards one of a small set of possible profiles (you can easily imagine the "authority" profile, or the "scarcity" profile in the case of Cialdini's influence strategies). However, nowadays I see profiles as the collection of estimates of the effectiveness of different types of messages (including the uncertainty associated with these estimates) based on all the data we have available. For a computer to personalise a message it doesn't need to know that you belong to the "authority profile"; rather, it needs a good statistical model to predict which of the possible means available is most likely to be successful. I have largely moved away from human-interpretable models, towards "black-box" machine learning models, merely because of their effectiveness. This is a change I see in many areas of personalised communication.

Persuasion profiling also changed my perception of scale. I was used to thinking about personalisation on a relatively "small" scale: we would have different messages for males and females, or for introverts and for extraverts. Persuasion profiling highlighted for me that we do not need to limit ourselves to such "group personalisation", rather we can use all of the data that we have available about a person (including all the historical messages she or he responded to), to construct a message that is based on numerous factors (image size, price, argument type, text length, etc.). When adopting such an approach, simple pairwise AB testing of messages quickly turns out to be extremely inefficient, and we need to resort to novel evaluation methods; an exciting topic of research.

Finally, in some ways I believe the future of persuasion profiling is bright. I still think - as we noted in one of our first articles on the topic - that your browsing behaviour when purchasing products on the web might eventually be used to learn which means work for you, and this information could subsequently be used in your eHealth exercising coach to improve your health. This would be great. In other ways, however, there is a grim outlook: the business incentives currently seem aligned in such a way that only large corporations, without the conscious consent of users, use persuasion profiles to unconsciously sway consumers into buying more products. This aim is not high on my list of socially desirable communication research outcomes.

A SCIENTIFIC PERSPECTIVE

Over the last decade, scientists have wracked their brains over persuasion profiling and its effectiveness. These smart heads – mainly data analysts and psychologists – made a path for our understanding of the technique. We pick up where they left off.

As aforementioned, persuasion profiles are effective because they take into account the individual differences in susceptibility to persuasion. Dividing markets into 'homogenous' segments of people (also known as *market segmentation*) is not the most effective targeting method anymore since it is possible to track the behaviour of each individual person. Instead of a handful of segments, millions of profiles can be formed. But how do they function? When it comes to persuasion profiling, the techniques to make people comply are not selected and executed by a human persuader, but by a computer. The computer exposes people to several persuasion techniques and remembers the successes and failures. These processes of experimenting with techniques, learning from the past, and applying the most successful and personalised persuasion techniques, are the skills of the smart salesman mentioned earlier.

COMPUTER FLATTERY

While reading this, you might wonder whether people respond differently to the application of psychological principles to computers, compared to human beings. One interesting laboratory experiment[3] to highlight here is a study on people being polite to computers, that is to say applying good manners and being nice to others. Participants were asked to assess the performance of a computer after they had completed some tasks on it. Half of the participants assessed the performance of the computer on the same computer and half of the participants on another computer in the same room. The results indicated that if people assessed the performance on the same computer, their responses were significantly more positive than those using another computer. Without knowing it, the participants were actually 'polite' to the computer.

Another experiment showed that flattery of the computer affected people's responses in a positive way. The media equation, as a result of experiments like these, states that people treat new media as if they are real people. In other words, when a computer uses your persuasion profile to persuade you, it can be seen as a social actor. Computers apply 'social rules' in interactions with human in order to affect attitudes and behaviour. Keep in mind that the memory capacity of the salesman is limited, whereas computers have an infinite storage. They do not forget anything. Back to the functional triad of Fogg and colleagues, persuasion profiles could be considered as social actors if we viewed them from the perspective of internet users. From the perspective of marketers, they could be considered as a tool. They simplify the process of consideration and give an answer to the question of how to present commodities and services to each person.

NON-CRITICAL PROCESSING

So, persuasion profiles unconsciously track, evaluate, and direct behaviour by causing click-whirr responses. This invisible nature of the technology has consequences for the cognitive processing of information generated by persuasion profiles. The highly integrated nature of the technology means that we are not aware of its persuasive impact. As a result, the processing of information selected by persuasion profiles will be less critical, causing a relatively large impact.

STABLE SUSCEPTIBILITY TO PRINCIPLES

One of the criticisms of persuasion profiling is that the effect of a certain persuasion strategy on a person differs per product category. Because of that, persuasion profiles might not be capable of predicting the success of persuasion strategies for a wide range of products. The reasoning is that, for example, one might be susceptible to other strategies of influence when buying a cake or life insurance. It all depends on the persuasive context. A study by Kaptein and his colleague Eckles shows something different. They asked people to participate in two separate experiments, one in an online bookshop and one in an online music store. After several visits to the stores, the effectiveness of different persuasion strategies was measured for each person. The participants were not told that the two experiments were related. The analysis of the results revealed that there was a reasonably strong stability in the susceptibility to various principles of persuasion, no matter what the product was.

PERSONALISED PERSUASION USING PERSONALITY TRAITS

The Cialdini principles of influence are not the only psychological principles that can be personalised. Instead of using his principles as a foundation for persuasion profiling, you can also use other persuasive techniques. For example, psychologists determine people's personalities by using questionnaires designed to reveal aspects of individual characters. The analysis of these data consistently shows five (known as the *Big Five Personality Traits*) different dimensions of personality, which are openness, conscientiousness, extraversion, agreeableness, and neuroticism[4]. Research shows that advertisements that match with someone's personality traits are more effective, matching Cialdini's principles with persuasive techniques. One study[5] tested the effectiveness of matching personality traits. The researchers constructed five different advertisements promoting a cell phone with a few lines of text highlighting the motivational concerns associated with the personality traits. For extraversion, it stated: *"With Phone X, you'll always be where the excitement is"* and for neuroticism it said: *"Stay safe and secure with Phone X"*. The perceived effectiveness of the advertisements increased if the advertisement matched the personality traits, which were also measured. Not the personality traits themselves, but the appeals that connect to them are then personalised. Like the reasoning behind persuasion profiles, it shows that people are not a homogeneous mass and that they differ in their receptions.

As you can see, there are multiple ways to use persuasion profiling. We have discussed two options, based on Cialdini's principles and the 'Big Five Personality Traits'. Its adaptiveness forms part of the power of persuasion profiling; it makes it relatively easy to use.

FUTURE AND ETHICS

In the public and scientific debate, worries are being expressed about the use of adaptive persuasive technologies like persuasion profiling. A frequently used example in discussions, to point out the expected impact of new media on society, is Orwell's novel *1984*[6] in which he envisioned a dystopia of telescreens that were able to spy on people in their living rooms and broadcast messages in support of the ministry. We use computers to look at the world and they are able to look into our lives to see what we are doing and thinking. Moreover, intelligent technology is integrating into our lives; it is already in our mobile phone, television, and watch, and over time it will be everywhere. Some scientists[7] speak of a new economic system, which is called *surveillance capitalism*. This system depends on the global architecture of computer mediation and produces a new expression of power, the *Big Other* (another expletive to express worries about the impact of new media). This power can alter human behavioural patterns through monitoring and automated personalisation. We are not only being watched, but we are also being directed by technology in this new economic system. Imagine what would happen if behavioural information like search behaviour via Google, actions on Facebook and demographics for each individual were combined with the learnings from persuasion profiles. The salesman's dream would come true because he would know what people desire and how he must sell it.

YOUR PERSONAL PROFILE AS A WEAPON AGAINST PERSUASION

In the era of the internet of things, in these times of blurring borders between public and private, surveillance and hidden persuasion, it is important that people become skilled in interacting with smart technologies. In order to survive in the information age it is important that people acquire social intelligence – the ability to search for and evaluate information in complex social and technological environments. We have just discussed the potential hidden influence of persuasion profiles, but they could actually also contribute to our critical thinking in complex environments. Imagine that you have access to your own persuasion profile. You could learn from your own behaviour, even those actions that you were not aware of! *"Do I really copy other people that much when I make decisions? Next time I will think twice."* Kaptein argues that persuasion profiles could increase our autonomy when they teach us how we evaluate information and make decisions. As mentioned earlier, we can look at the threats of technology, but we can also look at the opportunities that technology could bring to society. One example[8] of adjusting persuasive techniques is the personalisation of three social influence strategies. The system in this example matches each student's susceptibility to one of the social influence strategies: social comparison (compare the performances of students on one course with the performance of other students); competition (using a leader board to provide students with a means to compete with each other); or social learning (by showing aggregate grade ranges and how many students have each grade range). The application of the right strategy to the right person should lead to stronger motivation for students to engage in online learning activities in order to improve their overall performance in educational courses.

So it seems that our thinking and actions can be predicted more accurately, especially when persuasion profiles will be combined with other forms of behavioural targeting in the future (means & ends). This gives us two challenges: a scientific and a societal one. The societal challenge is to make people skilled in interacting with ubiquitous intelligent technology. Continuing to search for ways to safeguard our free will and improve the quality of life, using technology, is the scientific challenge.

CLASSIFICATION

★★★★★ ★★★★★ ★★★★★ ★★★★★ ★★★★★

References and notes

1 We highlight the principles of authority and scarcity. Other principles are: reciprocity, commitment & consistency, social proof and liking. For a comprehensive theoretical explanation and discussion of the professional applicability of all the 6 principles of influence, read: Cialdini, R.B. (2001). Influence: Science and practice. Boston: Allyn & Bacon. In a more recent book, Cialdini introduced a seventh principle of persuasion, which is unity: when you emphasise the shared identity (e.g., ethnicity, family, religion and political affiliations) in an attempt to influence someone, the likelihood of compliant behavior increases. Read: Cialdini, R.B. (2016). Pre-suasion: A revolutionary way to influence and persuade.

2 Maurits Kaptein (2015) wrote a nice popular scientific book about persuasion profiles. Read: Kaptein, M. (2015). Persuasion profiling: How the internet knows what makes you tick. If you are interested in more scientific work on individual differences in effects of online persuasion, read: Kaptein, M., & Eckles, D. (2012). Heterogeneity in the effects of online persuasion. Journal of Interactive Marketing, 26(3), 176-188. doi:10.1016/j.intmar.2012.02.002

3 Reeves, B. & Nass, C. (1996). The media equation: How people treat computers, television, and new media like real people and places. Cambridge University Press.

4 These could be remembered with the acronym OCEAN. The British behavioral researcher Daniel Nettle wrote a nice book "Personality" which provides an overview of the Big Five Theory. Read: Nettle, D. (2007). Personality: What makes you the way you are? New York: Oxford University Press. Do you want to determine where you fall on the scale of the personality traits? There is an online inventory that helps you find it out within 10 minutes: http://www.personalityassessor.com/bigfive/.

5 Hirsh, J. B., Kang, S. K., & Bodenhausen, G. V. (2012). Personalized persuasion tailoring persuasive appeals to recipients' personality traits. Psychological Science, 23(6), 578-581.

6 Weir, T. (2014). Today is the new 1984: Big Brother is not only watching you – he is selling to you. In C.J. Pardun (Ed.), Advertising and Society: An Introduction (pp.169-174). West Sussex: Wiley Blackwell.

7 Zuboff, S. (2016). Master or slave? The fight for the soul of our information civilization. Public Affairs.

8 Orji, F.A., Vassileva, J., & Greer, J.E. (2018). Personalized persuasion for promoting students' engagement and learning. PPT@PERSUASIVE.

#10 LOCATION-BASED ADVERTISING

Location-based advertising allows companies to approach consumers individually, on the basis of their current location, dynamically and in real time[1].

Suppose you are looking for a new pair of jeans from a certain brand and in a certain colour, but you are a little short of cash. When you park your car in the parking lot of the shopping centre, your smartphone beeps, and shows a nice overview of retailers who sell pairs of jeans of the brand you like. You choose to visit a specific retailer, and when you approach the store: another beep. A pair of jeans in your size is currently available in the store in the model and colour that you like. You decide to go in. Exactly in front of the shelf with the pairs of jeans that interest you, you get another message, customised to your specific need: an extra sale on the regular sales price in your size, only if you decide to buy them right now. The ad says 'especially for you' and the offer also feels like it, considering your cash-flow problem! Although you feel slightly uncomfortable about being tracked, you decide to buy it.

DEFINITION AND KEY FEATURES

When we frame location-based advertising (LBA) as only beneficial, as in the example above, it seems like an innovation that is hard to resist, making the ultimate dream come true: no more ad overload, because the ads are specifically tailored to your needs, at the moment that you want them to show up. However, when you ask 10 people around you whether they would allow advertising to appear on their smartphones, even when it is tailormade, many will say 'my phone is off limits for advertisers'! Is LBA an innovation to account for ...

LBA IS LOCATION- AND TIME-BOUND

An increasing number of retailers are offering their own mobile apps, often incorporating a digital version of their loyalty programme card. Consumers might appreciate the convenience and possibility of checking for special offers or for information about developments around the brand, and retailers get unique information about their customers, such as their purchase behaviour, links to their social media accounts, and most importantly, their location. Many apps require consumers to provide access to location services in order to function properly. This means that retailers know where their customers are and can target them accordingly with location-based mobile ads.

As well as being location-bound, LBA is time-bound because information about the location is sent through in real-time, which makes it possible for advertisers to further tailor their messages. In our example, only consumers who are standing in front of a specific shelf with the desired pairs of jeans from certain brands receive the tailored ads, not the ones who are standing in front of shelves with other products. The central element of this innovation is that personal online data are tied to an offline context using location detection. LBA can only be practised successfully when consumers have opted in, meaning that they have downloaded the app of a company, permitting the advertiser to access the location data on the GPS system of their smartphone.

LBA IN PRACTICE

The practice of mobile behavioural advertising, which involves monitoring and analysing online customer behaviour and their location in order to provide behaviour-based personalised advertisements, is on the increase. Some marketers consider mobile marketing as the next step in the evolution of marketing, and accordingly, mobile expenditure is on the rise. Several companies experiment with a specific form of mobile marketing, LBA, inside and outside stores, for instance Hunkemoller, Starbucks, Shell, Dr. Pepper and Coca cola in The Netherlands. The expectations of marketers about the potential of LBA are highly strung, but most of them have a 'just wait and see' attitude.

LBA IS A PROMISING INNOVATION?
On the one hand, practitioners believe that LBA is a promising innovation, not only for selling products, but also for approaching consumers in real-time, made possible by their smartphones, which they always carry with them. LBA can increase traffic in their stores and brand awareness. Consumers are actively involved with the brand, when they view the LBA. It allows advertisers to target groups on the basis of their socio-demographic traits. LBA might also attract new customers and visits to websites.

On the other hand, there is scepticism. Mobile marketing faces a serious challenge as LBA might arouse feelings of intrusiveness and may be perceived as spam. For instance, when consumers are shopping, they do not want to be disturbed by ads on their phones. A bigger problem may be that consumers feel that their privacy is being invaded and they are therefore not willing to share their location in real-time, or their personal data. They may not like the idea that they are constantly being traced, and their data collected and stored.

GEOGRAPHICAL AREA OF INTEREST

Several retailers using LBA are experimenting with proximity and message content. As in our example, a crucial parameter for the success of LBA seems to be distance. At what proximity should advertisers predefine the area within which they fire their ads at consumers? One can approach customers far away from where the offer is optimally relevant: say at home, in a car park in front of a shopping centre, OUTSIDE a specific store, or when customers are standing in front of the shelf with the desired product INSIDE a specific store. The virtual demarcation of a geographical area of interest outside a store is called geo-fencing. Inside a store in front of a specific shelf, this demarcation is realised using Bluetooth and iBeacon technology. In fact, iBeacons are devices in stores that can send a Bluetooth low-energy signal. This technology offers a much higher level of precision than geo-fencing.

LBA may be used for different goals, such as "Real-World Retargeting". The iBeacon tracker connects to the consumer's smartphone and reads out a unique number. These identifiers are used by advertising networks to target consumers. Consumers who have visited a store, but have not purchased anything, can be retargeted on a later time. Edwin Metselaar will now show how people's locations can be used to target them with advertisements and he will explain the phenomenon of real-time bidding.

REFLECTING ON LOCATION-BASED ADVERTISING

By Edwin Metselaar
Technologist
Mobile Professionals

For the last couple of years it has been possible to use the sensors of a smartphone for advertising purposes. Next to location, you can also use things like the connection type (WiFi vs 4G) or the accelerometer to see if someone is moving, or other sensors. This chapter has mostly described the use of close-proximity technology, but there are other ways to implement LBA. One of these is through real-time bidding (RTB) on the basis of the location of consumers. I will explain briefly how this works.

SELLING DATA IN AN ONLINE AUCTION-BASED SYSTEM

A publisher (like a newspaper or a game) that wants to make its in-app traffic available for external advertisers can automatically sell this traffic (also called inventory in digital advertising). The traffic consists of impressions (chances that a consumer will see an ad in the app) that can be sold in an online auction-based system. Publishers can implement a piece of software that sends signals to an advertiser that an impression is available. Next, multiple advertisers can select to bid on that particular impression. Because the publisher app that tries to sell the impression can have access to the sensors of the smartphone (when the user has approved this of course), the app can send information from these sensors to the auction system in order to sell more valuable impressions. In many cases, more data (such as location data) can mean more value. Advertisers respond to the received information and place a bid when they think it is useful for their advertising campaign to buy those impressions. I will describe some use cases of this technology below and will give you some ideas for how to apply this technology in your communication strategies. Finally, I will also describe some of the potential issues and pitfalls to take into account.

EXTEND LBA WITH THE POWER OF REPETITION

The first and most straightforward form of LBA in the context of RTB is to use it to target smartphones that are currently present in a certain geographic area. This is comparable to what people have been doing since the dawn of advertising with billboards in the streets. Actually, I was once asked to show ads only when people were inside very specific bars. I just advised the advertiser to put up a poster in the bar. Hopefully people in a bar are looking more around them than at their phone. It is usually not worth the extra communication and targeting effort of reaching such a small amount of people with LBA. This aligns with the results of scientific research, which are discussed in the next paragraph.

However, because you can retarget phones that you have already seen in your campaign, you can now also target phones that have been in a certain geographic area in the past. This second approach to LBA makes it quite a lot more powerful, and something that cannot easily be done in another way. You can extend the initial LBA with the power of repetition, which increases the chance that someone will be influenced by the communication. This was recently used in a campaign targeted at festival-goers. A music festival had been organised with thousands of visitors. An LBA campaign was targeted on phones in that area.

Later when people were at home, they could be reached again with references to the festival, hopefully triggering a positive association with the brand that ran the campaign.

DIGITAL OUT OF HOME (DOOH) ADVERTISING

A third approach and innovation in this area is to combine LBA on smartphones with Digital Out Of Home (DOOH advertising). When you detect that your LBA campaign on smartphones is reaching quite a lot of consumers in a particular geographic area, you can decide to dynamically change the digital billboards that are present in the neighbourhood of the phones that have been shown the initial ad. You can greatly increase the number of times someone sees the ad by doing this. The combination of LBA and DOOH is not yet used a lot, but I expect this multi-channel location-based approach to become very popular in the near future.

MESSAGES DEPENDING ON THE LOCATION

A final and more intricate way of using location is by dynamically showing a different message depending on the location. You can think about communication for a beverage in areas near the beach with ads that use images with sand and beach chairs. Consumers who are in the cities will be shown other creatives that show the same beverage being consumed in a square or garden. To take it one step further, you can couple external sources like temperature, wind, and rain to the ads. The weather can be quite different in different parts of the country, so when you know the location, you can check the weather on that spot and use that signal to send a different message. An ice cream commercial usually works better when it is hot and a commercial for a food delivery service works better when it is raining at the location of the device.

SUSPICIOUS DATA

Because an advertiser values impressions with more information higher then impressions without it, you can guess what happens. Publishers in this ecosystem have an incentive to gain as many impressions as possible with location-based information, even when they in reality do not possess such information. There is no easy way for advertisers to see if the location information is actually correct, but they need to pay higher prices anyway. One of the most common cases is that instead of using the GPS module or location services of the device to get the location information, the IP address of the device is used and mapped with a list of cities/IP addresses. Then the centre of the matched city is set as the location of the phone. So in this case, the advertiser thinks that someone is in the centre of a city, nearby a potential shop, but in reality they may be on the outskirts of that city, nowhere near that shop. These locations based on IP addresses and mapped to a city centre are called 'centroids'.

If you had access to the raw data in the advertising platform that you use, you could detect this. Unfortunately, most advertising systems let you only select locations without showing how the targeting exactly works. This way it is very hard to determine whether the location data used is of any value and worth the premium price. Another issue that I often encounter is that locations are represented by more digits behind the comma then are actually technically possible with current GPS technology in smartphones. This indicates suspicious data. It is often indicative of a faulty application of the GPS technique in the app, or it is a 'calculated' instead of a measured location. These and other issues can be overcome, but it requires a trustworthy technology partner who can explain and maybe even show exactly how they handle these types of cases.

Summarising: Be creative in the use of LBA, combine it with other communication technologies and make sure you know what is going on behind the scenes so you will not pay extra for sub-par targeting.

A SCIENTIFIC PERSPECTIVE

Scientists have become interested in LBA during the last decade. This has opened up promising avenues for cooperation between science and practice, because the basic scientific questions are interesting for both parties. How do people process LBA? And what are the effects?

LBA MIGHT RAISE CONSUMERS' SELF-EFFICACY

When ads appear on the display of consumers' smartphones they feel that their daily flow of life has been intruded and they are conscious of the persuasion attempt. In an instant they will decide to look at the ad, or avoid viewing it altogether. When they decide to view it, they will conclude that the ad is tailor-made, perfectly fitting their goals like a glove, thus optimally relevant for them, which may lead to systematic processing of its content, and subsequent favourable effects, such as a positive attitude and buying behaviour[2]. LBA might also raise consumers' self-efficacy because it helps them to make choices in a swift way.

DISTANCE DOES MATTER IN THE ACCEPTANCE OF LBA

Research has shown positive effects of LBA. When using LBA it is important to determine whether those ads are really relevant to the context of consumers when they receive them[3]. They are interrupted in their activities by the buzzing of their smartphones, 'so the offer had better well be worth the disturbance!' It is of utmost importance that the firing of ads with the right message happens exactly at the location where consumers are most receptive to them, for instance in a supermarket in front of the shelf with the desired products.

As expected, privacy is an issue, but more so in private situations, and less in the public domain, as in a supermarket. When consumers receive tailor-made location-based messages that also match their goal, such as an ad for an article on their grocery list[4], the trade-off between losing privacy and gaining relevancy weighs in favour of the latter. This is also caused by the mindset of consumers. When they are shopping, they act like consumers. Therefore they experience ads that are fired to them in stores as more congruent with this goal, than for instance at home, causing the ads to be less intrusive and more effective when received in a supermarket. This means that distance does matter in the acceptance of LBA.

DISPLAYS MAY BE AS EFFECTIVE AS LBA

The concerns of communication professionals about consumers' feelings of intrusiveness are justified. Consumers often perceive the tracking of their behaviour on mobile devices as intrusive and as an erosion of their privacy[5]. This is problematic, because perceived intrusiveness can have detrimental effects for brands[6]. Another critical note is that LBA does not always have an edge on traditional advertising. LBA outperforms traditional displays in supermarkets, but only when it is tailored to the specific goal of consumers, aligning with the products on their grocery list, and when it is important to draw their attention. When a location-based mobile ad just shows a general sales promotion for a desired brand, displays are just effective as LBA[7]. Maybe even more effective, because the sound of the smartphone disturbs people and causes irritation, especially when it does not differ from the usual sound of, for instance, an incoming WhatsApp message.

A LITTLE CHALLENGE TO DECIPHER LBA REDUCES FEELINGS OF BEING INTRUDED

Does message design matter? Little research has investigated how location-based mobile messages should be designed to maximise their effectiveness and avoid undesired outcomes such as feelings of intrusiveness. Openness in mobile ad design decreases consumers' feelings of intrusiveness and consequently increases their purchase behaviour. This means that a little challenge for consumers to decipher LBA helps to reduce feelings of being intruded, but ads should not become too complex[8].

Finally, usability is an issue to think about when designing LBA campaigns. For instance, coupons offered in LBA should be easy to cash in.

In all, research shows indeed that relevancy does the trick and facilitates the processing of LBA, that this relevancy is fuelled by designing tailor-made messages, and that the design of the message matters. Once the consumer has opted-in to receive location-based messaging, and has decided to view a location-based ad, the chances for effective communication are optimal.

FUTURE AND ETHICS

The rise of LBA in the past decade does have a downside. Intrusiveness may soon become an even bigger problem as LBA becomes more popular among advertisers.

OVERLOAD OF LBA FIGHTING FOR ATTENTION

Let's go back to the supermarket example. Academic research focuses on the effects of a single LBA campaign, but what happens if you get several LBA messages fired at you when getting your groceries? Then we would get an enormous overload of LBA fighting for attention, leading to feelings of intrusiveness, which influences effectiveness negatively. This calls for self-regulation of LBA advertisers, otherwise LBA will die an early death. Furthermore, consumers' awareness of privacy infringement by companies increases as a result of public debate, for instance about Facebook's privacy policy. Their privacy seems at stake as advertisers know more about them, who they are, what they do, why they do it, and how they do it. Negative effects of LBA may even affect the relations that consumers experience with brands. Research has shown that negative experiences of consumers with LBA can be detrimental for their perceived brand ethical value, which may enlarge advertisement avoidance and diminish the quality of the brand-customer relationship[9].

Another problem for advertisers is that people shut-off location detection and Bluetooth on their smartphones because of the already mentioned privacy concerns but also because of a diminishing battery power when continuous tracking of the smartphone is possible.

INVESTING IN IBEACON TECHNOLOGY

To fully develop this innovation, marketers should invest further in optimally tailoring their ads to specific consumer interests, based on recurrent purchases at the same or similar locations. Here, an investment in iBeacon technology might be beneficial, as this Bluetooth-based technology allows consumers to be targeted considerably more precisely than the more common geo-fencing approaches. LBA can be combined with real-time marketing, customising the offer depending on the weather, or an event going on. In addition, a more "active" consumer role seems to evoke more positive brand responses, which could be further stimulated by offering consumers a more encompassing "ad experience," including, for example, elements of gamification, augmented reality, interactive banners, digital storytelling, and ads that are framed as questions and are a little open to interpretation.

SYNERGY BETWEEN OFFLINE AND ONLINE ADVERTISING

The beauty of LBA is that it offers a synergy between offline and online advertising. In potency, LBA is a powerful innovation that makes life easier, for instance, providing tailored information when you want to buy a pair of jeans and are a little short of cash. When companies and brands convincingly show consumers the added value of LBA, they will allow them to use privacy-sensitive information such as their location. The punch line is to gradually introduce consumers to LBA, to experiment with it, and to research it. The future will show whether marketers will be able to develop LBA into an instrument that will succeed in providing relevance instead of feelings of intrusion and privacy invasion.

CLASSIFICATION

★★★★★   ★★★★★   ★★★★★   ★★★★★   ★★★★★

References and notes

1   Bauer, C. & Strauss, C. (2016) Location-based advertising on mobile devices. A literature review and analysis. Management Review Quarterly, 66, 159–194.

2   Jagoe, A. (2003). Mobile location services: The definitive guide. Prentice Hall, Upper Saddle River, NJ.

3   Banerjee, S., & Dholokia, R. R. (2008). Mobile advertising: Does location based advertising work? International Journal of Mobile Marketing. 3(2), 68-74.

4   Van't Riet, J., Hühn, A., Ketelaar, P. E., Khan, V. J., Konig, R., Rozendaal, E., & Markopoulos, P. (2016). Investigating the effects of location-based advertising in the supermarket: Does goal congruence trump location congruence? Journal of Interactive Advertising. DOI: 10.1080/15252019.2015.1135089.

5   Gupta, S. (2013). For mobile devices, think apps, not ads. Harvard Business Review, 91(3), 70–75.

6   Ketelaar, P. E., Bernritter, S. F., van't Riet, J., Hühn, A. E., van Woudenberg, T. J., Müller, B. C., & Janssen, L. (2017). Disentangling location-based advertising: The effects of location congruency and medium type on consumers' ad attention and brand choice. International Journal of Advertising, 36(2), 356-367.

7   Aguirre, E., Mahr, D., Grewal, D., de Ruyter, K., & Wetzels, M. (2015). Unraveling the personalization paradox: The effect of information collection and trust-building strategies on online advertisement effectiveness. Journal of Retailing, 91(1), 34-49. https://doi.org/10.1016/j.jretai.2014.09.005.

8   Ketelaar, P. E., Bernritter, S. F., van Woudenberg, T. J., Rozendaal, E., Konig, R. P., Hühn, A. E., ... & Janssen, L. (2018). "Opening" location-based mobile ads: How openness and location congruency of location-based ads weaken negative effects of intrusiveness on brand choice. Journal of Business Research, 91, 277-285.

9   Mpinganjira, M., & Maduku, D. K. (2019). Ethics of mobile behavioral advertising: Antecedents and outcomes of perceived ethical value of advertised brands. Journal of Business Research, 95, 464-478.

#11 GAMIFICATION

Gamification stands for the application of techniques and elements that are typical for games, but in a non-game environment.

In a theme park in The Netherlands, called the Efteling, lives a family who is always hungry. They don't like meat, bread, or fish but love to gobble up paper. 'Papier hier!', which means 'paper here', they shout repeatedly when you pass by. If you feed them with paper rubbish, they give you a friendly 'thank you'. Humpty Dumpty (in Dutch: Holle Bolle Gijs), always hungry for 'paper' makes the children in the park enthusiastic to put their paper trash in his mouth. Some children are even so excited that they collect paper and ask random passengers for rubbish to feed Holle Bolle Gijs, keeping the Eftelings' environment clean.

DEFINITION AND KEY FEATURES

In 1896, marketers sold postage stamps to merchants, who in turn used them to reward loyal customers. This antique example is seen as one of the first applications of gamification. Gamification has been used in various ways since then. In the sector of communication professionals, gamification is described as a development in which elements from video games are used in environments that are not game related, in order to stimulate the motivation and ultimately the behaviour of users in those environments. In the elaboration of this definition, strong emphasis is placed on two central characteristics of gamification. Firstly, there must be a clear connection between parts of the (online) gaming world and parts of the physical offline world. Secondly, gamification is about the application of elements from games, not about fully developed computer games or role plays. It is important to mention that gamification distinguishes itself from other game-related concepts, such as advergames and serious games. In both advergames and serious games, there is a fully developed game, whereas gamification uses game elements in a non-game environment.

A more recent example of gamification is Starbucks, which rewarded its customers with a free latte if they had visited five different Starbuck locations. McDonalds also made use of gamification by encouraging its customers to create their own burger. Some winning entries were put on the menu for a short time. Gamification is also used frequently in non-commercial areas: in Sweden, a speed camera lottery was introduced to reduce the average speed of motorists on the motorway. Everyone who complied with the speed limits automatically got the chance to win the money coming from the speeding tickets. In the United Kingdom, an insurance company uses gamification to encourage young people to drive safer. The safer the young people drive, the more discount they receive on insurance premiums. Gamification is also used in the workplace to make monotonous work, such as working on the assembly line, more fun.

These are just a few examples. Think of a boring task that you have had to perform today, or this week. How could the use of a game element have made this task more fun? By thinking carefully about this important question and finding an answer, you are laying a foundation for the gamification of the task. This is an essential feature of gamification; through the gameful design of (digital) communication processes you are better able to involve people and let them do things. The users are often deliberately called 'players' by gamification designers. Typical game elements that are often used in gamification include progress indicators, rankings that allow comparison with other players, and feedback for the players with regard to the completed tasks.

GAMIFICATION IMPROVES THE USER EXPERIENCE

In the marketing industry, gamification seems to be seen as the method to increase customer engagement and improve the user experience. As more and more organisations wonder how they can involve customers, citizens, or patients in certain matters, the demand for gamification solutions is increasing. This is underlined by the worldwide value of the gamification market. In 2015, the market value was 1.65 billion dollars[1] and it is expected that the market value will rise to 11.1 billion dollars in 2020. Within the sector of communication professionals, it is certainly believed that gamification is an excellent method by which companies can offer their target group an improved service or user experience. In addition, the increased availability of technologies and connectivity, for example in the form of smartphones, facilitates the use of gamification.

GAMIFICATION IN PRACTICE

From the moment in 2002 when the term 'gamification' was used for the first time, it received more and more attention. The results of the annual trend research of the IT research and advisory firm Gartner showed that gamification was at the peak of its hype in 2011[2]. Gartner predicted that 70% of 2000 global organisations would do something with gamification in 2014. But one year later, Gartner stated that: "*by 2014, 80 percent of current gamified applications will fail to meet business objectives primarily because of poor design*"[3]. The enormous popularity of gamification therefore seemed to be accompanied by considerable scepticism. Sceptics argue that gamification is used too simplistically, with potentially many negative consequences as a result. This scepticism was fuelled by the different gamification applications that did not live up to expectations due to 'bad' design or were outright harmful to the organisation. A company that used meaningless gamification is Zappos. The shoe retailer thought it was a good idea to reward its VIP members with badges for regular shopping and writing reviews. Apart from the fact that the badge might look cool, the purpose and meaning of these badges were totally unclear. Nobody knew when you got them or for what, and users were thus left confused.

UNDERSTANDABILITY IS KEY

Burke, lead researcher at Gartner, attributes the defective application of gamification to a faulty design[4]. The mistake most companies make, according to Burke, is that they place too much emphasis on the hobby horses of gamification, such as point systems or rankings. This makes gamification too simplistic and superficial, with the result that it is simply not interesting for the target group. Kleinberg[5] adds that *"in order for your game – or your gamified non-game experience – to be engaging, people have to understand how to play it."* He states that many gamification applications often forget the basic condition – understandability – with all the negative consequences that it entails. A lack of concrete business objectives and objectives for a gamification project lead to inferiority.

The global market value of gamification (and its expected increase) indicates that the industry welcomes it. Burke states that almost all sectors can benefit from gamification, because it can contribute to achieving three business objectives: changing behaviour, the development of skills, and facilitating innovations[6]. The potential to change behaviour and thereby generate more direct or indirect revenue is the reason for many companies to apply gamification[7]. A subtle example is the way Linked-In entices its users to fill in their profile data. A bar indicates what percentage of the profile is already filled in. By specifying what needs to be done to get this to a higher percentage, Linked-In persuade users to fill in all the data in a playful way. In other words, clever choices for the design of the environment in which users interact affect the decision-making processes of individuals. In the next part, Jeroen van Mastrigt theorises further about gamified infrastructures and societal implications.

REFLECTING ON GAMIFICATION

By Jeroen van Mastrigt
Partner & Strategist
WeLoveYourWork

Recent studies from the field of happiness economics show that most activities people engage in on a daily basis, such as working, studying, commuting, and care, have a negative effect on their happiness. There are, on the other hand, activities that positively contribute to our happiness, such as arts, sports, or being in nature. These generally make up only a small percentage of the day and are often considered a playful 'waste of time'. This not only leads to a loss of happiness, but also losses in productivity and burn-outs, with enormous costs.

Over the past decades, academics and designers have been creating more engaging and effective ways of studying, training, organising, or working through the application of games, play, and game design principles outside the context of entertainment. This field is known as applied game design and encompasses categories such as design for serious games, exergames, advergames, and gamification.

REAL VIRTUALITY

For several decennia the paradigm of the 'virtual world' has been dominant in this domain. The governing idea was that a player would step into an engaging virtual world, learn about and/or practise with certain concepts and after that return to the real world with his or her newly acquired knowledge and skills. Since the introduction of the idea of gamification (around 2010) the discourse has shifted towards a paradigm of 'real virtuality': game design principles are integrated within the real world itself, for instance to motivate, nudge certain behaviour (such as receiving currency for undertaking real life activities, for example unlocking abilities in Pokémon Go by walking).

The advent of the Internet of Things will, it is believed, make way for a perfect gamification infrastructure, enabling the realisation of an engaging, motivational virtual layer on top of reality. Superimposing 'virtual' systems of rulesets and mechanics onto reality comes with under-appreciated social responsibility. If you can engage and nudge people into showing healthy, sustainable, effective behaviour, or steer their opinion in a positive way, you can also probably nudge them into showing unhealthy, addictive, non-sustainable behaviour, or steer their opinion in a negative way. And who decides what is positive or negative? Is there is an inherent asymmetry in knowledge that can be designed and therefore exploited? What is the procedural rhetoric underlying these gamified systems? Are people engaged in these gamified realities aware that they are part of a game? And can a system with real-world consequences still be considered virtual or a game? What about the consequences of virtual characters generating and spreading fake news to influence opinions? Most people will agree that the Chinese social credit system, a government initiative for developing a national reputation system, punishing people (slowing your internet speed, banning your children from the best schools, denying loans) because they show 'unwanted behaviour' is perceived as neither positive nor fun in the West. But by what calculus can we evaluate the extent to which our own solutions can be contextualised and evaluated to ensure that they remain non-coercive and inclusive? We could, for example, consider insurance companies giving you perks and bonuses for the steps you take to be suitably responsible, but is this the thin end of the wedge?

Innovation strategists, system designers, and interaction designers working in the applied game domain are still mainly focused on simulation, immersion, and connecting humans as effectively as possible to systems, working on orchestrating design elements to create extrinsic motivation, starting from a user-centred design perspective.

A PROFESSIONAL PARADIGM

But in the age of real virtuality we need to thoroughly rethink the profession of applied game design. This could begin with considering the intrinsic motivation of people and their potential happiness; thoroughly understanding the ethics and procedural rhetoric involved in applying game design elements; and co-designing algorithms and systems. Often this will involve redesigning services or organisations instead of marrying new elements and technology to an older way of organising. Therefore, the profession of applied game design in the age of real virtuality will need to evolve from the metaphor of being an interior architect, to that of an urban planner (that is, moving from orchestrating elements within a given context towards co-designing systems within the context of other systems). This means not simply using a user-centred design approach to effectively connect people to systems, but designing new systems from scratch around the intrinsic motivation and the autonomy of people, and in doing so creating true agency. And not simply having a focus on design and psychology, but also on enabling sovereignty and the conservation of the self by design, sustaining freedom by designing economies and rules, starting with philosophy, ethics, anthropology, and smart urbanism. This will play a pivotal role in realising what the Japanese call Society 5.0: a human-centred society focused not on the Quantified Self, but on the new spaces for our qualified selves.

A SCIENTIFIC PERSPECTIVE

To understand the effect of gamification, it is important to have a clear scientific definition. Let us first compare gamification against other game-related concepts such as serious (applied) gaming, also discussed in this book. In order to provide insight into this distinction, Detering and colleagues have designed a model (see figure 1 below). In essence, this model divides the 'playing field' into two axes: the *entertainment goal* (gaming vs. playing) of the product and the extent to which game elements are part (whole vs. parts) of a system. Whereas playing denotes a more free-form, expressive, improvisational, recombination of behaviours, gaming captures playing structured by rules and competitive strife towards goals[8]. Gameful design (gamification) is located in the top right corner of this model.

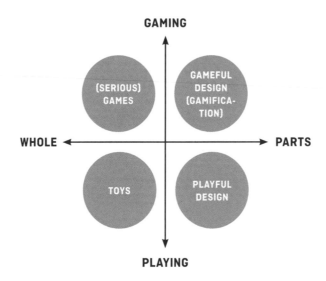

Play- and game-related concepts, distinguished by two axes (Deterding et al., 2011)

Let's take the speed camera lottery in Sweden as an example. The rule to win a sum of money is clear: players must stick to the maximum speed. Game elements are integrated into the physical world, bounded by rules with a clear goal. Now that gamification is scientifically defined, which processes underlie its operation? First of all, the effects of gamification are often explained on the basis of the self-determination theory[9]. This theory states that intrinsic motivation comes from the gratification of three psychological basic needs. Gamification motivates players to show certain behaviour by responding to: competence, relatedness, and autonomy. 1) *competence*: people like to control the result of their actions and to experience mastery; 2) *relatedness*: people have a universal desire for interaction and connection with others; and 3) *autonomy*: the human urge to make choices for ourselves, to act freely, not being under pressure. By satisfying these psychological needs, people are motivated from within, rather than by extrinsic motivation where the motivation comes from outside. Take, for example, the involvement of employees in a company: intrinsically motivated employees work hard because they find fun and honour in doing their job as well as possible. In extrinsically motivated employees, however, the motivation comes from outside: they look forward to a promotion, a pay rise, or maybe just a pat on the back. By integrating game elements into daily practice that satisfy the three basic needs, the engagement of employees could be increased by intrinsic motivation.

DIFFERENT ELEMENTS FULFIL DIFFERENT FUNCTIONS

That gamification influences motivation has been confirmed by numerous studies. However, gamification was often treated as a generic construct, neglecting the fact that different game-design elements fulfil different functions. In an experimental study[10], a digital warehouse was simulated where participants were given the task of picking orders (using a packing slip to find materials and supplies and prepare them for shipment to customers or for internal use). To investigate gamification this was a suitable task because in itself it is not a stimulating or motivating task so it has potential for improvement, using game design. In the experiment, different configurations of game-design elements were varied and then analysed to investigate their effect on the fulfilment of basic psychological needs. It emerged that meaningful stories, teammates, and avatars affect experiences of social relatedness while badges, leader boards, and performance graphs positively affect competence and satisfaction.

PROCESSING GAMIFICATION

The PCMC model of Buijzen and colleagues[11] can be used to explain the effects of gamification from an information-processing perspective. Game elements are often changeable and interactive. As a result, they require a relatively large amount of cognitive capacity from users. Moreover, the user who acts freely (but on the basis of rules) and receives feedback on his own actions (autonomy) is the centre of a gamified design. A well-designed gamification application responds to the (intrinsic) motivations of customers, which leads to the allocation of more cognitive resources. This causes prominently advertised brands or products, for example, to remain in the *top of the mind*, which may allow customers to stay loyal longer through more engagement.

GAMIFICATION AND ITS DIFFERENT FUNCTIONS

Within Foggs' Functional Triad, gamification can be interpreted as a tool with which an organisation can influence its target group's decisions. An example of this is an app with gamification applications that stimulate diabetes patients to pay more attention to their blood sugar levels[12]. In addition, gamification can be used to simulate experiences as a medium. A great example of this is Into D'Mentia[13], an experience built in a mobile container to create understanding about people with dementia. The simulation starts with a visitor who goes to a door with a bunch of keys and there are groceries at that door. As the visitor wants to go inside, he or she has to find the right key between the foreign keys in the key bunch. When the visitor finally has opened the door, the voice says: "Finally you are there, now put the groceries in the fridge." Once the refrigerator is found, it appears that five packs of milk and four packs of ham are already in it, which is strange because the moment the visitor looks into the bag with groceries, a lot of milk, and a pack of ham are also found there. In the experience, tricks are played with the visitors' minds, so that they are left with confusion. This confusion is the procedural rhetoric of the gamified experience, to create empathy around dementia. Many people leave the set-up in tears. After the experience, people state that they better understand what their parents or the person they care for is experiencing. Now consider yourself, reasoning with the self-determination theory, which psychological basic needs are invoked here? How do they influence the meaning that visitors derive from the experience?

So, all in all, does gamification work? Juho Hamari, a professor of gamification, analysed 24 empirical studies with his colleagues on the effect of gamification applications on motivation and behaviour[14]. No less than 21 studies showed an effect of gamification on behaviour, in different contexts: from commerce to education and from health to sustainable consumption. So, the answer is yes, gamification works.

FUTURE AND ETHICS

Several factors make it plausible that gamification will be used more often in the future: technology becoming cheaper, success stories, and the prevalence of the game medium[15]. Nevertheless, the increasing use of gamification is accompanied by criticism. Some critics think[16] that the large-scale use of gamification creates a façade that does not realise its promises.

The application of gamification would privilege the media-wise user in the current 'techno-utopia'. This seems to correspond with what Lievrouw calls network literacies; in her view, individuals should have media-related competencies if they want to join the complex online communication networks of today. However, we do not agree with the view that gamification is only effective for media-wise users because effective gamified designs to stimulate attitudes and behaviour are based on people's intrinsic basic needs and competencies. A well-gamified design is just as powerful in its simplicity.

EFFECTIVE AND ETHICAL?

One of the most outspoken critics is Bogost. He states that marketers and large organisations simplify and exploit gamification to make 'an easy' profit[17]. According to Bogost, gamification designers use the human tendency to want to play, in a devious way to generate turnover. The gamification designers exploit this tendency to stimulate certain emotions, such as joy, surprise, pride, and so on. This in turn can increase the involvement of individuals in the organisation, with the ultimate goal of selling products or services. Sceptics[18] are also critical about the effectiveness of gamification because companies use gamification too superficially. Many companies rely on achievement badges for completing a task, without giving any context to it. Users drop out, so that responding to intrinsic motivation is impossible in advance. Or, because of the tunnel vision of companies over the competitive element, the users are only concerned with acquiring and propagating social status. There is then a danger that the desired positive behavioural change will be reflected in a negative behavioural change. The Israel Defence Force (IDF) in 2012 showed how far gamification can go with a heavily criticised application in the fight against Hamas. By killing enemies, members of the IDF could earn badges and go up in rank.

GAMIFICATION USED FOR GOOD

Inducing positive emotions is characteristic of positive technology, technology designed to improve the quality of our lives. Games could make boring things more pleasant and fun. Fortunately, we have seen that gamification applications can be used for the welfare of people. They ensure that people keep to the permitted speed on the road, watch their blood sugar level, make people better understand people who suffer from dementia, and help to keep the environment clean. The interactive nature of games is suited to subtly influencing users. Encapsulated in the game design, users are confronted with the moral values of the designer. We believe that it is important that explicit reflection on the persuasive role of gamification is part of the maker's moral responsibility, whether this is conscious or unconsciously motivated by the designer.

CLASSIFICATION

★★★★★   ★★★★★   ★★★★★   ★★★★★   ★★★★★

References and notes

1   Statista. (2015). Gamification market value worldwide 2015-2020. Retrieved from:
    https://www.statista.com/statistics/608824/gamification-market-value-worldwide/

2   Gartner. (2011). Gartner predicts over 70 percent of Global 2000 organisations will have at least one gamified appli-
    cation by 2014. Retrieved from: https://www.gartner.com/newsroom/id/1844115

3   Gartner. (2012). Gartner says by 2014, 80 percent of current gamified applications will fail to meet business objec-
    tives primarily due to poor design. Geraadpleegd op 24 januari 2018, van
    https://www.gartner.com/newsroom/id/2251015

4   Gartner. (2011). Gartner predicts over 70 percent of Global 2000 organisations will have at least one gamified appli-
    cation by 2014. Retrieved from: https://www.gartner.com/newsroom/id/1844115

5   Kleinberg, A. (2011). Gamify your marketing. Retrieved from
    http://mashable.com/2011/07/18/gamification-marketing/#t.FdbR4ZEqqK

6   Gartner. (2011). Gartner predicts over 70 percent of Global 2000 organisations will have at least one gamified appli-
    cation by 2014. Retrieved from: https://www.gartner.com/newsroom/id/1844115

7   xix Thorpe, A. S., & Roper, S. (2017). The ethics of gamification in a marketing context. Journal of Business Ethics,
    1-13. https://doi.org/10.1007/s10551-017-3501-y

8   Deterding, S., Dixon, D., Khaled, R., & Nacke, L. (2011, September). From game design elements to gamefulness: de-
    fining gamification. In Proceedings of the 15th international academic MindTrek conference: Envisioning future
    media environments (pp. 9-15). ACM. http://dx.doi.org/10.1145/2181037.2181040.

9   Ryan, R. M., & Deci, E. L. (2000). Self-determination theory and the facilitation of intrinsic motivation, social devel-
    opment, and well-being. American Psychologist, 55(1), 68-78. http://dx.doi.org/10.1037/0003-066X.55.1.68

10 Sailer, M., Hense, J. U., Mayr, S. K., & Mandl, H. (2017). How gamification motivates: An experimental study of the
    effects of specific game design elements on psychological need satisfaction. Computers in Human Behavior, 69,
    371-380. http://dx.doi.org/10.1016/j.chb.2016.12.033

11 Buijzen, M., Van Reijmersdal, E.A., & Owen, L.H. (2010). Introducing the PCMC model: An investigative frame-
    work for young people's processing of commercial media content. Communication Theory, 20, 427-450. doi:
    10.1111/j.1468-2885.2010.01370.x

12 Rose, K. J., Koenig, M., & Wiesbauer, F. (2013). Evaluating success for behavioral change in diabetes via mHealth
    and gamification: MySugr's keys to retention and patient engagement. Diabetes Technology & Therapeutics, 15,
    A114. http://dx.doi.org/ 10.1089/dia.2012.1221.

13 More information: https://www.ijsfontein.nl/en/projecten/into-dmentia-2

14 Hamari, J., Koivisto, J., & Sarsa, H. (2014, January). Does gamification work? A literature review of empirical studies
    on gamification. In System Sciences (HICSS), 2014 47th Hawaii International Conference on (pp. 3025-3034). IEEE.
    doi: 10.1109/HICSS.2014.377

15 Deterding, S. (2012). Gamification: designing for motivation. interactions, 19(4), 14-17. doi:
    10.1145/2212877.2212883

16 Chang, E. Y. (2012). Technoqueer: Re/Con/Figuring posthuman narratives. University of Washington, Ann Harbor.

17 Bogost, I. (2011). Gamification is bullshit. Retrieved from http://bogost.com/blog/gamification_is_bullshit/

18 Bogost, I. (2011). Gamification is bullshit. Retrieved from http://bogost.com/blog/gamification_is_bullshit/

#12 REAL-TIME COMMUNICATION

Real-time communication is communicating to the right people at the right time by picking up on a relevant recent happening, and using this happening to instantly communicate a commercial or social message.

Suppose you have a keen eye for fashion. What seemed weird to others was unique styling for you. Then suddenly your styling is trendy and popular. As frustrating as losing your unicity may be, how cool is it that everyone is following your example? Isn't it kind of funny that everybody starts hyping something that seems so normal to you? Ikea must have felt that way when high-end luxury brand Balencia launched a bag that was so similar to Ikea's characteristic blue shopping bag that customers began to notice. A hilarious scandal that quickly went viral on social media. Ikea did not hesitate for a moment and took control of the online discussion with a fast and humorous response. Instead of just pointing out the resemblance, Ikea positioned itself as the real designer, and gave people directions on how to recognise the original Ikea shopping bag[1] – and, by the way, the Ikea bag only costs £1, instead of £1600 for the Balencia bag!

Strategically responding to recent, relevant events the way Ikea did with the Balencia bag is a form of real-time communication (RTC). It has been used for a long time, at least since the mid 90s[2], but digital media make using RTC easier than ever and enables companies to keep up with their customers' fastmoving interests and communication. This changes the use of RTC and makes it a relevant innovation for this media landscape.

DEFINITION AND KEY FEATURES

Generally, two types of RTC are distinguished. The first one is event-driven, like the case of the Ikea bag. This type is usually applied on social media and can refer to a broad range of things like big events, news, company crises, or holidays. The second type of RTC is *data-driven*. This approach is more personal, because it uses data of previous purchases or likings to create relevant advertisements. This is usually called behavioural targeting, which is discussed as a separate chapter. While in many ways these are very different types of communication, there is also an overlap.

While data-driven communication is named after its use of personal data, this does not mean that event-driven communication does not use any data. Both types of RTC often use contextual data such as time, location, and temperature to make the message as relevant as possible, to the people that receive it, amongst others, by using it for tailoring.

WORD-OF-MOUTH

Real-time communication is mostly based on earned media[3]. Thus, an ad like this is extremely dependent on the opinion of consumers. They will only share the message if they like it well enough – which in this busy media landscape can be translated to: if they absolutely love the ad, for example, because it is outstandingly funny or has a very relevant message. The consumers decide whether the ad becomes a success or not. A nuance in this statement must be made. Most of the time, companies use paid media to 'get people talking'. This way, the company does have some control. It can influence whether people will see the ad, but not whether they will talk about it, and how they will talk about it. Therefore, successful RTC is always a strong collaboration between the company and consumers.

This brings us to a unique element of RTC (specifically real-time advertising): the opportunity to be shared by consumers. Advertisements are rarely shared. In fact, even the best advertisements are often avoided. Real-time communication ditches that bullet. The best explanation for this is that when there is news or a big event, most people turn to (social) media for more information. So, if a company is talking about what they want to know, at the place where they are searching for it, at the moment that they are doing so, the ad is as relevant as it can be. And the chances of it being shared are optimal.

REAL-TIME COMMUNICATION IN PRACTICE

Real-time communication is used by marketers and other communication professionals to strengthen the engagement between the company and the consumer[4]. Especially in commercial contexts, the fact that RTC enhances the loyalty of the consumer is important. Their loyalty is enhanced, because they feel more connected to the brand, which leads to more positive associations[5]. Also, in every field of communication, RTC makes senders more relevant, because they join the conversation that the consumer wants to have, and in fact is already having. Adweek investigated RTC and found that this form of advertising leads to a large number of views when it goes viral on social media[6]. And as Les Binet and Peter Field point out in their report on marketing effectiveness in the digital era[7]: reach is still the most important factor for success.

An argument often raised by practitioners as a reason to use RTC is the idea that it is cheap. Since it largely or completely consists of earned media, the costs of producing and distributing RTC are relatively low. Practitioners emphasise, however, that if a company wants to use RTC regularly, it should invest in the monitoring of relevant subjects and events, knowing the target group by heart and hiring creatives that can handle the time pressure. This is an investment in structure, time, and money. Thus, even though making RTC is relatively cheap, one needs to invest in it first. Also, it is important to think of the 'conversation fit' before implementing it. Asking the questions "Does it make sense for your company to use RTC?" and "Does it make sense for your company to react to this event or subject?" can help.

An illustrative example: when Suarez bit another football player during a major game, the whole world was shocked about this radical behaviour. Snickers brilliantly used this shock to communicate their usual brand message through social media at the most relevant moment they could have chosen. Snickers satisfies hunger. That is the message behind every Snickers ad. And this time they added a little extra: it is even more satisfying than Italian. The double meaning behind 'Italian' is another great element of this ad: Italian food is very popular, and Suarez chose a bite of Italian meat on the football field as well.

Practitioners are cautious about RTC because of its unpredictability. At the same time, they are enthusiastic, because its concept fits perfectly with the recent developments in the needs of consumers: speed and actuality[8]. In the age of social media, we are used to knowing everything that goes on in the world within the day. And what is important today can be completely different tomorrow. That is why companies have trouble communicating relevant messages. People change fast, along with their needs and wishes. Real-time communication follows that trend by responding to a topic while it is still relevant.

TAILORING

One of the interesting developments in RTC is tailoring to people's identities. Let's take targeting sports fans for instance, when the subject is related to the result of a sports game. Another option for personalisation is to tailor the message to a context, like attendance of an event, or knowledge of the subject. For instance, when the message is a reaction to a news story, one could target the ad to people who, according to the data of the news site, have read a recent article on the subject. Tailoring the message can help to reach more people who are genuinely interested in the message, which makes it more likely that the viewer will share the ad, which results in more penetration in the target group.

Now that we have discussed the use of RTC by practitioners in general, Ralf van Lieshout takes over to discuss the development of RTC, including its future. He uses his own experience, but also other examples from the field, to illustrate his story.

THE REALITY OF REAL-TIME COMMUNICATION

By Ralf van Lieshout
Brand Strategy Director
Greenhouse Group BV (WPP Company)

In an over-complex digital media and marketing landscape, we run into the risk that a few (successful) examples become the definition of an entire line of communication tactics. They can even become a strategy in themselves like the infamous 'viral' once was. In the context of social media, 'reactvertising' has become the definition of Real-Time Communication (RTC). The famous Oreo 'dunk' in the dark' tweet has led a lot of agencies and brands on a wild goose chase after their own moment of RTC fame. Some were successful, most were not.

During the 2013 Super Bowl final, a power outage caused the game to be suspended. Oreo's social media team (with the help of their agency 360i's) quickly responded: 'Power out? No problem. You can still dunk in the dark'. The tweet got massive retweets and earned world-wide reach. The day after the Super Bowl, the Huffington Post posted that "one of the most buzz-worthy ads of the Super Bowl on Sunday wasn't even a commercial – it was a mere tweet from Oreo during the blackout."

I'm convinced that the dynamic development of social media platforms, combined with the fast rise of data-fuelled communication technology, makes RTC a future-proof communication tactic - you might even say the communication tactic of the future. In order to explain this we have to look at the bigger picture first. I will use the slope of tactical effectiveness as a guideline.

Phase 1 started 10 years ago, when social media were a playground for brands. Paid-media options were limited so brands would focus on how to get the most organic and earned reach. The brands that built most experience in phase 1 and/or the ones with budgets to hire the best creative teams, were the most successful in phase 2; the 'dunk in the dark' phase.

As people flocked to social media during phase 3, brands followed suit and the social networks started to tune their algorithms, leaving brands with far less organic reach and more paid-media options as an alternative. With increased competition and less organic reach, relying on the effects of reactvertising became an uncertain and less effective tactic.

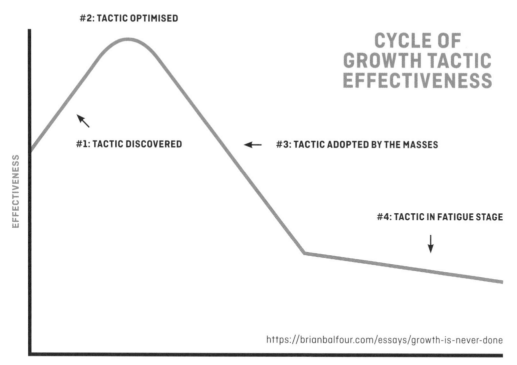

#2: TACTIC OPTIMISED

CYCLE OF GROWTH TACTIC EFFECTIVENESS

#1: TACTIC DISCOVERED

#3: TACTIC ADOPTED BY THE MASSES

#4: TACTIC IN FATIGUE STAGE

EFFECTIVENESS

TIME

https://brianbalfour.com/essays/growth-is-never-done

In phase 4, the current phase, most brands work with editorial plans. They make conscious decisions on how and when to use 'reactvertising'. Most often this is only incidentally. Mainly brands with the means to support high-end creative execution and/or brands that have 'fun' as a core value in their brand DNA (for instance many beer brands) consistently use reactvertising as a primary social media tactic to build their brand.

We are at the dawn of a new phase 1 where RTC is much more than reactvertising. This new phase is fuelled by contextual data and technology. This gives brands the opportunity to move from purely event-driven RTC to a combination of data- *and* event-driven RTC. Technology makes it possible for brands to connect with different (public) data sources and to use these sources to dynamically and in real-time create and push messages to multiple digital touchpoints. From mobile ads, to display, to social media and digital out of home. Here are some examples.

For their campaign on their Managed Investment Service, Dutch bank ING aimed to communicate that their product would give consumers less stress (less 'grijze haren', which means less grey hairs). Their TVC featured a dad looking at his daughter's' Facebook timeline. These things can cause a lot of stress, but luckily, ING's Managed Investment Service does not, leaving the dad with one less thing to worry about. The agencies responsible for this campaign (JWT Amsterdam, Mindshare Amsterdam and Greenhouse Group) wanted to bring this theme closer to their target audience with high relevance.In order to do so, they created real-time social content and digital out-of-home communication. Social content an Dynamic Digital Out of Home screens featured messages based on hyper local, hyper actual events. For instance; '4538 Grey Hairs due to your train delay between Amsterdam and The Hague' on Amsterdam CS. Or '8932 Grey Hairs because of the tree-policy Amersfoort' – when, of course in Amersfoort, there was some political debate about the chopping of some old landmark trees.

Another great case of the creative use of data-fuelled RTC is Canal+ France's 'The Young Pope'. They used Artificial Intelligence to access the 39,000 verses of the Bible and to respond in real-time to people who posted 'sinful' messages on Facebook and Twitter. According to agency Havas Cognitive, AiMEN has generated over 2.4 million impressions. More than 800,000 messages have already been posted by AiMEN.

Because of the element of surprise and the high relevance of the message, most campaigns that use these technologies show above-average ad recall and engagement rates. This is the steep learning curve of phase 1. Currently, creating these kinds of campaigns is still quite an endeavour. Few agencies and brands have the means and technological know-how to create such campaigns.

During phase 2, these parties will benefit most from their first mover advantage. But as the technology behind these types of campaigns becomes mainstream in phase 3, a new level playing field will emerge. During this phase, the most creative (rise above the noise) and the most efficient (get the most results out of the tech investments) will be most successful.

I question, however, whether after phase 3 we will end up in a phase 4 of slow decline. Instead I believe that this will be a new baseline for communication technology, not only to build awareness and engagement, but also to drive conversion and increase customer service levels. In every phase of the customer journey there is an opportunity to use RTC. Already there are numerous cases of AI-fuelled chatbots that serve customers in real-time, or – the other way around – 'real' call centre agents who are supported by AI with template-based answers that can then be personalised and sent to customers. Dutch Royal Airways KLM is a good example of a front-running company in this field.

For years marketeers have been looking for scalable ways to build brands over different digital touchpoints using a combination of technology, data insights, and creativity. Real-time communication can do just that!

A SCIENTIFIC PERSPECTIVE

The unpredictability of RTC makes it hard to research. Also, the effects are short term, the subjects differ every time and one can rarely predict the use of RTC. Its use depends on events that have yet to happen. Think back to Suarez for instance. Who could have thought he would bite another football player? Research on similar communication techniques and strategies shows that there is a lot of potential for techniques that respond to events and use the speed of social media[9]. It strengthens positive attitudes and the bond with the audience. Also, it can give relevance a boost. Since RTC also leads to more positive associations[10], using the technique can also have financial benefits: companies that use real-time marketing have a ROI (return-on-investment) that is higher than companies that do not use the technique[11]. This can be explained by the positive associations evoked by RTC. After all, the more associations one has with the brand, the more often that person might think of the brand – in different situations, locations, and contexts – which creates more entry points for buying the brand's products or using its services[12].

Another reason why RTC is an effective strategy is because of the human urge to keep an eye on the world to survive[13], which is called the surveillance function of the news[14]. One more explanation for the success of RTC lies in the way people receive the news. Since RTC has a high chance of being shared, most people will receive the ad from friends and family. People prefer hearing news from personal contacts[15], versus companies from which we feel an emotional distance. This can partly be explained by the fact that people in our own circle usually share the same point of view, which means that our image of the world is usually confirmed, which in turn makes communication easy and pleasant. So, RTC is a win-win situation for both the consumer and the sender.

PROCESSING REAL-TIME COMMUNICATION

Real-time communication is focused on emotions and associations, and the message is simple; usually a short quote with a striking image. Therefore, little cognitive elaboration is needed to understand the ad. Consequently, the message is not criticised. There is, however, a small amount of effort needed to connect the message to a central theme. Therefore, we can conclude that we process RTC in a heuristic way[16]: with a small amount of effort, we process the information emotionally, based on heuristics that ease the cognitive load of making a decision. This explanation of the processing of RTC is closely related to the Evaluative Conditioning theory, which states that when a known brand is repeatedly evoked in a positive context, a person will in time associate the brand with these positive cues, even if the context is absent. In other words, it leads to a positive brand evaluation[17]. The Ikea and the Snickers ads are both great examples. They used humour to create a positive context, made sure the message was strongly related to the brand, and became a great success.

ETHICS AND FUTURE

Because RTC is focused on news and events instead of people, in its original form there are few privacy issues tied to this technique. However, RTC is getting more personal and uses data to tailor the message more often. Tailoring the message based on the data of the target group, however, may give rise to some privacy issues. Data that is acquired without the consent of the consumer is not ethical, and consented data is rare. Additionally, with the recently implemented GDPR laws in the EU, acquiring this data is not even legal in most cases. We advise taking these arguments into account when considering the use of tailoring, or while researching the use of RTC.

THE ETHICAL VERSION

There are ways to use tailoring without crossing ethical boundaries, by using contextual data instead of personal data. The #comeonin campaign by the Sydney Opera House illustrates this well. The opera house is the most Instagrammed icon in Australia. However, out of all the people who post a photo of the building, only 1% actually enter it. That is why the opera house started a campaign[18] to invite people to come on in. They used computer vision and public data, namely the geo location and hashtags on Instagram, to track people who were near the Sydney Opera House and had just posted a picture. They created personal welcoming messages, inviting them to come on in. They created unique experiences for everyone who was invited. Some got to try on real costumes, others were invited to attend a private soundcheck, and so on. Of course, they all posted about their unique experiences on Instagram again, which resulted in over 5 million people seeing another side of the opera house: the inside.

CONCLUSION

As we have argued above, RTC fits the current use of media well. It is timely and relevant. It has a quick development phase and can therefore easily keep up with fast-moving consumers, with even faster social media consumption. The biggest challenge for RTC is therefore not on the consumer side, but in company structures. Consumers 'live in the moment', but companies still work with periods of a quarter – or even a whole year[19]. Marketing budgets are usually set in stone, long before the opportunity for real-time marketing comes along. A company can preclude this, by using real-time as a business model as well. This means agile working: fast, flexible and nimble[20]. It gives companies the opportunity to connect an advertisement in real-time with consumers. This way, one knows the trends in the target group, which will improve the business and future (real-time) marketing.

CLASSIFICATION

★★★★★   ★★★★★   ★★★★★   ★★★★★   ★★★★★

References and notes

1   Find a more detailed description and three other great examples on: https://bigmarketing.co.uk/4-examples-of-brands-getting-real-time-marketing-right/

2   Huff, T. (2014). The history of real-time marketing in 500 words. Retrieved from: http://www.socialmediatoday.com/content/history-real-time-marketing-500-words

3   Earned media is publicity that is earned through word of mouth or attention by news media

4   Frankwatching, (2015). Real-time social media marketing: de magie van de inhaker. Retrieved from: https://www.frankwatching.com/archive/2015/04/14/real-time-social-media-marketing-de-magie-van-de-inhaker

5   McKenna, R. (1995). Real-time marketing. Harvard Business Review, 73(4), 87-95.

6   Adweek (2013). Does real-time marketing work? Retrieved from: http://www.adweek.com/news/advertising-branding/does-real-time- marketing-work-153089

7   Binet & Field's report 'media in focus', about the effectiveness of marketing in a digital era is very much worth reading. It gives you relevant insights with good argumentation, based on strong data.

8   Reid, C. (2014). Real-time marketing can keep businesses successful - But how? E-ContentMAG, 6-10.

9   1) Aguirre, E., Mahr, D., Grewal, D., de Ruyter, K., & Wetzels, M. (2015). Unraveling the personalization paradox: The effect of information collection and trust-building strategies on online advertisement effectiveness. Journal of Retailing, 91(1), 34-49. 2) Bronner, F., & Hoog, R. de. (2014). Social media and consumer choice. International Journal of Market Research, 56(1), 51-71. 3) Doyle, S. (2006). Real-time technologies in marketing - Interaction management. Database Marketing & Customer Strategy Management, 12(3), 272-278.

10 McKenna, R. (1995). Real-time marketing. Harvard Business Review, 73(4), 87-95.

11 Meerman Scott, D. (2010). Real-time: How marketing & PR at speed drives measurable success. Retrieved from http://www.davidmeermanscott.com/documents/Real_Time.pdf

12 Sharp, B. (2010). How brands grow: what marketeers don't know. Oxford University Press

13 Shoemaker, P. J. (1996). Hardwired for news: Using biological and cultural evolution to explain the surveillance function. Journal of Communication, 46(3), 32-47

14 Lasswell, H. D. (1960). The structure and function of communication in society. In Schoemaker, P.J. (1996). Hardwired for news: Using biological and cultural evolution to explain the surveillance function. Journal of Communication, 46(3), 32-47

15 Hermida, A., Fletcher, F., Korell, D., & Logan, D. (2012). Share, like, recommend. Journalism Studies, 13(5-6), 815-824. Doi: 10.1080/1461670X.2012.664430

16 This argumentation is based on the PCMC model. Read more about this model via: Buijzen, M., Van Reijmersdal, E. A., & Owen, L. H. (2010). Introducing the PCMC model: An investigative framework for young people's processing of commercialized media content. Communication Theory, 20(4), 427-450. DOI: https://doi.org/10.1111/j.1468-2885.2010.01370.x

17 De Houwer, J., Thomas, S., & Frank Baeyens, F. (2001). Associative learning of likes and dislikes: A review of 25 years of research on human evaluative conditioning. Psychological Bulletin, 127(6), 853-869.

18 Watch the case film on: https://vimeo.com/159130469

19 Silberbauer, L. (2015). Lego social media chief: Oreo set a dangerous precedent for real-time marketing. Marketing. Retrieved from http://www.marketingmagazine.co.uk/article/1354227/lego-social-media-chief-oreo-set-dangerous-precedent-real-time-marketing

20 Forbes. Retrieved from: https://www.forbes.com/sites/stevedenning/2016/08/13/what-is-agile/#4b36498126e3

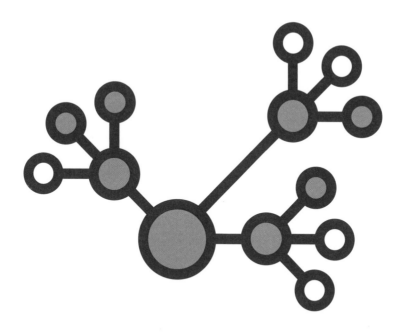

#13 GO VIRAL

Viral messaging anticipates the natural inclination of people to share messages through word-of-mouth, creating a multitude of exposures.

"I've been called out by everybody: Homer Simpson, Mike Tyson, and Vince McMahon." Like everybody is going crazy over this thing. I'm challenging President Obama!" On top of one of his famous towers, Donald Trump accepted the Ice Bucket Challenge. The challenge encouraged nominated participants, from celebs to ordinary people, to be filmed having a bucket of ice water poured on their heads and then nominating others to do the same. Its aim was to promote awareness of the disease amyotrophic lateral sclerosis (ALS, also known as motor neuron disease) and encourage donations to research. These videos were posted on social media and the challenge to do the same or to donate to research on ALS was put to friends and acquaintances via social media. It went viral on social media during July and August 2014. The challenge was so successful that it provided the template for online viral marketing for years after.

DEFINITION AND KEY FEATURES

Viral marketing implies that consumers are talking about a brand or service. It is a form of consumer-to-consumer communication, based on the idea that consumers like to share experiences, either good or bad. The central element is the organic spreading of messages. Different media are integrated to add to the buzz, with the ultimate goal being that consumers talk about a brand or service or news item, increasing attention. The resulting buzz is not a matter of luck; it results from a deliberate strategic and well-thought-out message. The use and passing along of this form of user generated content created by ordinary consumers has grown quickly during the last decade.

SOCIAL MEDIA FACILITATES THE SPREAD OF ELECTRONIC WORD-OF-MOUTH (EWOM)

Viral marketing is not a new phenomenon. In the early days, when the circus arrived in town, it was customary to take a parade onto the streets in order to get consumers talking, to create a buzz. Likewise, there were the well-known Tupperware parties in which product demonstrations at the homes of housewives got consumers talking about brands and products, creating enormous buzz, and increasing sales with no complementary marketing actions. Related concepts are word-of-mouth and viral communication[1]. Word-of-mouth is the chit-chatting between consumers and it does not have to be related to marketing[2]. There is little doubt about the decisive role that word-of-mouth plays in the success of products and brands. Word-of-mouth can be a very powerful tool as a large number of consumer decisions in marketing are influenced by word-of-mouth communication because fellow consumers are seen as more credible and trustworthy than the companies that send out commercial messages. Not only purchasing behaviour, but also consumer expectations, feelings and attitudes before and after the product purchase[3] are heavily impacted by word-of-mouth messages. A big difference between the traditional word-of-mouth, and the digital E-word-of-mouth is that nowadays several social media are available to create buzz by spreading shares, reviews, retweets, and clicks.

THE CONSUMER BECOMES THE SENDER

Viral communication is a strategy in which consumers are encouraged to pass along messages to friends, colleagues, and family via digital media in order to sustain exponential awareness of these messages[4]. The sender is always identifiable, and there is always a pass-along opportunity. This way, the consumer becomes the sender of commercialised messages, without becoming aware of it. Two decades ago, consumers spoke with six offline friends on average about a campaign, and that was it. Nowadays a consumer shares a post with a lot of friends online, with one push of a button. And you can do this at any time of the day, using your smartphone. Therefore, institutions nowadays try to reach their target group online, aiming for them to communicate on- and offline, reaching other consumers. The messages can be conveyed in viral games, brand pages, movies, or online video, et cetera.

VIRAL MARKETING IN PRACTICE

There are several examples of successful cases that were deliberately set up to create a buzz around a brand. A well-known spontaneous happening that turned out to be a carefully staged action to create buzz was the Oscar selfie of Ellen Generes. During the Oscar ceremony of 2014, Ellen took a selfie with several celebs. It went viral and became the most retweeted tweet in history, creating enormous buzz. However, the main sponsor of the Academy Award show, Samsung, had the whole thing orchestrated because in front of 43 million viewers, Ellen not only coincidentally took a Samsung smartphone out of her pocket to take the selfie, but the brand was mentioned over 40,000 times on social media and the ads promoting Samsung drew more attention during the ceremony.

About ten percent of consumers are really active and responsible for spreading messages among other consumers, making them a primary target group of marketers. They deliberately organise viral marketing by employing buzz agents or brand pushers to trigger a buzz. These 'early adopters' create a buzz and subsequently a snowball effect by word-of-mouth, assuring an exponential epidemic growth of a viral message, spreading among consumers who will likewise share these messages with other consumers in their social networks.

THE VIRAL CONCEPT HAS TO CREATE A 'WOW' EFFECT

In times of advertising clutter and ad avoidance of consumers, marketers use viral marketing to create reach and brand awareness. Viral messages will stick in consumers' minds and have more persuasive power, because they receive these messages from people they are strongly tied to, such as family and friends, instead of a company with whom they mostly experience a weak tie. There are several inspirational ideas among communication professionals about how to make a message stick into the minds of consumers, facilitating viral marketing. They all boil down to the fact that the concept has to create a 'WOW' effect. It has to make them smile or cry, or teach them something. This added value maximises the chance that consumers will pass along the message.

VIRALS HAVE A LIMITED SHELF-LIFE

Although viral marketing has become more popular as a tool among marketers, they remain cautious about using it. Most of them agree that a main goal of viral marketing is awareness of the brand or message. Going a step further, there is a common belief that viral marketing generates sales, but there is no hard evidence that it does so, because return on investment is hard to establish. For instance, there are no numbers available about whether the buzz that arose from the publicity stunt of Samsung during the Awards ceremony led to increased sales. A big disadvantage of viral marketing is that one cannot control how consumers will talk about the brand or organisation. If they talk in a negative way this might harm the intended informative or persuasive goals. Another point of attention is the limited shelf-life of viral marketing. Once a campaign has generated its buzz, it loses its power. It can only be used once. And there is always the risk that consumers do like a campaign but choose not to share it, thus limiting the chance of buzz around a brand.

Going back to the Ice Bucket Challenge in our example, there was no big marketing campaign to start it off. It relied in the beginning entirely on ordinary individuals, seeing other ordinary people participate in the challenge. Soon the action was taken over by celebrities, facilitating organic reach. Identification was easy as people watched their friends get involved in something they saw as equally worthwhile. And people got to see big names take part in something they were a part of too. The success is also explained by the authenticity of seeing the proof of the challenge in the videos. Although the challenge only had a short life, as is the case with all viral campaigns, the Ice Bucket Challenge was wildly successful, raising millions of dollars for research for ALS and substantially raising awareness of the disease.

In sum, besides a 'sticky message', the success of viral marketing is determined by consumers, who have to be eager to pass along messages, not by the senders who just send those messages. In the next paragraph, Fleur Willemijn van Beinum will share valuable insights on how to successfully implement viral communication as a marketing strategy.

HOW TO DEVELOP AN EFFECTIVE VIRAL CAMPAIGN

By Fleur Willemijn van Beinum
Global Content Director a.i. & Interim Consultant

Given the successful examples above, the main question is how to get to the execution of viral marketing. Often heard is "I want to go viral" by the Marketing Manager. Now it is time to wake up from the dream and get real about going viral: it is not that easy and takes strategy, time, money, balls, and some luck.

CREATING VALUE FOR YOUR AUDIENCE
'Choosing' to go for a viral message in your communication strategy can be driven by different objectives, from sales to awareness. (Direct) sales are a long shot and if this is your objective, it is often shown in the message and not appreciated by your audience, hence it has a small chance of success. Being realistic, the main objective is and should be 'leaving

a positive impression' with your audience and gaining as much reach as possible for the lowest spending. Create awareness, get goodwill, and grow your likeability as a brand, the basics for brand growth. Just remember, it is about creating value for your audience, it is about them, not about you.

LESS IS MORE AND KEEP IT SIMPLE

To develop an effective viral, you need a solid content strategy with a long-term objective; it is not a 'one off' that develops brand growth on its own. Next to that, the viral needs to be in line with the brand and products, to be recognisable as what the brand stands for, and to reflect the 'why' of the brand and its products. Simply put: the message you want to spread needs to make sense for the brand and be logical for your audience to connect to your brand. You need a top-notch creative: surprise and stand out. Most of the time, 'less is more' and keep it as simple as possible to be understandable and recognisable for the majority of people. If you make it complicated, a receiver has to make an effort to understand the meaning and capture the message. Then you are missing out, because people are often not inclined to undertake such an exercise.

DARE TO STAND OUT

Quality in creativity does not come cheap. You need to benefit from your strong relationship with your creative agency with digital skills and stay in line with the media budget. The best virals take time, planning, strategy, and a brave mindset. Dare to stand out and make your message worth sharing by being different. Keep in mind: input is output. If you want that quick-business-problem-fix with your viral without spending quality thinking, time, and budget, more often than not you are set up for failure.

RESERVE ENOUGH MEDIA BUDGET

To generate reach and be visible, social media is the way forward. You have to "pay to play" to boost your (organic) content at Facebook, Instagram, or any other social network. Hence, you need a media budget. Of course the exceptions confirm the rule and a few lucky ones did manage to go viral without a media budget. Do not count on such luck and do not be frugal. Do spend a small to medium media budget to create that first visibility in social media, to kick-start your viral and give it the best chances possible to succeed.

WEBCARE: CREATE AN ESCALATION AND CRISIS COMMUNICATIONS PROCESS

Please, do not forget about having your webcare in place. Having your message out means that people will and do react to it. Have your webcare team ready to react swiftly and be spot on, especially if it is a bit more daring viral. Two suggestions to prepare your webcare team accordingly: set up a list of frequently asked questions or expected questions in advance to respond quickly to consumers or press, and create an escalation and crisis communications process for when the 'shit hits the fan' and the viral explodes or goes in another direction than that expected.

Best is a dry run with the worst and the best scenario possible, to get the details into your webcare team to respond to feedback from your audiences. It also is a lot of fun to do and the outcome can be used to further sharpen the viral message.

ADD VALUE FOR THE RECEIVER

Already mentioned, this is the big 'no brainer'. Every piece of content you produce has to add value for the receiver. It is not about you as a brand or your products; it is about whether you make your audience smile or cry, touch their hearts, or teach them something special and unique: tips, tricks, hacks, knowledge, skills, or anything else – as long as it is not about your product features or brand.

One or the other way, virals must be worth sharing. A very easy suggestion for this: think about your own behaviour on digital, when do you share something with your friends? What makes you tick and want you to spread that message? Think again, 'did you ever hit the 'share now' button' just because you were asked to by the brand?

YOU STILL NEED A BIT OF LUCK AND FORTUNE

However excellent your creative product, your push with the media budget, and your preparation with the team, you still need a bit of luck and fortune. It can be that people just do not want to share it. You may be too explicit, too outspoken or too obvious in their eyes and they just 'don't feel like sharing'. And maybe you will never know the reason why they do not want to share it. Another option is that however brilliant your viral, something else happens that takes all the attention at that specific moment. Imagine you push your viral, and a natural disaster happens; an earthquake shakes up the world and is in the heart and minds of everybody... You cannot plan for this.

EASILY DIGESTIBLE AND SHAREABLE RESULTS

Make sure you set up easy-to-digest reporting, including a production and media budget, with target lines based on your Key Performance Indicators (KPIs). Practical tip: copy paste the visual trendline of the results and a few bullet points in an email to be read on the mobile, not a PowerPoint deck, or even worse, a login to a dashboard. Present the result on a golden plate, easy to digest and easy to share. Practise what you preach. Send out these results immediately and continuously. Do not make the mistake to only report afterwards; do it also during the viral to show your own pride and passion for your work.

Last not least, have fun. Please, do not forget to have fun creating the viral. This shows off in the creative viral and in the results :)

A SCIENTIFIC PERSPECTIVE

Only ten percent of consumers, so called opinion leaders, are active in spreading viral messages. The two-step flow of communication theory may shed some light on the diffusion of innovations, such as the spreading of viral messages. It takes place in two steps: from mass media to opinion leaders and then from opinion leaders to the rest of the population, the opinion followers[5]. While the mass media provides both opinion leaders and opinion followers with information in the first step, opinion leaders use this information to exert influence on the followers' opinions in the second step. The opinion leaders' appraisal of the viral messaging is thus of great importance for the success of virals. Viral messaging functions like a social actor[6], because the consumers who pass messages along implicitly say that the content of these messages is highly likeable, thus enforcing social proof[7], which makes consumers feel good because they like sharing positive experiences.

RELEVANT MESSAGES CAUSE A BUZZ

Part of the success of viral messaging is determined by the way that viral messaging attempts are processed. Do consumers actively process a persuasive message once they recognise it, or are they influenced more by the message context, such as a nice viral? Probably more overt viral messaging will be processed more systematically[8] than average persuasion attempts. This is because we are likely to allocate more cognitive resources to conspicuous, novel, and surprising content that is recommended to us by our acquaintances. Consumers pay attention to it for subsequent processing, then they actively share it and are willing to talk about it. The moment the message is relevant for people, buzz might arise. There is a great chance that the message will be scrutinised. However, when the message is hidden, information processing might happen more heuristically. This may also happen when the source is familiar because that diminishes that chance of systematic processing because one might focus less on the persuasive intent. And when the message is embedded in a context that takes up too much attention because of a surprise or WOW effect the chance that a hidden message is processed becomes even smaller.

HUMORISTIC AND SURPRISING VIRAL MESSAGES ARE PASSED ALONG MORE OFTEN

Academic research has predominantly focused on the motives to pass along viral messages. This behaviour strongly depends on who the sender is. When the strength of the tie with a sender who is trustworthy is high, as with friends and family, this enlarges the chance that a message is passed along, compared to when the tie strength is weak, as with companies[9,10]. To a lesser degree, enjoyment of the message plays a role, as does the strength of the relationship a consumer experiences with the advertised brand. Humoristic and surprising viral messages are passed along more often than shocking or sexually explicit viral messages. Obviously, senders do not want to be associated with shocking or sexually explicit messages. Another study showed that future-framed marketing that features product preannouncements positively influences consumers' product interest and pass-along behaviour[11]. This could be explained by the optimistic bias, the tendency of people to overestimate the likelihood of positive uncertain future events. Therefore, this positive uncertainty and novelty stemming from future products would stimulate imagination, interest, and word-of-mouth in turn.

Finally, research investigating the motives to pass along news items found that positive news is passed along more often than negative news[12]. While common wisdom suggests that people would rather spread negative than positive news, (surveillance function of the news: people constantly monitor the world around them for danger), it appeared that amusing content elicits a higher level of arousal and activation compared to sad news.

The traditional paradigm of the sender-receiver model lies way behind us. Nowadays consumer groups can organise themselves at high speed and form a unity. Viral messaging is made possible by the fact that consumers are always connected, in real time, 24 hours a day. Consumers become the senders of information, are more in control of communication, and are crucial for the brands' well-being. Advertisers are losing track of what consumers are buzzing about and how, quite rapidly.

DEVOTE ATTENTION TO FOLLOW-UP ON VIRAL MESSAGES

There are a few aspects that communication professionals should care about when using virals in the future. They should make more use of social media monitoring. Who listens to my brand and in what way? The whole target group or just a part? Do early adaptors attend to the messaging or the whole target group? How do consumers think about my brand? How would they talk about it with friends and family, and can I get them to talk about my brand? How can I exert influence on this interactive process? This information is very important for marketers in order to allocate attention and money to create buzz around a certain brand. Another development is that marketers will have to look for suitable brand ambassadors for their brands – preferably consumers who are authentic and are willing to become a representative for a certain brand. Also important is the support that buzz campaigns should get in the form of other media, such as display advertising or public relations, because they can hardly exist on their own. Communication professionals should also devote attention to the follow-up on viral messaging. As the content is an important denominator for success, marketers should always pre-test campaigns. Lastly, the branch is definitely in need of objective parameters for the success of virals because good benchmarks are missing. Technological developments will facilitate the distribution of marketing messages around the globe by creating better fora. The creation and maintenance of social relations, offline as well as online, will contribute to the well-being of people[13], offering opportunities for viral messaging for the coming years.

TRANSPARENCY IS NEEDED IN BUZZ MARKETING CAMPAIGNS

An ethical issue to discuss is that the objective behind viral messaging remains often implicit, and thus covert, and therefore consumers do not always recognise the persuasive intentions of the communicators. The fact that viral messaging contains hidden messages or information incites the idea that consumers should be warned.

Otherwise people are not conscious of the fact that they are being influenced. In contrast, some of the virals do overtly communicate their intentions. The Verbal Buzz Marketing Association (VBMA) and the Word of Mouth Marketing Association (WOMMA) plead for a law favouring transparency in buzz marketing campaigns. This law would make consumers conscious of the fact that they are being influenced and are part of a marketing campaign. Most companies are not in favour of this law, because it might jeopardise the outcome of their campaigns.

A last word of caution for marketers is that some organisations will be tempted to copy successful viral campaigns. However, viral messaging is not a matter of remaking or imitating successful campaigns. Instead they should think carefully about what the drivers are behind their brands in order to create their own unique buzz moment.

CLASSIFICATION

★★★★★ ★★★★★ ★★★★★ ★★★★★ ★★★★★

References and notes
1   Ketelaar, P. E. & Schaerlaekens, B. (2015). Viral marketing: More than the online version of word of mouth. Journal of Euromarketing, 24(1), 5-19.
2   Nyilasi, G., (2006). Word of mouth: What we really know – and what we don't. In J. Kirby and P. Marsden (Ed.), Connected marketing (pp. 161-184) United Kingdom: Butterworth-Heinemann.
3   Bone, P. F. (1995). Word-of-mouth effects on short-term and long-term product judgments. Journal of business research, 32(3), 213-223.
4   Thevenot, C., & Watier, K. (2001). Viral marketing. Georgetown University, Communications, Culture & Technology Program, 1-15.
5   Rogers, Everett M. (2003). Diffusion of Innovations, New York: Free Press.
6   Fogg, B. J. (1999). Persuasive technologies. Communications of the ACM, 42(5), 26-29.
7   Cialdini, R. B. (2001). The science of persuasion. Scientific American, 284, 76–81.
8   Buijzen, M., Van Reijmersdal, E., & Owen, L. H. (2010). Introducing the PCMC model: An investigative framework for young consumers's processing of commercialized media content. Communication Theory, 20, 427 450.
9   Ketelaar, P. E., Janssen, L., Vergeer, M., van Reijmersdal, E. A., Crutzen, R., & van't Riet, J. (2016) The success of viral ads: Social and attitudinal predictors of consumer pass-on behavior on social network sites. Journal of Business Research, 69 (7), 2603–2613.
10 Van Noort, G., Antheunis, M. L., Van Reijmersdal, E. A. (2012). Social connections and the persuasiveness of viral campaigns in social network sites: Persuasive intent as the underlying mechanism. Journal of Marketing Communication, 18 (1), 39-53.
11 Thorbjørnsen, H., Ketelaar, P. E., Van't Riet, J., Dahlén, M. (2015). How do teaser advertisements boost word of mouth about new products? For consumers, the future is more exciting than the present. Journal of Advertising Research, 55(1), 73-80.
12 Berger, J., & Milkman, K. L. (2012). What makes online content viral?. Journal of marketing research, 49(2), 192-205.
13 Riva, G., Banos, R. M., Botella, C., Wiederhold, B. K., & Gaggioli, A. (2012). Positive technology: Using interactive technologies to promote positive functioning. Cyberpsychology, Behavior, and Social Networking, 15(2), 69-77.

#14 ONLINE REVIEWS

Online reviews are a way for consumers to express and share their opinions with the world about products, services, and people.

Imagine that you are travelling in England and it is night and you still need accommodation. On Google maps you find a nice family hotel nearby. Before you decide to call to see if there is a room available, you check some online reviews and the first goes like this: *"Do not stay in this absolute dump of a hotel, and I use the term hotel very loosely. I cannot convey strongly enough how disgusting this place is. Bloodstained headboards that have clearly been up since the World War (the first one), rude staff, windows that won't close, no hot water, broken furniture, dirty utensils, broken light fixings, and actual poo in the kettle. Pretty sure I'm going to end up with some sort of rash or disease due to sanitation conditions similar to those of a homeless crackhead. In summary, this place is a complete hole."* Would you take this extremely negative review seriously and look a little further? Or would you ignore this review and give the hotel a chance? In this chapter you'll learn about the factors that play a role in the evaluation of online reviews.

DEFINITION AND KEY FEATURES

Online reviews are reviews or ratings based on personal experiences. In addition to practical information about a product or service, which is often shared by the selling organisation, potential new customers can also keep the experiences of other customers in mind when making a choice to purchase or not. It can be argued that the internet makes the buying process easier, because it offers the possibility to interact with millions of others with different knowledge and experiences. Online reviews are therefore a form of electronic word of mouth and consumer-to-consumer (C2C) communication. You can leave a review online to formulate an opinion for others. As the name implies, online reviews are published online, making them easy to search for. Many websites, including selling companies such as Amazon and product and comparison sites such as TripAdvisor, make it easy for consumers to share and find a review. Online reviews are therefore a way to quickly find out about the opinions of others about a product or service. Although the term 'online reviews' generally refers to reviews on webshops and specially created review websites, consumers can also share their experiences in reviews via blogs and social media. In addition to products and services, it is also possible to assess other persons. An example of this is reviewing colleagues on professional social media like LinkedIn; read more about this in the chapter on personal branding. In conclusion, the definition of online reviews is wide. It is a form of information about products, services, and people, based on their own experiences.

ONLINE REVIEWS IN PRACTICE

In practice, it is noticeable that online reviews are widely used, first of all by the fact that many webshops utilise the possibility to leave reviews. Webshops featuring different brands give consumers the chance to leave their comments under the 'reviews' section, and to express their evaluation in a summary rating in a number or in stars. Brands themselves also make use of reviews on their sites: Samsung product reviews can be found on the Samsung website. Media are also used more frequently to share reviews. For example, more and more organisations are allowing consumers to share their experiences and complaints on Facebook: the service moves to public messages instead of private chats. For example, on the Facebook page of the Dutch airliner KLM, under the 'community' tab, the company responds to messages from customers in which clear opinions emerge from bad and fantastic experiences.

Within the marketing industry, the influence of online reviews is estimated to be large. Online reviews offer a wide range of benefits to companies[1]. First, it is said that online reviews on a third-party site mean a free form of advertising and content. These 'advertisements' mainly consists of reviews that potentially increase confidence in the company. Companies or products that are often reviewed, will also be assessed by search engines as being more relevant and therefore get a good position on the search engine result page. Online reviews also offer the opportunity to improve products or services and to adapt to customer needs that are publicly expressed.

One of the problems for companies is that online reviews are written by third parties, so companies have limited control over the content. Think of the horrible review in the introduction, if that had been said publicly about your company, what would you have thought? The paradox is that the absence or a very low number of negative reviews can have negative effects on a company. This is based on the fact that customers have more confidence when negative reviews are also found. When this is not the case, people suspect that reviews are fake or that the negative reviews are censored[2]. Negative reviews, in other words, can increase the credibility of the company. The information is assessed as more reliable when there are varying opinions. However, when only a few reviews exist, just a couple of negative reviews may result in a strong negative image. In addition, reviews should always be current and up to date, otherwise the reviews and the company seem to be irrelevant. Fake reviews are really a problem in the business. Amazon, for example, deletes thousands of fake reviews[3]. These false reviews can be either positive about the reviewed company or negative about the competition, as in the case of Samsung, which was fined US$340,000 by Taiwan's Fair Trade Commission for paying people to post negative online reviews about products from HTC, while praising Samsung's[4]. Pratik Dholakiya will now give his expert view on how online reviews can be a medium that customers trust as much as their close family and friends.

REFLECTING ON ONLINE REVIEWS

By Pratik Dholakiya
Founder & CEO
The 20 Media

A customer review is a review of a product or service made by a customer who has purchased and used, or had experience with, the product or service. Honestly, that's all the backstory you need on something as omnipresent as online reviews. You've read them, you've written them, you've trusted them, and you've made purchases based on them. You know well enough that the opinions of your customers are a force to reckon with. All that you need now is a way to get this force to streamline with your business goals and work in your favour.

THE STATE OF ONLINE REVIEWS

We've come a long way since the first time customers began reading what other customers who had already bought a product had to say about it on Amazon. Today, customers trust reviews more than advertising media. A bright local survey found that 84%[5] of consumers trust online reviews as much as recommendations from friends. Also, positive reviews make 73%[6] of customers trust a local business more. A study by Review Trackers found that customers prioritise good reviews[7] over a discount deal. Clearly, reviews are big and impactful. However, consumers today are smarter, savvier, and more informed. They take positive reviews with a pinch of salt, pay more attention to the number of reviews than just a plain all-star rating, and smell a fake review from a mile away. The modern, empowered customer is no one's fool and the only way for a business to thrive is to garner honest positive reviews, and as many as they can.

CREATE A GOOD FIRST IMPRESSION

No matter how much data, stats, and hard numbers you have at hand, at the end of the table is a consumer who is human. And to humans, emotion reads stronger than any amount of hard facts. That is why when it comes to online reviews, there are some intriguing psychological principles at play, and understanding these will give you a much deeper understanding of how customers interact with or respond to online reviews.

It's not the overall rating, but the number of reviews that form a customer's mindset. Ten 5-star reviews, or a hundred 4-star reviews? Your answer is as certain as mine, isn't it? A study published in Psychological Science[8] expounded that people trust products that have the largest number of reviews. Understandably, customers gravitate towards a product that lots of people are buying and reviewing, even if some of the reviews are bad. In fact, especially when some reviews are bad, as a few bad reviews make the entire experience more authentic and believable[9]. So businesses should focus on encouraging more customers to share their earnest feedback about their product. The more reviews you can garner, the more new customers will trust your brand.

Early positive reviews can mitigate the effect of negative reviews later. Another study[10] found that customers who read an adequate number of positive reviews about a brand early on, tend to develop a forgiving fondness towards that product. So even if a few bad reviews tumble in later, these customers are likely to ignore them and maintain a positive outlook about that brand. Similarly, early negative reviews can have a lasting impact, foreshadowing positive reviews later, and hurting your business. Businesses must therefore work hard to create a good first impression, and motivate their early customers to become brand advocates. Needless to say, this must only be done by providing them with a quality product and stellar service.

THE ONLINE REVIEW ECOSYSTEM

Reviews older than a month or two tend to lose currency with customers. Only the most recent reviews are successful at motivating users to trust your brand. 44% of consumers will not find a review relevant[11] if it was written more than a month ago. With the way e-commerce has exploded lately, customers now have more options than they can count. They will only buy the latest and the best products, and a product that hasn't seen much action in over a month is considered archaic. This shows just how crucial it is for businesses to seek reviews as an ongoing process.

Negative reviews are a platinum opportunity. So you think you have had a negative review that will break your reputation? Well, not necessarily. Negative reviews could in fact help you form a more trustworthy connection with your customers, if you begin responding to these negative reviews and resolving customer issues. An article in the Harvard Business Review[12] chronicles how the ratings of hotels on TripAdvisor began to improve when they began responding to negative reviews. Customers are happy to see the human side of a business that can be vulnerable to errors. But a business that is eager to make amends and do right by their customers is easily forgiven and happily accepted.

Your customers will want to play sleuths and be mighty good at it. Transparency is the lifeblood of the online review ecosystem. With concerns over paid reviews and biased opinions rising, customers often want to drill down into the deeper reality. Businesses that aim to offer transparency must allow customers to access detailed data about the reviewers – how long have they been reviewing, how often do they review, and are they biased towards anything? Those are some of the questions that customers like to ask.

KEY TO A BRAND'S REPUTATION

Despite becoming a top-notch influencer of public opinion, online reviews remain a largely unregulated, un-moderated territory. Companies have frequently been caught buying and selling biased reviews. The ethical side of this ecosystem is largely questionable as customers have little to no power over companies publishing biased online reviews on their site. Businesses need to be reverent of public opinion and commit to publishing honest, unpaid reviews only. Incentivising customers for a positive review, with a discount or a coupon, for example, must be discouraged. Only then will online reviews continue to be a medium that customers trust as much as their close family and friends.

You would be hard pressed to find a person who doesn't Google a hotel and read reviews before checking in, or one who doesn't run their local business through a search engine before contacting them. Online reviews have become a pre-game ritual and hold the key to a brand's reputation. So while businesses must work hard to build a strong repertoire of positive reviews, they must also remain reverent of the ecosystem and follow ethical practices to ensure transparency in online reviews.

A SCIENTIFIC PERSPECTIVE

The effects of online reviews have been extensively empirically investigated, which gives us a good idea of how they influence consumers in purchasing processes. One study shows[13] that online information is deemed more important than offline information, and that ratings in particular, expressed in a number of stars or a numeric score, are important for the degree of perceived reliability. In addition, the study shows that ratings have a direct impact on the intent to buy a product and on the perceived quality of a product.

Scientists have also examined what characteristics of a review are important for potential customers who consult reviews. Research has been carried out into[14] online reviews for hotels and other tourist products, using the elaboration likelihood model (ELM), which makes a distinction between factors that are peripherally processed (without much thought) and centrally processed (critical and reasoned). As in the aforementioned study, the researchers found that the strongest influence is based on product ranking. This dimension is a peripheral cue because it does not require complex information processing. The second peripheral cue, the amount of information, proved not to exert any significant influence on the behaviour of consumers. The central cues highlighted the different quality requirements of the information that the review held. It was found that the accuracy of the information, additional information, and relevance were the strongest central predictors of information adoption in online reviews. The topicality of the reviews was a little less important and the completeness and comprehensibility were not at all important.

Personal features of the readers of online reviews also play a role in how reviews affect attitudes and behaviour. Researchers have investigated[15] to what extent more and less sceptical consumers differ in terms of cognitive processing of the information from online reviews. The researchers also made use of the ELM and against their expectation it was found that more sceptical consumers were not influenced by the quality of the information, the credibility of the source, or the number of reviews. They mainly ignored the content of the reviews and made use of their intrinsic beliefs to judge products. In other words, they were biased and indifferent to the message quality. Less sceptical consumers were again mainly led by the peripheral cue of the number of reviews. Another study[16] found that the consumers' knowledge about the product or product class, derived from prior experience, study, or training, affects how consumers evaluate online reviews. When, as in the study, a consumer has little expertise on cameras, he or she is more affected by online reviews than a person who has a lot of knowledge about and experience with cameras.

On the basis of data from the online retailer Amazon, researchers also investigated[17] whether certain features of reviewers affect buying behaviour. One of these dimensions is the quality of the reviewer, which is measured according to how helpful the reviews of the single reviewer are evaluated by other users. Reviews of reviewers who are 'high quality' are generally evaluated as very helpful and the opposite applies to 'low quality' reviewers. In addition, the researchers make a distinction between high and low exposure. This involves the number of reviews that the reviewers write, with those who write many reviews being classed as 'high exposure', and vice versa. Reviews have been found to weigh more heavily when they are written by high-quality and high-exposure reviewers. Thus, whether online reviews affect readers not only depends on the characteristics of the review itself, but also on the reader and the reviewer.

FUTURE AND ETHICS

We have been able to see that peripheral cues such as the average ranking and the number of reviews play a significant role in assessing products, services, and people. Knowing this, you may wonder to what extent online reviews really contribute to the well-informed nature of consumers. And we didn't even take false reviews into consideration. The question can also be asked whether people are still thinking for themselves, or whether they simply believe everything that others say on the internet, creating a *bandwagon effect*. This means that beliefs and ideas increase the more they have already been adopted by others. If many people assume something, it is attractive to agree with those people. They hop on the brand-wagon, regardless of the underlying evidence. In addition, it may be questioned whether consumers are honest in their reviews, or whether they consciously or unconsciously let certain prejudices weigh. After all, brands arouse certain associations in the brains of consumers.

On the other hand, online reviews ensure that consumers have a voice. You can ask yourself whether suppliers of products and services provide objective information. Online reviews are mainly intended to facilitate a new digital information flow from user to user without the influence of companies. It creates less consumer dependence on commercially produced content such as advertisements. If people are better informed, it can work towards happier and healthier people because they can make better choices, be it over purchasing consumer products or recommending a potential colleague through reviews on LinkedIn. Looking at the changes to the internet over the last decade, it is particularly salient that the internet has become interpersonal and interactive[18]. As more and more is being communicated via social media and fora, this line can be expected to continue, and the internet will become even more interactive. For online reviews, this means they will play an even bigger role. Moreover, social media is increasingly used as a customer service platform[19]. Customers leave complaints and compliments in public messages on Twitter, for example. Since social media has been increasingly used by companies in recent years to get in touch with their consumers, it is to be expected that online reviews will continue to play a major role, probably even more than ever.

CLASSIFICATION

★★★★★ ★★★★★ ★★★★★ ★★★★★ ★★★★★

References and notes

1 Thompson, A. (2014, October 15). The pros and cons of online customer reviews. Retrieved from https://www.irpcommerce.com/en/gb/IRPStrategyCenter/The-Pros-and-Cons-of-Online-Customer Reviews/sc-55.aspx

2 Thompson, A. (2014, October 15). The pros and cons of online customer reviews. Retrieved from https://www.irpcommerce.com/en/gb/IRPStrategyCenter/The-Pros-and-Cons-of-Online-Customer Reviews/sc-55.aspx

3 Retrieved from: https://www.marketwatch.com/story/10-secrets-to-uncovering-which-online-reviews-are fake-2018-09-21

4 Chang, J. M. (2013, October 24). Samsung fined over fake reviews criticizing HTC. Retrieved from https://abcnews.go.com/Technology/samsung-fined-paying-people-criticize-htcs products/story?id=20671547

5 Retrieved from: https://www.brightlocal.com/learn/local-consumer-review survey/?SSAID=314743&SSCID=21k3_2trr2

6 Retrieved from: https://www.brightlocal.com/learn/local-consumer-review-survey/

7 Retrieved from: https://www.reviewtrackers.com/online-reviews-survey/

8 Retrieved from: https://www.psychologicalscience.org/news/releases/people-favor-highly-reviewed products-even-when-they-shouldnt.html

9 Retrieved from: https://blog.reevoo.com/ebook-bad-reviews-good-business/

10 Coker, B. (2012). Seeking the opinions of others online: Evidence of evaluation overshoot. Journal of Economic Psychology, 33 (6), 1033-1042 DOI: 10.1016/j.joep.2012.06.005

11 Retrieved from: https://www.brightlocal.com/learn/local-consumer-review-survey-2015/

12 Retrieved from: https://hbr.org/2018/02/study-replying-to-customer-reviews-results-in-better-ratings

13 Flanagin, A. J., Metzger, M. J., Pure, R., Markov, A., & Hartsell, E. (2014). Mitigating risk in ecommerce transactions: perceptions of information credibility and the role of user-generated ratings in product quality and purchase intention. Electronic Commerce Research, 14(1), 1–23.

14 Filieri, R., & McLeay, F. (2013). E-WOM and accommodation. Journal of Travel Research, 53(1), 44-57 doi:10.1177/0047287513481274

15 Sher, P. J., & Lee, S. (2009). Consumer skepticism and online reviews: An Elaboration Likelihood Model perspective. Social Behavior and Personality: an International Journal, 37(1), 137-143. doi:10.2224/sbp.2009.37.1.137

16 Ketelaar, P. E., Willemsen, L. M., Sleven, L., & Kerkhof, P. (2015). The good, the bad, and the expert: How consumer expertise affects review valence effects on purchase intentions in online product reviews. Journal of Computer-Mediated Communication, 20(6), 649-666.

17 Hu, N., Liu, L., & Zhang, J. (2008). Do online reviews affect product sales? The role of reviewer characteristics and temporal effects. SSRN Electronic Journal. doi:10.2139/ssrn.1324190

18 Lievrouw, L. A. (2012). The next decade in internet time: Ways ahead for new media studies. Information, Communication & Society, 15(5), 616-638.

19 Gummerus, J., Liljander, V., Weman, E., & Pihlström, M. (2012). Customer engagement in a Facebook brand community. Management Research Review, 35(9), 857-877.

#15 ONLINE VIDEO ADVERTISING

Online video advertising is the use of paid audio-visual content in an online environment

Amsterdam is known by many for its vibrant culture, openness, curiosity, and free-thinking minds. These qualities are not only applicable to a city. They can also be seen as a state of mind. Based on this insight, fashion brand Scotch & Soda launched the 'From Amsterdam, From Everywhere' campaign[1]. In this online video campaign, we see a visual representation of this mindset. We see travellers, discovering different raw landscapes with great curiosity. Different video lengths are used for specific platforms. Based on 4 long videos, 92 short variations have been made for YouTube, Facebook, and Instagram. The creative strategy is built around the brand personality of the Explorer: *'Scotch & Soda dares us to imagine where 'everywhere' could lead; asking if you'd go there, even if it means exposing or having to redefine yourself. By celebrating those who set out to find new roads the brand continues to explore themes of curiosity and discovery'*. Just like the city where the brand started – Amsterdam.

One of the unique elements of the digital media landscape is the eruption of video content, like the campaign described above. We see our media consumption shifting from text to video more and more. An average media consumer in 2018 watched more than one and a half hours of online video content per day[2]. Now, businesses have picked it up as well. No less than 85% of businesses in 2018 regarded video as an important part of their marketing strategy[3].

DEFINITION AND KEY FEATURES

Online video advertising is an innovation that we all come across. Therefore, its description is rather simple. Online video advertising is the use of paid audio-visual content in an online environment. It has many different forms, which we will discuss in detail later. Online video advertising is often confused with online video marketing. There are two distinctions. First, online video advertising is always a form of paid media. Online video marketing, on the other hand, is a form of owned media.

Second, online video advertising is used in the first phase of the consideration process, while online video marketing is applied later on in the customer journey. Online video advertising can have several goals: building brands, generating sales, or raising awareness of a certain subject.

ONLINE VIDEO ADVERTISING IN PRACTICE

There are many different forms of online video advertising. We will shortly discuss a few forms. Firstly, when watching video content, one is often exposed to *pre-rolls*. These are short ads that play before the video content you actually wanted to watch. These are most common on YouTube. Mid-rolls are a version of these. As the name already gives away, mid-rolls are placed in the middle of the content, instead of in front of it. These can be found on YouTube as well, but Facebook has also started using them. A clear benefit of this type of video ad is that the receiver is motivated to watch the video content it is connected to, which makes it more likely that the ad will be watched fully. But its biggest disadvantage is connected to the same reason. Since the receiver is motivated to watch the content that the video ad comes in front of or interrupts, he/she is likely to be annoyed by the ad. Therefore, some pre-rolls are skippable. This means that after a few seconds, the receiver decides whether the ad is interesting enough to finish watching it, or not. The length of these ads differs, but recently YouTube added a new format: 6 second videos. This format is completely tailored to mobile audiences. They are much more motivated to watch a short piece of content, because of its brevity and directness[4]. Besides, being able to share a message or story in a very short time perfectly fits the spirit of the digital age.

A second example of an online video ad is part of a huge trend that came with the development of social media: short, temporary content. The limited access gives the content a form of exclusivity. Only the people who check out the content within 24 hours get to see it. After that time, and also once you've seen it, it is gone. Snapchat started with this form. Now Instagram, Facebook, and WhatsApp have also implemented their own versions of short, temporary content. Not long after this content appeared, so did ads in this form. Due to the lack of an official term we will call them *Disappearing Ads.* Instagram Story Ads are an example thereof. These ads blend in well with other Instagram Stories, since they have the same format (the same rules) and are placed between other Stories. This means that there is little disruption for the receiver.

Disappearing Ads are not the only way to blend in. While these ads blend in because of their format, *companion video ads* blend in because of their message. They add to the content they are placed with. So, for instance, when an instruction video is placed on YouTube about how to build a website, one could place a companion video ad about the tool the receiver can make the website with, or an ad from a company that builds websites for you. They add to the content that the receiver is motivated to watch, so they are not intrusive. Also, the ads are usually smaller than the video the receiver is watching, which can also make them less intrusive than many other forms of advertising[5].

As you see in the list of examples above, there is a broad and rich scope of approaches to online video advertising, on many different levels. We have listed a few pros and cons, but the reality is that there is not one single type of video advertising that is generally best. The best choice is dependent on your objectives, options, target group, and budget, to name a few factors. And even then, there are more factors that influence the effects of online video ads. We discuss below a few important factors and debates that are influential with regard to online video advertising.

INSPIRE AND TOUCH

As an advertiser, grabbing the attention of the consumer is crucial. Without it, you cannot inspire, you cannot bond and most importantly, you cannot sell. In the current media landscape, grabbing attention is quite difficult, because there are a lot of other advertisers competing for that same attention. Therefore, one must stand out. One way to do so is by adding relatable emotions to the advertisement. Relatable emotions are needed for brand building. And online video advertising is a powerful channel for brand building[6].

These days, most online videos are very short. This makes it challenging to transfer an emotion or feeling to the customer. Therefore, it is helpful to know which emotions are relatively easy and clear to transfer in a short period of time. Pre-testing research[7] suggests that the following five emotions lend themselves best to short video formats: hilarity, surprise, knowledge, arousal, and fear. Other, softer emotions such as warmth, pride, and inspiration are more difficult to evoke in short video formats, because they take more time to build up. However, because these emotions are more difficult to evoke, they also stand out more in the overloaded media landscape.

To really inspire and touch people, creative and cinematic quality is essential. Although not substantiated from research – there is no criterion for creative and cinematic levels –

every topper in the field claims that this is what really matters and that it is possibly more important than the medium, the length, technical possibilities such as personalisation, and use of data.

THE DEBATE: SHORT OR LONG?

While the trend towards shorter video advertisements is clear, practitioners are not entirely in agreement when it comes to the most effective format. While most results show that shorter online video ads are more effective, the most remarkable examples are usually a lot longer: up to short documentaries that are fifteen minutes long. Nike is one of those extraordinary brands that manages to fight the trend and grabs our attention with powerful, long content. The dilemma seems to be: how long can I hold the attention of the consumer? Nike proves that consumers are willing to spend more than a few seconds on advertisements, as long as they are inspiring, relevant, and entertaining. Unfortunately, Nike is one of the top brands of this world, and not many companies can match this power brand. Perhaps the guideline should be: make the video as short as possible, unless the message is so impactful and outstanding, that a long format is beneficial to enrich the experience for the consumer. Relevance, inspiration, and entertainment then are preconditions for this to happen.

The trend for shorter online video ads has a lot to do with the rise of social media. Most online video ads are watched in a social media environment. On social media, content is scrolled through in seconds. So, in order to fit in with the speedy consumption of media content, online video ads become shorter as well, because if the media experience of the consumer is disrupted, it will cause irritation and the consumer is likely to scroll it away.

PLEASE BE SILENT

On social media channels such as Instagram, Facebook, and LinkedIn, suddenly starting sounds are seen as annoying, and therefore these channels are usually scrolled through with the media sound switched off. In fact, 85% of Facebook videos are watched without sound[8]. This means a great change for advertisers. For instance, full conversations between people are hard to transfer to a consumer who is watching a silent video on a mobile phone. In order to make it understandable, the advertiser must use fast-moving and small subtitles. This means that the consumer must either focus completely on the subtitles and not see the rest of the ad clearly, or miss parts of the message and story. Therefore, practitioners and researchers of this subject advise using only functional subtitles, which provide necessary context to the message. Ideally, no text is needed at all. The power of video is mostly in its use of images.

Not all channels are predominantly used in silent mode. YouTube, for instance, is usually consumed with the sound on. Multiple versions of the ad can be created, so the ad will fit both YouTube consumers and Facebook consumers, for instance.

Above we discussed several factors that one should take into account when using online video advertising. Next, Jan Heuvel explains how he implements online video advertising and what he feels are impactful factors to consider in that process.

ONLINE VIDEO ADVERTISING CAN BE IRRESISTIBLE

By Jan Heuvel
Director Strategy & Innovation at SAMR Marketfinders
and co-founder of Spotton Media

My definition of marketing is very simple. Marketing is the art of seduction. To seduce you must be irresistible. Sounds logical and simple, yet most marketers do not succeed. I also see this in online video advertising. In particular, the product properties or the functional customer benefits are emphasised. The psychological or social benefits and a creative strategy are often lacking or the advert gives over to bad humour. Not to mention the quality of the execution – direction, casting, camera work, editing, and many other disciplines make or break a commercial. Now that anyone can shoot a movie at any time, the quality is decreasing rapidly, without being aware of it.

HOW TO BECOME IRRESISTIBLE

If you want to be irresistible as a brand, product, or service you have to be crystal clear, personally relevant, fully credible, distinctive, and inspiring. The first three are hygiene factors. To be distinctive one has to jump out and to become irresistible you have to inspire people, which is only possible if you know how to touch people emotionally.

Scientists disagree about what emotions actually exist. My analysis of hundreds of commercial propositions reveals roughly nine emotions that can inspire people: joy, honesty, connectedness, recognition, ecstasy, energy, surprise, reward, and security. Many online video commercials mainly revolve around joy (e.g. showing a happy family), reward (20% discount!) and security. As a result, many online commercials look alike and are unable to make the difference.

LEADING PEOPLE THROUGH THE FUNNEL MATTERS, NOT JUST VIEWS

The days of just focusing on the number of views are over. Meaningful performance indicators next to views are completion rate, drop-off point (the number of seconds after which people stop viewing), reach in the target audience, viewable CPM (cost per mille), cost per acquisition, engagement (likes, comments and shares) and fraud (views from bots). The goal is to lead your target audience through the funnel of awareness, consideration, preference, and behaviour. Online video, different from a TV-commercial, allows you to build in calls to action such as watching another video or making an appointment directly in the web shop.

Video offers room for creative storytelling, personalisation, and interaction. Combine this with focus on the right target group, high-quality execution, and continuous optimisation of your commercial by analysing views and engagement drivers. Think of text in the video, facial expression, colour, objects, and associations, such as 'feminine' for the colour pink. Analysis of the presence of these elements and their nature in specific frames not only provides insight into success and failure factors in general, but also specifically for your video commercial.

PERSONALISATION

The ultimate point of irresistibility is that people get the feeling 'this is about me'. In the chapter Behavioural targeting, this phenomenon is analysed in depth. Personalised video uses information from a data source, and displays that information within the video content. Many companies already collect this data. Nevertheless, the personalisation of online video commercials is still in its infancy, often limited to showing the viewer's name in the commercial. Yet if you have the data, you could 'coincidentally' show the specific type of car the viewer is driving even though the commercial is about a new type of Audi. It has the chance to become the next level in video advertising.

Technically, personalisation can go very far, but just as you do not have to become too personal with strangers, you'd better avoid coming too close to people with online video advertising[9]. If you show that you know someone is looking for a new washing machine, you are too close for many people. Consumers value personalised videos mainly later in the buying process or if they are already customers, but not in the orientation phase. At that time, personalisation is too intrusive for most consumers. Yet, a specific form of personalisation, interactive video, is usually appreciated at that first moment, because they can then make choices themselves. The brand Maybelline has a video you can personalise with a single click to your own skin type and character, after which you will see a nice tutorial. In order to achieve a similar effect, you do not have to make it so technically complicated. When you target specific audiences, you can also make two or three variants of the same video. For example, a campaign for security systems that we made with exactly the same images and texts, but with young and older actors, proved to be particularly effective in the corresponding age groups.

WHAT SHOULD YOU PAY ATTENTION TO IN PRACTICE?

When writing the script, specify exactly where a personalisation element should appear. Make sure that the data on which the personalisation is based is really correct and the creative representation is taken for granted, not artificial. If, as a simple example, you want to show someone's name in your commercial, make sure that it looks natural instead of just being stuck in. If you want to bring out a specific product characteristic for someone, make sure this happens emotionally in the right flow of your story. Otherwise you detract from the illusion that your commercial was made especially for the viewer. Avoid extending your commercial by bringing in personalisation – the shorter it is, the greater the chance that the commercial will be watched.

CONCLUSION

Bring your functional message in a powerful emotional context, with a creative-strategic story and high-quality cinematic quality. Use data for personalisation where possible and acceptable. Why? You want your online commercial to be so irresistible that people like to look at it – not because they feel obligated to do so.

A SCIENTIFIC PERSPECTIVE

Online video advertising is a means of getting a message across. For advertisers, it is mostly a marketing tool, but one can also see it as a medium. Through the ad, the information and the emotion of the message that the advertiser wants to tell reach the consumer. Research tells us that online video advertising can be a very smart marketing tool (or medium) for advertisers to use. We will discuss an impactful study to illustrate this.

A large research study by IPA[10] shows that online video, and online video advertising in particular, is very effective. The impact of online video advertising is bigger than that of non-video formats, and campaigns that include online video tend to be more effective than those that do not. Online video is particularly effective for brand-building purposes. This has to do with its video format as well. Another medium that is very effective for brand building is TV. Combining these two media makes the most effective campaigns. TV gets mass reach and online video advertising extends this reach to a younger, less TV-orientated generation, and allows them to discuss and share the content, which takes it further in a fast way. Besides, online video advertising is not only effective, it is also efficient. It achieves impressive business results on relatively small budgets, according to the IPA research.

EASY PROCESSING

One of the reasons why online video advertising is so effective is that it is easy to process. In fact, people process images 60,000 times faster than text[11]. We remember them better as well. A stunning 85% compared to 10% for things we have been told and 45% for written messages[12]. This can be explained by the human tendency to avoid cognitive load. Because of it, we prefer information that is easy to process. A reason why video is easy to process is that the images that we usually form in our heads while reading a text are already presented to us in video. So, our brains have less work to do.

How online videos are processed depends on a number of aspects. Research[13] into the relationship to the number of camera changes and the amount of newly introduced information, shows clear connections here. Increasing the number of camera changes in videos slightly increases recognition if a small amount of new information is introduced. That is, if there are relatively few new visuals shown between different cuts. For instance, when the camera standpoint of a quiet park is varied a few times, every variation adds a little bit of information to the video. But, when the video transitions from a loud club in one image, to a silent park in the second, and a busy boardroom meeting in the third, a large amount of information is introduced per camera change. As the amount of information introduced by these camera changes increases, and the number of camera changes increases as well, recognition decreases significantly. Following the PCMC-model[14] we can conclude that because of the little elaboration that is needed to process short, clean online video ads, the ad is usually not processed in a systematic manner. That is, unless the subject is familiar and/or relevant to the receiver. This may cause the ad to be processed systematically, because more resources will be allocated to the message, since the receiver is more motivated to process the message and will recall earlier memories, which leads to the allocation of mental resources. However, usually people are not very motivated to process advertisements. Online video ads do not go by unnoticed, though as we stated earlier, 85% of video messages are remembered, thus it is unlikely that video messages will be processed automatically. Therefore, we conclude that most times, online video advertising is processed heuristically. This means that the message is processed emotionally, via heuristics that ease the cognitive load.

There is a difference in processing between younger and older people. Research[15] shows that younger adults outpace older adults in information memory as the pacing of media messages increases and this difference is even larger for arousing compared with calm messages.

AROUSAL

A second reason why online video advertising can be effective is its ability to arouse emotion, through storytelling. Storytelling can influence thoughts about brands and ads, as well as attitudes and behaviour towards them. Read all about this in the scientific storytelling chapter.

Thirdly, the digital environment of online video ads, and the data that surrounds it, makes it possible to thoroughly target the ads to the exact target audience. This increases the efficiency of the ad.

FUTURE AND ETHICS

Online video advertising is gaining popularity, and it is influencing other parts of the media landscape. For instance, the online trend of short videos is being picked up by TV as well. TV commercials are also starting to use shorter video formats more often[16]. This shows that we are getting used to the short video formats that online video ads have taught us.

Another trend that is a little obvious, is the trend towards mobile-first communication. Forrester discovered that mobile is forecast to account for an enormous growth in spending on online video advertising in the next couple of years[17]. This has implications for online video advertising as well. Of course, already every online video campaign has to be mobile proof. But with the trend towards mobile-first we also see more vertical video formats, for instance: videos that are especially shot in a way that is most impactful for mobile viewing. This implies that even in the production phase of an ad, mobile is the mindset.

TARGETING AND PERSONALISATION

Thirdly, online video ads will be targeted even more specifically in the future. With more and more data becoming available, we expect that in a few years a brand will know so much about us, that they can target their ads to us, based on preferences and earlier purchases (as many already do), but they will also time exactly when someone is hungry, how long they usually wear the same clothes, what their regular time for household chores is and when and where they meet up with friends. These data can then be used to target needs and wishes at the exact time and place that they are most relevant. And all of this will be done automatically, by algorithms and machine-learning processes. In a similar matter, data will be used to personalise online video ads more often, as Jan Heuvel has already described.

While precise targeting and personalisation make sure that online video ads will become even more relevant to us as consumers, and more efficient for advertisers, they also pose some ethical issues. To target precisely, personal data is needed, which is hard to acquire without intruding the consumers' privacy. Personalisation of videos also has its risks. Again, personal data is needed, and additionally personalisation can scare consumers off.

NEW VIDEO FORMATS

As the trends described above show, online video advertising is in constant development. This development does not stop at optimising elements of online video ads. It is also about integrating other techniques. For instance, AR content is gaining popularity. In fact, following a survey in 2018[18], 82% of the technology-minded respondents stated that developers are focusing on creating more collaborative and social experiences for VR and AR, and 81% claimed that developers will also focus on creating AR tools and apps for smartphones. This creates opportunities for online video ads, to add new layers of reality and therefore intensify the experience.

Concluding, online video advertising is a popular technique, with lots of opportunities to grow with the digital media landscape. First of all, because of the applicability of data to target and personalise online video ads, but also because it can be the base for new online video formats, such as AR and VR videos. With the integration of these new media techniques, online video advertising will keep its attractiveness.

CLASSIFICATION

★★★★★ ★★★★★ ★★★★★ ★★★★★ ★★★★★

References and notes

1   Check out the campaign on:
    https://www.campaignlive.co.uk/article/scotch-soda-from-amsterdam-everywhere-fw-2017-publicis-133/1443402
2   Wyzowl (2018). The state of video marketing 2018.Retreived from:
    https://www.wyzowl.com/video-marketing-statistics-2019/
3   Wyzowl (2018). The state of video marketing 2018.Retreived from:
    https://www.wyzowl.com/video-marketing-statistics-2019/
4   Media Expert video. Retrieved from:
    https://www.mediaexpertvideo.com/blog/2018/04/26/the-top-6-trending-types-of-online-video-advertising
5   Media Expert video. Retrieved from:
    https://www.mediaexpertvideo.com/blog/2018/04/26/the-top-6-trending-types-of-online-video-advertising
6   Binet, L., & Field, P. (2017). Media in focus: Marketing effectiveness in the digital era. Institute of Practitioners in Advertising.
7   Waring, R. (2018). How to engage consumers with short-form video. Retrieved from: warc.com
8   Digiday (2016). 85 percent of Facebook video is watched without sound. Retrieved from:
    https://digiday.com/media/silent-world-facebook-video/
9   Pöyry, E. I., Hietaniemi, N., Parvinen, P. M. T., Hamari, J., & Kaptein, M. (2017). Personalized product recommen-
    dations. In Proceedings of the 50th Annual Hawaii International Conference on System Sciences. IEEE Computer Society.
10 Binet, L., & Field, P. (2017). Media in focus: Marketing effectiveness in the digital era. Institute of Practitioners in Advertising.
11 Semetko, H.A. & Scammel, M. (2012). The SAGE handbook of political communication. Sage Publications.
12 Brain rules. Retrieved from: http://www.brainrules.net/vision
13 Hendriks Vettehen, P., & Kleemans, M. (2015). How camera changes and information introduced af-
    fect the recognition of public service announcements: A test outside the lab. Communication Research.
    10.1177/0093650215616458.
14 Buijzen, M., Van Reijmersdal, E. A., & Owen, L. H. (2010). Introducing the PCMC model: An investigative framework
    for young people's processing of commercialized media content. Communication Theory, 20(4), 427-450. DOI:
    https://doi.org/10.1111/j.1468-2885.2010.01370.x
15 Lang, A., Schwartz, N., & Mayell, S. (2015). Slow down you're moving too fast. Journal of Media Psychology: Theo-
    ries, Methods, and Applications. 1, 1-11. 10.1027/1864-1105/a000130.
16 WARC (January, 2019). Short-form ads are this year's big thing. Retrieved from:
    https://www.warc.com/newsandopinion/news/shortform_ads_are_this_years_big_thing/41517
17 Forrester. Found on: https://www.mobilemarketer.com/news/forrester-mobile-will-drive-72-of-growth-in-online-
    video-ad-spend/525203/
18 Perkinscoie (2018). Augmented and virtual reality survey report. Retrieved from:
    https://www.perkinscoie.com/images/content/1/8/v2/187785/2018-VR-AR-Survey-Digital.pdf

#16 DIGITAL STORYTELLING

Storytelling is the packaging of facts in an appealing context that unfolds through a narrative

Let us start this chapter about stories with a story, a story about a young boy who conquered the world, step by step. His name was John. He was just a local farm boy, but there was something special about him. A glint in his eye, a fire in his belly, a spring in his step. And one day, he went for a walk. This walk began when his father passed away. The year was 1819 and he was just 14 years old... Now, if you are interested in advertising, whisky, or both, you probably already know exactly who I am talking about: the one and only Johnnie Walker. A whisky brand famous for its constant drive to innovate, to 'keep walking'. For those who are not familiar with the story, Google it now[1], or re-freshen your memory with the most famous part of this story – its ending *"Two hundred years later and Johnnie Walker is still walking. And he is not showing any signs of stopping."*

DEFINITION AND KEY FEATURES

We started this chapter with a story, not just to get your attention, but also to make it easier to process the information we are providing here. That is why we have started every chapter with a story, that illustrates the innovation we are about to discuss. In fact, a lot of the information we receive in our life is presented as a story. These stories form the base of understanding new experiences, making decisions, and judging people, objects, and situations that are mentioned. Through stories we form general attitudes and beliefs towards all these story elements. In other words, we use stories to understand our own lives, the world around us, and our role in society[2].

Using stories to promote a brand is a popular classic marketing strategy. We would like to use Johnnie Walker to illustrate this fact. The brand has been striving on its story since 1820, although classic storytelling is constantly innovating. To discuss these new developments, we first lay down the basis.

There are two general ways to incorporate a story into a brand: building a corporate story or using narratives in advertising campaigns. Corporate stories are used to create meaning for a brand, to build a persuasive and consistent brand image. In this way, brands try to connect with their customers in a more personal and emotional way and take away some scepticism of consumers towards the brand and its advertising. The story of a brand is usually summarised in a brand mission and/or tagline. Johnnie Walker has "keep walking" as a summary of their brand story and innovative character. Another brand that understands the importance of a good mission is Philips, a Dutch technology company that operates worldwide. Since 1995 the brand has been working on a strong, consistent brand story, focussed on improving the world through innovation. That is when their first brand mission was introduced: "let's make things better", which evolved through "sense and simplicity" into its current line "innovation and you".[3]

Narrative advertising has a similar goal: marketeers try to build an attractive context around the persuasive message. By 'transporting' the consumer into the story, the consumer will ideally be distracted from the persuasiveness of the message, and therefore accept the message of the commercial in a non-critical way.

Corporate stories and narrative advertising are classic ways to integrate storytelling. There are more options however, such as using serious gaming to tell a story. In this way, information is not just shared, but the user is actually engaging in the story and influencing its course. Whereas corporate stories and narrative advertising are mostly found in marketing spheres, serious gaming is usually applied in other sectors, such as in education or food advising. Read all about this innovation in the Serious Gaming chapter.

TRANSPORTATION

Transportation into narratives is the most important process when it comes to storytelling. A good story is able to transport the consumer from reality, into the narrative world. In other words, the consumer stops thinking about his own life, and instead lets the story lead his thoughts to the narrative[4]. Being transported into a story has severe cognitive and emotional consequences and makes the receiver susceptible to attitude change with regard to the subject of the experienced story[5].

To create transportation into the narrative, the brand and/or product needs to be woven seamlessly into the story. Also, it is important that the story calls for a certain level of emotion and engagement from the consumer.

For emotion to be incited, the consumer needs to relate to the characters of the story. Identification is the first step. If consumers identify with the characters, they can be transported into the story, and can be persuaded by the message. It is therefore advisable to use characters that are easy to identify with. Most important is that the feelings or deeds of the character are relatable. If the receiver understands why a character feels the way he feels, and therefore acts the way he acts, the receiver can identify with the character.

THE POWER OF STRUCTURE

The power of storytelling depends, among other things, on the structure of the story. Research[6] shows that the structure of the story influences the way a person processes it. A person pays more attention to the story and experiences more emotional reactions when the main incident (the struggle of the character) is not instantly clear. This means that the story builds up towards the ending, and you need to continue with the story to fully comprehend it. Tricks such as plot twists help to keep the story interesting and the final message unclear until the end. Long-time television writer Doug Heyes says that there is only one rule for achieving proper plot structure: "What's happening now must be inherently more interesting than what just happened. The goal of structure – the goal of your entire story, in fact – is to elicit emotion in the reader or audience. If your story is increasingly compelling as you move forward, that's all you need to worry about"[7]. The well-known Christmas commercials by John Lewis are top class examples. They even won the PA Effectiveness Awards Grand Prix for their Christmas campaigns[8]. Therefore, we will discuss one of their commercials in full.

CASE: MAN ON THE MOON – JOHN LEWIS CHRISTMAS COMMERCIAL 2015

Little Lilly is bored and decides to look through the telescope. She zooms in on a perfectly bright and round moon. She keeps on zooming in until she sees a man standing there. An actual man! That is the start of one of John Lewis's best Christmas commercials. Accompanied by great, upsweeping music the story unfolds. The man on the moon is old and totally alone. Lilly enthusiastically tries so reach the man. She waves at him, makes paper planes of her letters and tries to shoot messages into the sky with her bow and arrow. But all efforts fail. The story shifts to Christmas evening.

Lilly seems to have forgotten about her man on the moon and is happily enjoying the company and gifts of her family. Then the plot twists again and we are back with the man on the moon. He is sitting on a bench that is turned to face the Earth. His head is bowed down in misery. Suddenly, a package flies at his feet. It turns out that Lilly did not forget about him after all. The package has colourful balloons attached to it. The man lights up completely when he sees it, and smiles broadly. We see him opening the gift, revealing a small telescope of his own. He immediately sets it to his eye and zooms in on Earth. After a little search he discovers Lilly's house and watches her waving at him. The man sheds a tear of happiness, and of course he waves back at her. The story ends with the message: 'show someone they're loved this Christmas'.

The commercial captures the core of one of our most profound emotions, loneliness, and seamlessly adds the simple solution to it: nothing more or less than a little bit of love. The story transports you into the narrative and makes you relate to the emotions of the characters. That the subject – loneliness among the elderly – is a very important issue in our current society makes the message even stronger. Also, all the necessary elements of a good story structure come back in 'man on the moon': a surprising opening scene to get your attention, after which the emotion is deepened with a heartwarming scene that outlines the conflict, followed by a plot twist and of course a happy ending.

The commercial 'man on the moon' was not the whole campaign; it was only the beginning of the story's integration into that year's Christmas promotions. John Lewis launched an augmented reality app that brought the story to life and allowed consumers to really interact with the story[9]. By pointing your phone at the John Lewis's Man-on-the-Moon-themed packaging and shopping bags, users were able to unlock a 3D interactive moon that contained daily facts, animations, a countdown to Christmas, and a Man on the Moon game.

The results? Between 2012 and 2015, 2453 million people watched the Christmas commercials, of which 'the man on the moon' had 1210 million views. John Lewis increased sales during the festive season by 16% on average. Besides that, it produced over £8 of profit for every £1 it spent, resulting in an annual market share that has increased to 29.6%[10].

THE BRAND

Another important factor that influences the power of storytelling may be obvious, but nonetheless of importance: the brand itself. For some brands and products, storytelling is easier to apply than for others. 'Significant Objects'[11], a literary and anthropological experiment, shows that even thrift-store objects can benefit massively from storytelling. The researchers asked over 200 great writers to write short purpose-written stories about the thrift-store objects. The objects were sold on eBay. While the objects were purchased for US$1.25 each on average, they were sold for nearly US$8,000.00 in total, showing that their value had increased a lot, while the only change was that their descriptions had changed from facts to stories.

THE NEW STORYTELLING

Now that we have discussed the basics of storytelling we proceed with the next step in the evolution of storytelling. As we argued before, storytelling is about as old as mankind, but things have not stayed the same since then. We still tell stories like we used to, but the way we tell them is changing and the role that stories play in our lives has expanded. The distinction between reality and fiction is blurring, because of our access to *digital storytelling*. Stories are even becoming a common mode for explaining and remembering data and facts. Through podcasts we have plenty of access to information – presented as stories. And webshops are not complete without a page labelled 'our story' or 'about us', containing the story of how their business started and their brand values.

For now, we will highlight another new development in storytelling that arose[12] as a consequence of the eruption of new media, in 2003. In this form, multiple media are combined to create a bigger story. All the media that are included tell their own story, but the stories combined form a bigger picture, so to speak. Concretely, *transmedia storytelling* represents a process wherein integral story elements are systematically spread over multiple distribution channels (media), creating a uniform and coordinated experience as a result. Ideally, every medium makes its own unique contribution to unfolding the complete story. With social media, augmented reality, and virtual reality we can go even further to optimise transmedia storytelling, namely to make the receiver part of the story by letting them participate in it.

The introduction of the movie 'The Hunger Games' is an example where transmedia storytelling was applied in pura forma. To support the story, fans could register themselves as citizens of 'the Capitol', which is the high-class community of the Hunger Games world. Simultaneously, a hashtag was introduced on Twitter, namely #whatsmydistrict. On the website, fans were assigned to an identity, profession, and district. Afterwards, people could join their district on Facebook, and in a similar way even more media were used to create a unique experience for the Hunger Games fans[13]. Creating a unique experience is crucial for users to be motivated to participate in the story. The district groups on Facebook are an illustrative example of deepening the experience. Knowing what district you are in might be fun to know for fans, but this way, they can actually influence their experience and are actively participating in it, interacting with fellow district-members, and forming a group similar to the actual Hunger Games characters. The challenge is to create a dynamic experience, with multiple entry points, so that everyone can follow their own journey. In the Hunger Games example, one could enter the experience through the website first, or through Twitter by seeing the hashtag. Ideally, even on the Facebook pages there is a link to the website saying, "if you want to know your district, go to the website and find out which group to join". To summarise: a transmedia storytelling concept is engaging, unique, and dynamic.

Next, Marc Oosterhout shares his vision and experience regarding storytelling. He believes that strong brands touch the right emotion, and use storytelling to create a position in the brain of the consumer.

BRAIN POSITION

By Marc Oosterhout
Founder & brand consultant
N=5

The essence of advertising is storytelling 'in a split second'. After all, an average TV commercial lasts only thirty seconds. And the attention paid to an Instagram post does not even come close to that. The average time is no more than six or seven seconds. In this ultrashort time, a brand has to tell their whole story. Besides, we live in a 'netflixitised' society where we live in our own bubble more and more – a bubble that it is harder and harder to get into, especially for advertising. Ads are more and more averted nowadays.

Advertising therefore has the primary task of standing out. Advertising must have an impact. It must agitate or thrill the receiver. It must tickle his brain. Even more, advertising has to create a position in that brain. To do that, advertisers primarily use emotion. Emotion is proven to be the fastest way to our brain. A lot faster than ratio. Therefore, we search for the right emotion for all the brands that we work for. In this way, we learned that Dutch people do not love the NS (The Dutch Railways), but they do love the train. Train romance is the emotion that we used to make the NS more sympathetic. And with success – the brand sympathy for NS has risen by about 25% in the last few years. Proof that emotional advertising works.

The right emotion is the one that truly aligns with the feelings of the brand's target group. That is what we must search for. For NS that was train romance. For a brand like Dove it is 'real beauty'. In a world where everything seems to be photoshopped and fake, we started to believe that beauty is always perfect, although really, beauty is in everyone. The images in advertising and fashion magazines are unreal, and maybe even hurtful. Dove fights that, with authenticity as their core emotion.

The best way to find this relevant emotion is to search for a conflict. Every brain is full of conflicts. The conflict between desire (what we want) and fear (what we do not want). The tension between desire and fear yields a perfect frustration. Emotion. That is how we know that lots of people have the desire to be a top athlete, but also fear that it is an unreachable goal. A source of frustration. Exactly that frustration is solved by Nike and its promise "If you have a body, you're an athlete". Beautiful. That is how you find the right emotion. When the right emotion is found, there is only one more thing of importance – creativity. Devise a story that appeals to the imagination, a way to enter the brain of the receiver directly, through the route of emotion. To create a brain position. The core of storytelling in advertising. Now, and in the future.

A SCIENTIFIC PERSPECTIVE

We can explain the success of storytelling through the way our brain works. Multiple studies have confirmed that our brain is a lot more involved with stories than with cold, hard facts[14]. When someone reads information, only the parts of the brain that process language are activated to decode the meaning of that information. But when someone reads a story, also the parts of the brain that the person would use if he would actually experience what he reads are activated. This makes the information provided a lot easier to remember; our brain does not divide story information much from experience information.

FUNCTIONS OF STORYTELLING

From the perspective of Fogg's functional triad[15], storytelling can be seen as a medium in the way that information and emotion are transferred through the story, to the consumer. It can also function as a social actor, as it connects consumers with the characters of the story. For marketers, storytelling can also be a tool to create a bond between the consumers and the brand, to create positive brand attitudes, or simply to sell more products.

EFFECTS

In this chapter, we will get into the levels wherein storytelling has influence and explain what processes these effects are based on. There is a lot more to learn about storytelling, but we believe this is the core.

We distinguish three levels of effects. The first one is affective effects, affective, emotion, and attitudes. Storytelling has a strong effect on this level since it is focussed on the emotions of the consumer. It is presumed that stories that evoke positive emotions in consumers result in positive brand attitudes[16]. Furthermore, research shows that when a consumer is 'absorbed' by a story his attitudes become consistent with the attitudes that are communicated in the story[17]. People love stories. So, presenting an advertising message through an attractive format like storytelling helps advertisers to evoke positive attitudes towards the advertisement.[18]

The second level of effects contains conative effects, which means action. A relevant evoked action is word of mouth. People like to share inspirational stories with others. So, when storytelling is applied successfully, a word-of-mouth-effect could occur and the story will be spread, and its effects will grow.

 third level, cognitive effects, is about the brain. It influences whether and how we think about a brand. Stories are easily remembered because they speak to multiple parts of the brain and are set up in the same way as our brain works: through cause and effect[19]. In other words, storytelling fits seamlessly with the way people process and save information in their brain, which enhances the remembrance and recognition of brands.

TRANSMEDIA STORYTELLING

For transmedia storytelling, discussing the effects is a bit more complicated, because of the interacting relationship between producer and receiver, content and receiver, and receivers as a dynamic group. In general, people prefer a uniform transmedia experience, whereby the stories in different media form a coherent whole. Amongst other effects that are discussed above, transmedia storytelling enhances engagement of the audience[20]. This mainly positive effect has the risk of dividing the public into 'true fans' and 'mainstream audience'. This makes it extremely difficult for producers to make the right content and to form a journey to the ultimate experience. For example, true Hunger Games fans will not be pleased if the experience lacks detailed hints to the books. But on the other hand, implementing story elements that the mainstream public does not know might confuse them, and therefore they lose their interest[21]. Because of these complicated factors, it is hard to say what exactly the effects of transmedia storytelling are. What we do know is that it can work really well. That is, if you find your way through the maze of your audience's wishes[22].

FUTURE AND ETHICS

Storytelling is a stable technique that will always play a role in the future, but its application and role will change. For example, the automatisation of companies' communication will make a lot of communication feel impersonal and cold, for instance because chatbots are not yet well enough developed to make them human-like. Storytelling will be the counterpart of this development. Its personal, emotional approach will stand out more, and make a difference by creating a bond with the consumer. That is, until machine learning is developed well enough to truly interact on an emotional level. In that case, machines might create a whole new dimension of storytelling, for example, by personalising the story, so that it fits the receiver best.

There are already examples of movies that can have different endings, depending on choices the consumer makes. With machine learning and enough data, this could be extended to personalised storytelling that predicts what fits the consumer without him/her even making a choice. Other new media such as augmented reality, robots, and voice assistants will also add new dimensions to storytelling, we presume.

With these new layers, the relatively innocent innovation will face ethical challenges. Data about users cannot freely be collected without permission. Also, it is important that your story is based on truths regarding the product involved. A story becomes unethical when certain elements are linked, which makes it look like one is the cause of another element, when this is not actually the case. Think of car commercials. Someone buys a new car from brand X and suddenly they find themselves in a beautiful environment, with a very happy family. Of course, stories are facts surrounded by an appealing context.

There is a thin line between a situation sketch and an unrealistic promise. Think about this: are we really better off if all brands in their own way tell the story that purchasing their products leads to a greater and happier world? Critics claim that brands are guilty of promoting a hedonistic culture with their stories and a focus on possessions or materials. On the other hand, it could also be argued[23] that the accumulation of material possessions is just a simple consequence of wealth and that the basic motive has always been there: people may not need many possessions but want them all the same. We advise to keep this in mind and not go too far. Have integrity when telling your story.

"Tell me a fact, and I'll learn. Tell me a truth, and I'll believe. But tell me a story, and it will live in my heart forever."

Ed Sabol, movie maker

CLASSIFICATION

★★★★★ ★★★★★ ★★★★★ ★★★★★ ★★★★★

References and notes

1 Type "Johnnie Walker - The Man Who Walked Around The World" into YouTube and you will find a short film of 6 minutes about Johnnie's story.

2 Escalas, J. E. (2004). Narrative processing: building consumer connections to brands. Journal of Consumer Psychology, 14, 168-180. DOI: 10.1207/s15327663jcp1401&2_19

3 Read more about Philips' brand mission on their website: https://www.philips.com/a-w/about/company/introduction.html

4 Green, M. C., Brock, T. C., & Kaufman, G. F. (2004). Understanding media enjoyment: The role of transportation into narrative worlds. Communication Theory, 14(4), 311-327.

5 For an example of research regarding the effects of transportation, see: Green, M. C., & Brock, T. C. (2000). The role of transportation in the persuasiveness of public narratives. Journal of Personality and Social Psychology, 79(5), 701.

6 Graaf, A, de & Hustinx, L. (2011). The effect of story structure on emotion, transportation, and persuasion. Information Design Journal, 19(2), 142-154.

7 For more information on how to build a strong story structure, check out "Structure of Plot: The Outer Journey" (April, 2015) on Writes with tools.

8 WARC (2016). John Lewis wins IPA Grand Prix. Retrieved from:
https://www.warc.com/newsandopinion/news/john_lewis_wins_ipa_grand_prix/37689

9 stinkstudios.com

10 Binet, L., & Field, P. (2017). Media in focus: Marketing effectiveness in the digital era. Institute of Practitioners in Advertising; McCarthy, J. (2018). Every John Lewis Christmas ad since 2006: a moon, a snowman, a bear, a hare and a penguin. Retrieved from: https://www.thedrum.com/news/2016/10/31/decade-john-lewis-christmas-ads-man-the-moon-snowman-bear-and-hare-and-monty-the

11 Significantobjects.com

12 Henry Jenkins introduced transmedia storytelling in 2003.

13 Ignition creative, 2014

14 An overview of research on processing and reacting on stories is given in 'Your Brain on Fiction' an article by New York Times: https://www.nytimes.com/2012/03/18/opinion/sunday/the-neuroscience-of-your-brain-on-fiction.html?pagewanted=all

15 The functional triad is a model made by Fogg, Cuellar and Danielson (2002)

16 Adaval, R., & Wyer, R. S. (1998). The role of narratives in consumer information processing. Journal of Consumer Psychology, 7(3), 207-245. DOI: 10.1207/s15327663jcp0703_01

17 Graaf, A, de & Hustinx, L. (2011). The effect of story structure on emotion, transportation, and persuasion. Information Design Journal, 19(2), 142-154.

18 Hsu, J. (2008). The secrets of storytelling. Scientific American Mind, 19, 46-51.

19 Woodside, A.G., Sood, S., & Miller, K.E. (2008). When consumers and brands talk: Storytelling theory and research in psychology and marketing. Psychology & Marketing, 25(2), 97-145.

20 Graves, M. (2011). 'Lost' in a transmedia storytelling franchise: rethinking transmedia engagement (doctoral dissertation). Retrieved from:
http://kuscholarworks.ku.edu/bitstream/handle/1808/9780/Graves_ku_0099D_11896_DATA_1.pdf?sequence=1

21 Graves, M. (2011). 'Lost' in a transmedia storytelling franchise: rethinking transmedia engagement (doctoral dissertation). Retrieved from: http://kuscholarworks.ku.edu/bitstream/handle/1808/9780/Graves_ku_0099D_11896_DATA_1.pdf?sequence=1; Smith, A. (2009). Transmedia storytelling in Television 2.0: Strategies for developing television narratives across media platforms. Film and Media Culture Department. Retrieved from: http://sites.middlebury.edu/mediacp/files/2009/06/Aaron_Smith_2009.pdf

22 Did you notice the between-the-lines-advice? Know your audience, it is important for every strategy, but especially for this one.

23 O'Shaughnessy, J., & Jackson O'Shaughnessy, N. (2002). European Journal of Marketing, 36(5/6), 524.

24 A quote by Tom French

#17 GO FIGURE

Open messaging does not offer ready-made interpretations but incites people to 'Go figure out' their own conclusion.

Elze and her friend Leila are waiting at a Chinese take-away. They both kill time by browsing through a car magazine. A Volvo ad shows up. It just features an empty egg box with nothing more than the logo of Volvo, leaving Elze confused about its intended meaning. However, Leila explains to Elze directly what the ad tries to convey: the egg-box protecting its 6 eggs is a metaphor for Volvo being a safe car to drive in and a spacious car accommodating up to 6 people. Does the fact that Leila is a fanatic Volvo fan have something to do with the speed and ability with which she managed to plausibly interpret this Volvo ad?

DEFINITION AND KEY FEATURES

Sometimes an image conveys more than a thousand words. For instance, a few lines in a face tell all about whether someone feels glad or sad. To transfer this emotion by text may be more complicated. The occurrence of visual campaigns with hardly any text referring to the product or service is on the rise[1,2]. Obviously, communicators expect positive effects from these open campaigns. Can these intriguing messages effectively transfer digital messages? In this chapter we will show that openness is a suitable strategy for digital communication formats.

We use the label *'openness'* to describe differences in the amount of guidance towards a certain interpretation[3]. A high level of openness means there is little guidance towards an intended interpretation, making an ad more susceptible to a variety of interpretations, while risking the lack of any plausible interpretation. Practitioners as well as academics have used several terms in advertising research that are related to openness, such as 'rhetorical ads' 'ambiguous ads', 'indirect ads', 'implicit ads', and 'unframed ads'. Although not synonymous, all of these terms are highly related to the concept of openness because they imply less guidance towards an intended interpretation, and indicate that research on the effects of openness in advertising is more common than studies that explicitly refer to open messaging[4].

Commercial messaging usually has an unambiguous purpose: to sell or promote a product or service, or increase brand awareness and positive ad associations. If this goal is not realised, the ad has failed. The question in this chapter is whether it is better to precisely guide the consumer towards the message, or to suggest one, leaving more room for consumers to create their own meaning. Open ads invite consumers to "think into" the ad and generate the message themselves, for example by posing a question that the consumer is supposed to answer. For example, a Dutch travel company advertises with people sitting in the water on the edge of a waterfall, without giving any comment about this peculiar situation, except for the caption: "What is your story?" A closed ad, on the other hand, would present a persuasive claim in an accompanying slogan[5]. For instance: visit the 'Iguazu waterfalls, a once in a lifetime experience'.

A MULTIPLICITY OF MEANINGS

Philosopher and university professor Umberto Eco[6] has offered a plausible theoretical framework for the concept of openness. He uses the term 'openness' to distinguish different types of text. Some open texts, such as music, can be regarded as unfinished texts; the author seems less concerned about how readers use the text or about the interpretations that readers infer from the music. Eco sees openness not only as a characteristic of the text but also as the result of the interaction between the message and its reader. To create an interpretation, readers use their own frames of reference, but at the same time they have to follow guidelines imposed by the text's lexical and syntactical structure. Hence, Eco argues that the experienced openness is affected by the reader as well as by the text. He argues that the theoretical concepts 'open texts' and 'closed texts' must be seen as the abstract ends on a continuum (texts with one meaning versus texts with an infinite number of possible meanings) rather than as a dichotomy. We should therefore regard texts not as open or closed, but rather as being 'more open' or 'more closed'.

THE FACT THAT AN AD IS AN AD REDUCES ITS OPENNESS

An advertisement in itself is a more closed text compared to texts such as music. Advertisements always communicate two central messages: (a) this is an ad for brand x, and (b) this ad conveys a positive claim about that brand[7]. According to the Persuasion Knowledge Model[8], and the ideas of other authors[9,10,11], consumers are aware of these goals and adjust their expectations of advertising messages accordingly, thus reducing their potential openness: "The very fact that we know that what we see is an ad … considerably helps shape our expectations about what it will communicate"[12]. The sheer adding of a brand logo in an image points to the fact that this image in fact is an ad, limiting the possible number of interpretations of that ad. In advertising, the openness of an ad is restricted not only by the expectations of consumers, but also by the intentions of the advertisers. However, ad-makers usually focus on conveying an ad's message effectively. They are not as much focused on the creative responses of receivers, which some artists try to maximise when they present their aesthetic works such as paintings or music.

BRANDS WITH STRONG ASSOCIATIONS REDUCE OPENNESS

As shown, brands play an important role in reducing the openness of ads. However, this is not the case for all brand types. Strong, familiar brands are able to anchor the meaning of ads, which we call 'brand anchoring'[13], which is not the case for weak, unfamiliar brands, for instance those that have just appeared on the market. Strong brand associations help consumers to understand the ad's message, because the brand provides a context for interpreting the ad, guiding the reader towards meaningful elements in it. These strong brand associations or schemas represent consumers' knowledge about brands, such as knowledge about brand benefits and drawbacks, about the image of a brand, about its users, and how the brand is positioned relative to other brands within a product category. Consumers can use the emotions, beliefs, and values that they have learned to associate with certain brands to create interpretations of an open ad. Therefore, strong brands reduce the experienced openness of ads and they often only need a picture to incite the many associations that people have stored in their memory about them. Weak brands do the opposite. They enlarge the openness of an ad and should be wary of using this strategy because people do not have these elaborate associations about them (yet).

Going back to the example, the fact that Elze has weak associations about Volvo explains why she could not interpret the Volvo ad. However, Leila was able to plausibly interpret the ad. She could easily 'think into' the intended interpretations because of her strong existing associations about Volvo.

OPENNESS IN PRACTICE

The use of openness in advertising is on the rise, and may offer a solution for standardising advertising messages across nations. The increasing globalisation incites international firms to approach their communication from a global perspective. Since global advertising can offer enterprises substantial financial benefits, advertisers are eager to adapt standardised global communication techniques. On the one hand, openness might be an advantageous strategy for global advertising because open ads are often highly visual and visuals are easier to standardise than text. A standardised advertising campaign is cost effective and enables brands to spread a consistent image throughout nationalities. Besides, an open ad without text may overcome the linguistic barrier in global advertising[14]. On the other hand, countries may differ in their susceptibility to openness, and their tolerance for ambiguity[15], because of cultural differences, making openness a less suitable strategy for cross-national advertising. Whether openness can actually open windows towards global advertising, we will read in the next paragraph by practitioner Kelly Philipse, who has experience in strategic advertising for ad agencies in several countries.

OPEN ADS AND THE IMPACT OF CULTURE

By Kelly Philipse
Strategy Director
TBWA\NEBOKO

The level of openness of an ad is often a topic of debate between ad agencies and their clients. But as we've read in this chapter, the openness of an ad isn't just about the brand's presence. The *messaging* – what the ad communicates about the brand or product – can also be more or less open.

OPENNESS BENEFITS FROM A HIGH TOLERANCE FOR UNCERTAINTY

Having worked in advertising in different countries and on a variety of global brands, it's interesting to note the cultural differences in tolerance towards openness in ads. I remember pre-testing a TV commercial for a margarine brand that we wanted to use across Europe. This particular commercial broke with the usual style of advertising for this brand, moving from a cold and scientific approach to a more light-hearted vibe. Contrary to the years before, this ad communicated hardly any functional benefits of the product and instead focussed on happy lifestyle imagery. The commercial tested outstandingly in The Netherlands; people saw it as a great step forward for this brand. We were thrilled. But then the ad was tested in Germany ... the contrast couldn't have been bigger. The Germans rejected the ad. They missed the health claims, they missed the functional information, they even missed the familiar doctor in the white coat. How can two neighbouring countries react so differently to the same ad? Germany is known to be a country with a high amount of uncertainty avoidance, whereas Dutch people display more tolerance for uncertainty[16]. Taking this cultural difference into account, it makes sense that the Germans prefer more product information in an ad than the Dutch.

OPENNESS CAN BE RISKY IN INTERNATIONAL ADVERTISING

While working at TBWA\Latin America, I noticed that Latin American advertising generally is quite explicit in its communication. This would hint to a preference for more closed ads. Latin American countries generally score high on Hofstede's uncertainty avoidance Index[17], meaning that they do not like openness because that leaves them insecure about an ad's intended meaning. Coincidence? Maybe… Although you could argue that openness in terms of conveying less verbal information in an ad can be an efficient advertising strategy for international campaigns, openness in the sense of limiting the amount of information in an ad can also be risky in international advertising. Cultures differ from each other in their tolerance for openness. My conclusion is that advertising and the successfulness of openness are simultaneously influenced by and a reflection of the culture it lives in.

ADS COMPETE WITH POPULAR CULTURE

There's another way that culture and advertising are intertwined, but in this case, I mean *popular culture*. Advertising competes with popular culture. How so? The media landscape has become so fragmented and people so overwhelmed with media choices that consumers block everything that is not worthy of their attention. The consumer is in charge; he or she chooses which content they'll pay attention to. Ads are usually not high on the consumer's wish list; Netflix series, make-up tutorials, and cat videos are. As an advertiser, you are not just competing with the other brands in your category. You're competing with everything that is fighting for the consumer's attention. You're competing with popular culture. And in this age of media abundance, the competition is fierce.

In order to compete with culture, ads need to become part of culture and play by its rules. That's where openness comes in. In popular culture, openness is liked. Where's the thrill in watching a horror movie when the creepy guy is always in plain sight? Where's the fun in a sitcom that explains every joke? Ads, in order to compete with culture, can be disguised as entertainment. And that means they'll look less like an ad, becoming more open. We're creating more and more other types of content besides ads for our clients. Online video formats, also an innovation in this book, are a great way for brands to engage with audiences and build brand preference, because they belong more to the world of pop-culture than to the world of ads.

OPEN AND CLOSED ADS FORM A POWERFUL TEAM IN DIGITAL MEDIA

The digitalisation of the media landscape plays a big part in the increase of this new kind of openness. Digital media allow brands to first entertain their audience with a game, or an episode, or any other type of content that is not obviously an ad – and thus can be seen as an open ad. Thanks to the opportunities that digital media provides, brands can subsequently serve a more closed ad to this already engaged consumer. The open and closed ads work together to get the consumer to act. The more open 'ad' warms the audience up to the brand and builds positive brand associations; the retargeting ad tries to seal the deal with a more commercial message and a clear call to action.

Whether or not an ad wants to look like an ad, the bottom line is that the ad needs to be worthy of a consumer's attention. Advertising doesn't have to be the annoying thing that interrupts entertainment, it can be entertainment. A little openness can help.

Several scholars have theorised about the effects of openness. Among other effects, openness may positively affect the attitude towards the ad[18,19]. Openness in ads may lead to a relatively positive attitude towards the advertisement when consumers: 1) experience pleasure in searching for an interpretation; 2) consider finding a plausible interpretation as a reward; 3) experience openness as pleasantly incongruent with their expectations of advertising; 4) view openness as an intelligent form of communication that they appreciate; and 5) when openness decreases counter argumentation.

ONLY EASILY UNDERSTANDABLE OPEN ADS ARE APPRECIATED

However, research establishing the effects of openness in advertising shows positive as well as negative results concerning attitude towards the ad and more negative results about interpreting and paying attention to these ads. Studies[20], also those conducted across nationalities[21], have revealed that open ads are more appreciated when they are easy to understand, and a strong brand helps them in doing that. Cross-national research has also shown that when uncertainty is associated with something positive, consumers may prefer uncertainty to certainty, because a little uncertainty allows consumers to imagine and speculate about potentially positive product benefits[22].

LOCATION-BASED ADVERTISING BENEFITS FROM OPENNESS

There are many digital contexts in which openness might be used and be even more beneficial than in traditional contexts such as ads in magazines. Research has investigated openness in the context of location-based advertising. As shown in the chapter Location-Based Advertising, it is a form of mobile marketing in which consumers are approached by advertisers exactly at the right moment, on the right spot, with relevant ads. Consumers sometimes experience feelings of intrusiveness when smartphone apps allow retailers to track the location of their customers and provide the opportunity to reach them, and disturb them, with location-based mobile ads. Can openness on location-based ads on smartphone ads reduce these feelings of intrusiveness?

Openness may significantly contribute to effective location-based mobile ad design because it may decrease feelings of intrusiveness. Open advertisements may encourage consumers to generate persuasive claims[23], and also distract from feelings of intrusiveness. The cognitive effort that is required to decipher an open ad may diminish consumers' capacity to develop resistance to it. Self-persuasion theory offers a related explanation of why openness may prevent feelings of intrusiveness. Research has shown that people generally fail to criticise self-generated information[24] and are more likely to accept a message claim when they have generated the persuasive arguments themselves[25].

OPENNESS PROVIDES FOR ENTERTAINMENT

Furthermore, the active role that open ads require the consumer to take, may fit better with an interactive medium like a smartphone than closed forms of advertising. Open advertisements are challenging for consumers to decipher[26], and the act of deciphering one may generate feelings of gratification[27] and entertainment. Authors[28,29] have argued that entertainment provides added value to the use of mobile phones. Ad value colludes with entertainment value, and entertainment is thus essential for communication between advertisers and consumers[30]. Although consumers predominately use their smartphones for private communication, they can appreciate persuasive communication when it is entertaining[31]. The study tested the effect of openness in ad design using a virtual reality supermarket setting and showed that openness in mobile ad design lowers perceived ad intrusiveness, which positively affects consumers' brand choice, via the attitude towards the ad[32].

Concluding, location-based advertising may profit from openness because it may diminish feelings of intrusiveness and because it is entertaining.

FUTURE AND ETHICS

The fact that the power of openness in digital communication lies in its subtleness underscores the importance of ad-makers in the process. They may use openness, but ads should always be relatively easy to understand, and not leave consumers confused about their intended meaning. They can use openness in different cultures but should study the susceptibility towards openness in these cultures beforehand. It is a risky strategy when open advertisements for strong familiar brands are also aimed at people outside of the primary target group who do not have these strong associations, or non-users of these brands. Especially risky is open advertising for weak unfamiliar brands, because associations are weak or not yet developed, making these open ads too difficult for anyone to comprehend.

OPENNESS AS A SOLUTION TO INTRUSIVENESS IN DIGITAL MEDIA

Using open ads in location-congruent settings in which an ad is offered on the right spot, for instance in front of the right shelf in a supermarket, offers marketers with a valuable and controllable instrument to reduce consumers' feelings of intrusiveness. Intrusiveness may soon become an even bigger problem as smartphones become even more popular. Consumers' awareness of privacy infringements has increased as a result of the recent public debate about Facebook's privacy policy. By targeting consumers with more open messages at a location in proximity to the advertised product, marketers can effectively sidestep the negative effects of intrusiveness and offer consumers a more valuable and convenient experience while still increasing profits. Although quite promising for interactive digital formats, an open ad strategy does seem like a risky undertaking. But, agreeing with the expert in this chapter: if done well, some openness can help.

CLASSIFICATION

★★★★★   ★★★★★   ★★★★★   ★★★★★   ★★★★★

References and notes

1   Van Gisbergen, M.S., Ketelaar, P.E., & Beentjes, J. (2004). Changes in advertising language? A content analysis of magazine advertisements in 1980 and 2000. In P.C. Neijens, C. Hess, S.J.H.M. van den Putte & E.G. Smit. (Eds.), Content and Media Factors in Advertising (pp.51-61). Amsterdam: Spinhuis Publishers.

2   McQuarrie, E. F., & Mick, D. G. (1992). On resonance: A critical pluralistic inquiry into advertising rhetoric. Journal of Consumer Research, 19(2), 180-197.

3   Ketelaar, P.E., van Gisbergen, M, S. & Beentjes, J. (2012) Interpretation of highly visual 'open' advertisements in Dutch magazines. Journal of Visual Literacy, 31(1), 23-52.

4   Ketelaar, P.E., Van Gisbergen, M.S., & Beentjes, J. (2008). The dark side of openness for consumer response. In E.F. McQuarrie & B. J Phillips (Eds.), Go figure: New directions in advertising rhetoric. Armonk, NY: M.E. Sharpe, 114-136.

5   Ketelaar, P. E., Gisbergen, M. S., & Beentjes, J. (2012). Interpretation of highly visual 'open' advertisements in Dutch magazines. Journal of Visual Literacy, 31(1), 23-52.

6   Eco, U. (1979). The role of the reader: Explorations in the semiotics of texts. London: Indiana University Press.

7   Tanaka, K. (1992). The pun in advertising: A pragmatic approach. Lingua, 87, 91-102.

8   Friestad, M., & Wright, P. (1994). The persuasion knowledge model: How people cope with persuasion attempts, Journal of Consumer Research, 21, 131.

9   Forceville, C. (1996). Pictorial metaphor in advertising. New York: Routledge.

10 McQuarrie, E. F., & Mick, D. G. (1996). Figures of rhetoric in advertising language. Journal of Consumer Research, 22, 424-438.

11 Phillips, B. J. (1997). Thinking into it: Consumer interpretations of complex images. Journal of Advertising, 26, 77-86.

12 Forceville, C. (1996). Pictorial metaphor in advertising. New York: Routledge.

13 Ketelaar, P. E., Van Gisbergen, M. S., Bosman, J. A., & Beentjes, J. (2010). The effects of openness on attitude toward the ad, attitude toward the brand, and brand beliefs in Dutch magazine ads. Journal of Current Issues & Research in Advertising, 32(2), 71-85.

14 Okazaki, S., Taylor, C. R., & Zou, S. (2006). Advertising standardization's positive impact on the bottom line: a model of when and how standardization improves financial and strategic performance. Journal of Advertising, 35(3), 17-33.

15 Phillips, B. J. (2000). The impact of verbal anchoring on consumer response to image ads. Journal of Advertising, 29(1), 15-24.

16 Hofstede, G. (2011). Dimensionalizing cultures: The Hofstede model in context. Online Readings in Psychology and Culture, 2(1), 8.

17 Hofstede, G. (2011). Dimensionalizing cultures: The Hofstede model in context. Online Readings in Psychology and Culture, 2(1), 8.

18 Philips, B.J. (2000). The impact of verbal anchoring on consumer response to image ads. Journal of Advertising, 24(1), pp. 15-24.

19 McQuarrie, E. F., & Phillips, B. J. (2005). Indirect persuasion in advertising: How consumers process metaphors presented in pictures and words. Journal of Advertising, 34, 7-21.

20 Van Mulken, M., Enschot, R. V., & Hoeken, H. (2005). Levels of implicitness in magazine advertisements: An experimental study into the relationship between complexity and appreciation in magazine advertisements. Information Design Journal & Document Design, 13(2).

21 Ketelaar, P. E., Maesen, S., Linssen, L., & Van Gisbergen, M. S. (2013). The cross-cultural effectiveness of openness in advertising for familiar and unfamiliar brands. Journal of Euromarketing, 22(1, 2), 5-23.

22 Ketelaar, P. E. Van' t Riet, J., Thorbjohnsen, H., & Buijzen, M. (2016). Positive uncertainty: The benefit of the doubt in advertising. International Journal of Advertising, 1-14, http://dx.doi.org/10.1080/02650487.2016.1231163.

23 McQuarrie, E. F., & Phillips, B. J. (2005). Indirect persuasion in advertising: How consumers process metaphors presented in pictures and words. Journal of Advertising, 34, 7-21.

24 Mussweiler, T., & Neumann, R. (2000). Sources of mental contamination: Comparing the effects of self-generated versus externally provided primes. Journal of Experimental Social Psychology, 36(2), 194-206.

25 Bernritter, S. F., van Ooijen, I., & Müller, B. C. (2017). Self-persuasion as marketing technique: the role of consumers' involvement. European Journal of Marketing, 51(5/6), 1075-1090.

26 Chang, C. T., & Yen, C. T. (2013). Missing ingredients in metaphor advertising: The right formula of metaphor type, product type, and need for cognition. Journal of Advertising, 42(1), 80-94.

27 Ketelaar, P. E., & Van Gisbergen, M. S. (2006). Openness in advertising: Occurrence and effects of open advertisements in magazines. Doctoral Dissertation Radboud Universiteit.

28 Blanco, C. F., Blasco, M. G., & Azorín, I. I. (2010). Entertainment and informativeness as precursory factors of successful mobile advertising messages. Communications of the IBIMA, 2010(2010), 1-11.

29 Watson, C., McCarthy, J., & Rowley, J. (2013). Consumer attitudes towards mobile marketing in the smart phone era. International Journal of Information Management, 33(5), 840-849.

30 Ducoffe, R. H. (1996). Advertising value and advertising on the web. Journal of advertising research, 36(5), 21-21.

31 Watson, C., McCarthy, J., & Rowley, J. (2013). Consumer attitudes towards mobile marketing in the smart phone era. International Journal of Information Management, 33(5), 840-849.

32 Ketelaar, P. E., Bernritter, S. F., van Woudenberg, T. J., Rozendaal, E., Konig, R. P., Hühn, A. E., & Janssen, L. (2018). "Opening" location-based mobile ads: How openness and location congruency of location-based ads weaken negative effects of intrusiveness on brand choice. Journal of Business Research, 91, 277-285.

#18 BRANDED CONTENT

Branded content is a form of paid communication where a brand message is integrated into an entertaining and/or informative context.

If you have hair on your head, you may recognise the struggle: taking a shower in the evening and waking up the following morning with greasy hair. So annoying. In a health magazine you read an article named 'How to get rid of oily hair: 3 ways to make your hair less greasy'. Tip number one in the article is to try not to touch your hair because both hair and fingers produce oil, which causes fatty hair. The second tip is to use a shampoo called Oribe because of the unique combination of natural extracts in the product that eliminates oil. It's relatively expensive but just one drop of it is already effective. The last counterintuitive advice is to wash your hair less often, because when you wash your hair every day, the scalp produces even more oil. If you struggle with greasy hair you may find the article interesting to read. Now ask yourself this question: if you knew beforehand that the producer of the product mentioned in the second tip also wrote the article and paid the magazine to place it, how would you have read and evaluated the same article?

DEFINITION AND KEY FEATURES

Branded content is one of those terms with various descriptions when scientists and communication professionals talk about it. The 'article' mentioned above is just one example of branded content. It's an advertisement because the owner of the product has paid for it but in appearance it is like an informative article. The key features of branded content are: (1) a brand message is produced in such a way that it seamlessly fits into an attractive context; and (2) the brand has paid for this integration into the context. The context we are talking about could be anything: a magazine, vlogging channel, review website, movie, or game. In other words, it is presented as 'normal' content produced with techniques that are used in popular entertainment or journalism.

Because branded content seamlessly fits into an (editorial) context, the commercial message feels less commercial because of the visually unobtrusive border between the commercial content itself and the content around it. This kind of advertising is a form of what is called *native advertising*: advertising without the obvious cues that enable people to recognise it as an advertisement. The word 'native' here refers to the coherence of the branded content with other content appearing on the platform. The degree of content integration may vary depending on the goals an advertiser has. A billboard along the track in a racing game is a form of in-game advertising (embedded communication) and a racing game fully produced by the brand on an online platform is branded content. The first form could help to increase the awareness of a brand, but if you want to convey a story and influence the attitude of people, then the first form is certainly not sufficient. The idea of branded content is that the more a consumer is entertained or informed with attractive content, the greater the influence will be. In order to offer this paid content a platform, advertisers cooperate with endorsers. That way you will not find branded content in the forced YouTube advertising block or in the Google ads section, but in a movie, game, or on a news platform.

New to this form of paid communication is that social media enables consumers to share branded content if it is relevant and interesting enough. The message could be recommended by both people who are aware and unaware of the commercial nature of the content. Social influencers on digital platforms (who are aware) could spread the word about beauty products in exchange for their salary and followers (who are unaware) share the message because they think it is relevant for their friends. In the chapter about influencer marketing you can read more about this.

Another form of branded content is paid content with the look and feel of a journalistic product. In this case, a brand cooperates with a publisher and uses the reputation of that publisher to increase the credibility of the persuasive message. The article about greasy hair could be considered as 'soft news' but there are examples of branded content about more serious topics. If you agree that independence is one of the greatest virtues of a professional journalist, do you see the contradiction here?

BRANDED CONTENT IN PRACTICE

It may seem that branded content is a young strategy but it has in fact been applied for decades. Brands have used popular songs, for example, for a long time to promote their products and services. 'Dumb ways to die' is a song that came with a video of funny and cute cartoon characters to raise awareness about rail safety, with the goal of reducing accidents and near misses at metro stations. Go watch it on YouTube if you haven't seen it and find out yourself why the video clip was a viral sensation. Practitioners believe that the key to effective branded content is that it has 'worth' beyond the marketing message. Successful branded content is produced with the audience in mind, not the 'consumer'.

The importance of valuable and attractive (branded) content becomes clear if we dwell on the current news and entertainment industry. We want to be informed because it is essential to know what is happening in the world and what friends and important (influential) people are thinking. Creators of successful branded content campaigns know that the audience is pickier, especially online: there is so much content[1] out there, that nobody has to watch, listen, or read something that is boring. In other words, when branded content performs poorly on likability, you know for sure that it won't create a huge impact. When branded content indeed has worth beyond the marketing message, like the cute and funny 'Dumb ways to die' song, people may choose actively to engage with the content. The act of choosing to interact with the content is crucial for its success[2]. Nowadays we live in a landscape where on-demand services are dominant. Consumers can freely choose (or at least we assume we can freely choose) *when*, but most of all what content we want to watch, view, or hear. We don't like to be told what we should buy or do, so we avoid commercial messages. When people consume branded content voluntarily, there is no question of advertising avoidance. Because it is the decision of the viewer, reader, or listener to consume the content, it is less likely that he/she will be suspicious about the implicit commercial message in the content.

ODDLY IKEA

Have you ever heard about ASMR video's? These are videos with recorded sounds (like pens writing on paper or tapping nails on tin objects) that cause pleasant chills and a so-called brain-gasm. You can find thousands of such videos on YouTube and Instagram of pens writing on paper, people whispering, or tapping nails on a tin object. People who are sensitive to ASMR (this stands for sensory meridian response and causes the pleasant feeling) have less inhibition in their sensory perceptions and when they hear such sounds, they translate that directly into images and feelings. Through the release of the 'cuddle hormone' oxytocin, dopamine is created, which means that when you hear the sounds, you want to hear more. We can hear you thinking: what has this to do with branded content? Well, the IKEA brand that sells ready-to-assemble furniture produced a series of ASMR videos called 'Oddly IKEA'. While a narrator with a hushed voice describes the merits of items in a dorm room, pillows are squished, bed sheets are gently stroked, fabric is scratched, and hangers are jangled. On YouTube it has over 2 million views and during the online campaign, sales rose by more than 5%[3]. This demonstrates that content that is worth watching and easy to share takes on a life of its own. Not because of the commercial offer in it primarily, but because of relevancy and attractiveness for a particular audience (people who are fond of ASMR). Some practitioners advise using journalists or skilled storytellers for that reason. Their expertise lies in producing fascinating, engaging, and authentic content. Instead of engaging content, marketers are fixated on the business model, which could lead to many fewer satisfying experiences if they are responsible for the content. Niels Cuijpers will now share his experience in creating successful branded content cases.

REFLECTING ON BRANDED CONTENT

By Niels Cuijpers
Brand- & Partnershipsmanager Scripted Content
EndemolShine Netherlands

Since we as humans exist, we tell each other stories. Because stories strongly appeal to the imagination, they are one of the strongest means of conveying a message. Branded content exists by the grace of the story and it makes the difference between effective and less effective branded content: do you have a good story to tell?

In my job, where I mainly focus on integrating brand stories into scripted film and drama productions, I see various forms of branded content. Product placement as one form of branded content is perhaps the most common form, but certainly not the most qualitative one. It is often a product that gets a somewhat forced place within the content because of the sales deal. That such product integrations are often noticed by people is clear, but is it for the right reason? Usually there is just one product integrated into a (television) episode or series, which makes it stand out. Compare it with a white rose in a field full of red. The problem with this prominence is that the advertising awareness is then activated ('someone is trying to sell me something'), which could lead to negative responses, such as negative brand associations. Standing out is just one thing, but branded content is of course much more than that. In my opinion, branded content concerns influence through storytelling, to create a positive attitude towards the brand. And all of this in a creative, organic, and qualitative way.

6 FACTORS FOR SUCCESS

Throughout the years, I have developed a lot of branded content cases and I have found six factors that, in my view, ensure successful integration. The better these factors are worked out, the more effective the campaign.

Credibility: To what extent do you tell a logical and true story around a product or brand? Are you building up a story gradually or does the plot just fall from the sky? What drives the story characters to use a certain product or to come in contact with a brand? By telling a story that is logical and credible, the consumer will be absorbed into the story more quickly, without rejecting the story through feelings of disbelief, which then has a negative effect on the integrated brand.

Match: Make sure there is a logical match between the brand values, product characteristics, brand story, and the story elements. As a result, you can unconsciously link the traits of a story character or element to the advertiser's brand in the consumer's mind.

Emotion: Good branded content integration must include an emotional story component. Emotions ensure that you stay enthralled and empathise with story characters; this binds you to the story and thus to the brand. By linking the brand integration to tension, love, sadness, or other emotions, it has a deeper impact on consumers.

Depth of the integration: What role do you let the brand or product play in your content (story)? Product placement is the simplest form. You let a product appear in your content in a logical way by simply displaying it or by showing the character using the product. Another much more extensive and efficient way is to integrate the brand values or the brand story into the storyline. You build the main story around the brand in such way that it is not directly about the product itself, but much more about the brand values or umfeld of the product. Or, in the case of drama production, a storyline that is told against the backdrop of the brandumfeld. If being together and escaping from the routines of everyday life are important brand values for a coffee brand, you can just show your coffee brand (product placement) but you can also let a story character open a coffee shop where all sorts of stories unfold about being together and escapism, of course linked to the cup of coffee that is being served. A brand story wrapped in a drama has more impact on the unconscious mind because it adds extra value and people are more inclined to digest that story.

Creativity and innovativity: What I mean by this is how original the integration is. Because that which is new, and which has never been done before, stands out and thus generates more impact. Creativity in branded content has to do with the originality of the concept within which the branded content is located. By linking other platforms and innovations, choosing surprising perspectives, or intertwining different perspectives, you offer the consumer an extra incentive to bind the content and the brand to them. In the example of 'WE x Nina', which I describe below, fiction and reality are interwoven; for the consumer the fictional story becomes reality and he or she could actually take part in the story. In another branded content integration in the Netherlands' most popular longest-running television soap, audio plays an important role. One of the main characters in the same television series writes and reads an audiobook and viewers are encouraged to actually listen to the book themselves in order to be informed of the story. These are two examples of extra dimensions added to the basic story that provide greater experience and the desired influence on the customer.

Quality: Quality, in my view, is about how the branded content campaign is developed and the links that are made with other digital platforms. Telling a (branded content) story on one platform is a waste of the investment. It is much more effective to create a complete 360⊗ concept so that the consumer comes into contact with your story via multiple touchpoints, because your story has been extended to the shop floor or other paid and owned (social) media channels. It is important to tell the story there where the target group is. With a younger target group, it is probably more effective to add digital channels like YouTube, Instagram, or an app as a platform.

Success does not come naturally and it is usually the cooperation between the advertiser and the producer that ensures acceleration. When all parties involved with the integration want to go the extra mile and have an eye for detail, and when the needs are intensively attuned during the process, it is possible to set something that goes beyond a regular collaboration.

WE X NINA

An example of a successful branded content case that meets all of the above factors is the WE x Nina Campaign in the Netherlands' longest-running soap opera 'Goede Tijden, Slechte Tijden'. One of the main characters, Nina Sanders, designed a fashion line for one of the advertisers (a fashion brand) of the series. Because the viewer had never seen that Nina was able to design clothing, it was completely inconceivable that she would create a fashion line out of the blue. To make the integration as credible as possible, a story was chosen that unfolded in a few weeks, in which she was discovered by a talent scout and eventually signed a fashion contract through a test collection. After that she started to design clothing in a credible way *(credibility)*. Because of the link between the brand and the young, trendy, and fashionable Nina Sanders, the brand values of the advertiser were positively influenced *(match)*. The main story that was told in nine weeks was about the loss of friendship, love, and self-confidence *(emotion)*, to which the task of designing a clothing collection was linked. Will Nina meet her deadline for her fashion line, despite the loss of a girlfriend, quarrel with her husband, and lack of confidence? The viewers saw Nina getting started in her own studio, so the fashion vibe hung around the story *(integration)*. The link between fiction and reality provided the necessary innovativeness in this case. The collection that she ultimately designed was actually for sale in all the advertiser's stores, making fiction a reality for the consumer. The link and translation to the shop floor, social media (paid, owned, and earned), an app, magazines, commercials, and outdoor advertising provided a consistent story for a wide reach and enormous impact. In the mobile app for the series, Nina gave clothing and styling advice and you could link directly to the relevant clothing article in the advertiser's webshop. By inviting influencers to the fashion show, the story about the new collection was spread via various social media platforms and also reached the young target group in a natural way. The project team that was responsible for this campaign was prepared to go the extra mile and made this case a successful 360° campaign *(quality)*.

I am not worried about the role of branded content when I look to the future. People are now overwhelmed with advertising and content. We do not have to be exposed to advertisements if we use On-Demand services and the range of drama series and films goes through the roof. In addition, the various digital (social) media channels that young people often use offer enormous possibilities to interweave the message in the content: think of branded content in Instagram Stories or in YouTube videos. In fact, only the medium changes; the interrelationship between content and brand, the core of branded content, remains unchanged.

A SCIENTIFIC PERSPECTIVE

From the functional triad perspective, branded content functions as a medium. It provides consumers with experiences, but within the experience, a persuasive message is transferred. This makes it a valuable instrument for marketers, complementary to the existing marketing communication. Scientific research on branded content shows that content likability is mutually correlated with brand likability. When consumers like the content itself, the impact of it also escalates. Another explanatory factor of impactful branded content is its perceived credibility[4] compared to commercials. The publication of content on 'independent platforms' like news sites brings a couple of advantages. First, the goal of media platforms is to deliver independent news so they are perceived as more reliable sources. The appreciation for the distributor of the content can spillover into the brand. Above that, the intentional exposure theory[5] states that people use media for its editorial content (like amusing videos or educational stories) and not for commercials; users are thus more open to editorial content and less open to commercial messages.

Now how do consumers process branded content? We have already mentioned that the public tends to be less critical towards branded content because of the intrinsic motivation of people to consume the content in question and a perfect fit of the content in a trustworthy context. When a person consumes content, he or she is not fully focussed on the branded content but more on the context in which the content is being offered. The more informative, engaging, and interactive the context, the more cognitive effort is needed to process the content and less cognitive capacity remains for the critical processing of the brand message.

Research shows that drawing attention to the commercial nature of content leads to more critical thinking. In one study[6] for example, the effect of warning people that a blog post contained branding was investigated. Students read a blog in which a blogger explained how she prepared a very tasty casserole, using a casserole mix, the brand of which was mentioned once. For half of the participants in the experiment, a disclosure was inserted in the middle of the blog, stating: *'Brand X paid for this blog to persuade you'*. The other half read the blog without the disclosure. It appeared that people show cognitive and negative emotional responses if they are aware of the commercial intentions of the maker of the content. In comparison to the blog post without a disclosure, readers of the content with the disclosure came up with more arguments against the advertised product and they experienced more feelings of anger and irritation while reading the content. This teaches us that people don't like to be fooled; be aware of that when you consider making branded content.

FUTURE AND ETHICS

Before the year 2000, film tape allowed media companies to capture large audiences through one channel. It seems unbelievable that consumers used just one channel to consume the news and with online streaming services now, films, music, and series are at our fingertips. Consumers have multiple choices over which platforms and devices they can use. On average, daily linear viewing of television decreases, the consumption of on-demand media products rises, and the problem of advertising avoidance grows. Because of this, brands must find alternative and creative forms of communication strategies like branded content. Based on the developments in the media landscape, it is expected that the amount of branded content will continue to grow in the future as it is seen as a necessary response to ad evasion. The presentation of Professor Hardy of the contemporary media and entertainment landscape is striking: *'Your Facebook feed says "Recommended for you" and "Sponsored". Your online magazine says "Paid Content", another in your Buzzfeed says "Promoted Content" and lists "12 Backpacking Hacks That Are Vital For Business Trips" in an article paid for by Holiday Inn Express. Buzzfeed may also list KFC as "Brand Publisher" for an article, "11 Things all Busy Families Should Make Time For", including KFC's Popcorn Nuggets ... From television product placement to mobile news feeds, brands are burrowing into media content.'*

To meet the interests and needs of consumers, brands will transform into media companies that operate in the field of media content and entertainment[7]. Media watcher Tom Foremski expects that companies in the future will have a do-it-yourself mentality when it comes to content and that they will create advertisements without the help of media agencies, in the form of branded content. In his words: every company is a media company.

BRANDED CONTENT GOES NATIVE

A positive ethical argument for the rise of branded content is that it could contribute to the hedonic wellbeing of people because consumption of attractive content leads to increased feelings of pleasure. But you can feel it coming: the implicit persuasive nature of branded content leads to worries. Lievrouw states that the markets in the field of media content and entertainment are distorted. More media content intrudes our daily life at home, in our families, spare time, work, and culture and this is certainly the case with branded content. Almost all forms of branded content are consumed in our spare time – think of implicit branding in online magazines, events, and movies. Lievrouw sees this intrusion as a negative consequence and for consumers it is also not desirable to tell them that they are being persuaded by companies all the time. People see it as manipulation of their free will or even as a misuse of power. Because of this ethical discussion, marketers and media agencies have called for a new branded content policy on Facebook and Instagram. Publishers are obliged to tag their partners in posts with branded content.

Another issue is that the appearance of branded content in journalism is not always appreciated by journalists. A study by the American Press Institute on graduated journalists and communication professionals found that two-thirds of them believe that branded content crosses ethical boundaries and will damage news organisations' credibility[8]. The New York Times uses a lot of branded content, mainly online. In the summer of 2014, the vice-president of marketing of the New York Times stated that consumers spent the same amount of time on branded content as on editorial content[9]. The cornerstone of a professional journalist's credibility is his or her integrity. People expect factuality and impartiality from the producer of a journalistic product[10] and you can wonder: does this hold true if a brand is involved in the production of news? Lievrouws' advocacy for learning network literacies could be a part of a solution. If internet users learn to distinguish commercial information from non-commercial information, this could protect them from unwanted persuasion. Elaborating on that, we believe that increasing persuasion knowledge enables us to recognise attempts of persuasion and accept the deal: because of the involvement of brands, we could play that game or read those articles. This makes branded content future proof as long as it has worth beyond the marketing message. For brands in journalism we foresee ethical challenges.

CLASSIFICATION

★★★★★ ★★★★★ ★★★★★ ★★★★★ ★★★★★

References and notes

1 Holt, D. (2016). Branding in the age of social media. Harvard Business Review, 94(3), 13.
2 Asmussen, B., Wider, S., Williams, R., Stevenson, N., Whitehead, E. & Canter, A. (2016). Defining branded content for the digital age. The industry experts' views on branded content as a new marketing communications concept.
3 Damian, F. (2018). The big business of making super soft sounds. Retrieved from http://www.bbc.com/capital/story/20180605-the-weird-whispering-videos-that-brands-want-to-cash-in-on.
4 van Reijmersdal, E. A. (2011). Mixing advertising and editorial content in radio programmes: appreciation and recall of brand placements versus commercials. International Journal of Advertising, 30(3), 425-446.
5 Lord, K. R., & Putrevu, S. (1993). Advertising and publicity: an information processing perspective. Journal of Economic Psychology, 14(1), 57-84.
6 van Reijmersdal, E. A., Fransen, M. L., van Noort, G., Opree, S. J., Vandeberg, L., Reusch, S., Boerman, S. C. (2016). Effects of disclosing sponsored content in blogs: how the use of resistance strategies mediates effects on persuasion. American Behavioral Scientist, 60(12), 1458-1474.
7 Lievrouw, L. A. (2012). The next decade in internet time: Ways ahead for new media studies. Information, Communication & Society, 15(5), 616-638.
8 API (2015). Facing change: The needs, attitudes and experiences of people in the media. Retrieved from: https://www.americanpressinstitute.org/publications/reports/surveyresearch/api-journalists-survey/.
9 Kemsley (2014.) Great news for native: The New York Times' sponsored content is as popular as its editorial. Retrieved from: https://contently.com/2014/05/22/great news-for-native-the-new-york-times-sponsored-content-is-as-popular-as-its-editorial/.
10 Westerståhl, J. (1983). Objective news reporting. Communication Research 10(3): 403-424

#19 PERSONAL BRANDING

Personal branding is presenting yourself as a brand to others, which evokes positive images and associations

When thinking of a brand, most people think of a company with a logo, slogan, and website. Information on brands is everywhere. We are inundated with hundreds of ads on a daily basis, so we are increasingly losing confidence in their sincerity. Today, we have more confidence in humans, which makes personal branding increasingly relevant *"It's important to build a personal brand because it's the only thing you're going to have. Your reputation online, and in the new business world is pretty much the game, so you've got to be a good person. You can't hide anything, and more importantly, you've got to be out there at some level"* - The Belarusian American internet personality Gary Vaynerchuk[1].

DEFINITION AND KEY FEATURES

Personal branding is the practice in which people market themselves and their careers as a brand. Someone devises a strategy for self-promotion to create a positive picture of the self in order to have them accepted by others. This results in certain expectations in the minds of others, when they see this person or hear their name. Developing a personal brand is similar to how companies put their product and brand into the market. A person tries to 'sell' himself in an attractive way to respond to demand from the market. As with companies, this is done by generating awareness and acknowledgement in others, aiming to identify and distinguish yourself from the competition. Instead of customers, personal branding involves employers, recruiters, colleagues, and relevant other professionals in the field.

Looking at major brands, we see that things other than functional aspects are being addressed. To be distinctive, the emphasis is often placed on emotional and expressive brand values. Think of Budweiser with their slogan 'The King of Beers'. The emphasis is not on the properties of the beer, but on the world of associations that has been created around it. A strong personal brand works in the same way: it does not only consist of functionalities, such as training, work experience, and certificates, but the focus is also placed on one's personality, passion, talent, vision, and dreams. Authenticity is important in this respect. An example of someone with a strong personal brand is Jamie

Oliver. He may not be the best cook in the world, but because of his personality and the fact that he is taking responsible initiatives like food education to combat childhood obesity, for example, he is well known and popular.

PERSONAL BRANDING IN PRACTICE

There are dozens of websites, blogs, books, and training programmes written by experts with tips on how personal branding can be deployed as a key tool to build a career. However, not all professionals are involved in personal branding. Proponents claim that there are several advantages. First, it gives someone the power to create a desired image of themselves. The individual can decide how he or she wants to be seen by others and manipulate the perception[2]. Secondly, by means of a strong personal brand, individuals can distinguish themselves in the market and thus gain a competitive advantage. With a strong brand you become salient and you are easier to remember and recognise, which increases the chances of success, such as getting selected for a certain job you applied for. An example of this is a student who builds a complete website around his own personal brand and then ensures that his CV reaches more than a thousand interested parties within one week. According to practitioners, personal branding is not only important for individuals, it may also have advantages for organisations. A company that wants to gain and hold talent attracts people by offering them the opportunity to work on their personal branding because this is in line with the need for self-development and deployment. When a company restricts its employees from doing that, there is a chance that they will look for another company that offers them this opportunity. Additionally, personal branding takes place within the context of the company where people work and is thus linked to the company's brand. This means that people are part of the brand story, which strengthens their bond with the company.

FROM SELF-HELP MANAGEMENT TO SELF-PACKING

In the communication industry, communicating with a particular strategy to be seen as influential and effective is not new. This is called self-help management. It is assumed that individuals in the business world can achieve successes by using self-management and self-improvement and this involves improving the competencies of an individual. With personal branding, the big difference to previous self-help strategies is that the focus of an individual is no longer on improving their own skills, interests, and motivations, but on self-packaging. It is not so much about skills and interests themselves, but more about the way they are organised, crystallised, and labelled. In other words, how they are branded.

The use of social media has grown in recent decades and is still growing. Social media is important for personal branding. Facebook remains popular among young adults, but younger people move on to Instagram and Snapchat where the focus is even more on the image instead of text. Research[3] suggests a positive relationship between interpersonal interaction, narcissism, and Instagram usage. Moreover, coolness, creativity, and Instagram as a means of documentation seem to be also important reasons for its usage. In this case, individuals use Instagram to promote the unique self and to increase their popularity. This shows that visual social media like these offer a chance for people to implement personal branding and for companies to respond to them. Through these channels one can communicate different personal characteristics and companies can offer products and messages that allow individuals to position themselves.

OPPORTUNITIES AT THE EXPENSE OF INVISIBILITY?

Not all people welcome the emergence of personal branding. First, sceptics claim that personal branding leads to a narcissistic I-culture that undermines loyalty to the organisation. Employees are more concerned about themselves and making their own brand more powerful and they therefore pay less attention to the organisation. Above that, organisations would be in danger of leaving employees with a strong personal brand linked to the organisation, taking a part of the brand with them. Another argument against personal branding is that it would take too long to build a personal brand. It would cost a lot of time and energy to maintain a personal brand. In doing so, a negative association can undermine a personal brand within a short period of time. Another point of criticism has to do with privacy. Information about the competencies and skills of a candidate and the perception of their possible fit with an organisation positively influence hiring, while use of alcohol or drugs, discriminatory comments an inappropriate photos negatively influence hiring[4]. To have a strong personal brand it is important to be visible, offline and online. As a result, there is a lot of personal information to find. But people who do not want this because of privacy considerations are lagging behind. Because of their online 'invisibility', they miss opportunities. Peopele may feel the compulsion to give (part of) their privacy up in order to make opportunities. Marjolein Bongers will now share some valuable tips in how to improve your professional LinkedIn profile.

PERSONAL BRANDING USING LINKEDIN

By Marjolein Bongers
Owner
House of Social Media

Do you want to increase the recognition of your name (personal brand awareness) and recruit more leads through LinkedIn? When people search for your name on Google, LinkedIn often appears at the top of the search results. It is therefore very important for your personal branding that you have a professional LinkedIn profile. I train people in the field of personal branding, in which LinkedIn plays a crucial part. Let me give you some practical tips that you will be able to use directly.

CHOOSE YOUR PROFILE

First of all, before you get started with optimising your profile, you have to think carefully about your personal branding. Which key words do you want to be found with, what is your expertise, and what can you help people with? Just like Google, LinkedIn is a large search engine. Companies spend a lot of money on Google Ads and SEO (search engine optimisation) so that they can appear as high up as possible on Google's search results, but they often forget SEO's power on LinkedIn. If you want to score in the search results of LinkedIn or to be able to be found in general, it is recommended that you use the right keywords in your LinkedIn profile. Add these keywords to your profile, as well as to your status updates and blogs.

Essential components of your LinkedIn profile are your profile picture and the headline, because these are the first things that visitors to your LinkedIn profile will look at. In addition, your profile picture and headline appear on the feed of LinkedIn every time you share content or interact. Thus, it is best to state your occupation or business in your headline. Stating solely that you are a CEO or a Manager at a particular company is not so informative. Write more about your occupation and the problems you solve. Part of your headline also appears in Google Search. So, use the given 120 characters of your headline well and do not forget to include the key words.

The strength of LinkedIn is not in the pages of companies, but in the personal profiles. Every day we see and hear many logos and advertisements. We have trained to avoid and become 'immune' to advertising. We no longer absorb it, unless it affects us emotionally. In other words, if you have a company page on LinkedIn and your content appears on the feed of LinkedIn users, they are more inclined to scroll past it when they see a logo than when you, your employees, or colleagues share this message from their personal profiles. People touch people; logos do not touch anyone anymore.

"Power is gained by sharing knowledge, not by hoarding it"

SHARE YOUR KNOWLEDGE

If you want to strengthen your personal branding, a professional profile alone is not enough. In order to work on your visibility, you also have to share your knowledge, for example in the form of updates, blogs, or vlogs. Do you want to add a link to a website in that update? This is possible, but you should know that your reach will be less, because LinkedIn wants to keep its users on its own platform. The best way to convey content is video, which is in line with the innovation online video advertising that is discussed in this book. Placing a video on LinkedIn works much better than a link to a website. However, note that you should be subtitling your videos. LinkedIn is a "silent" platform and takes care of square instead of rectangular video. Square video is much more prominent than vertical video and provides more interaction.

So far we have discussed what your profile should look like. Ultimately, it is of course the added value of the content you share and how active you are on LinkedIn that matter. Do not forget the power of hashtags in your messages. When you add a number of hashtags to a status update, you notice that your messages gain a higher reach. With a good strategy and regular posting of valuable content in the right way, LinkedIn will consider you an expert. And this will generate leads and ultimately sales.

"The best personal brands are authentic, so stay true to yourself"

LISTEN AND CREATE AMBASSADORS

Sharing valuable content is paramount if you want to show who you are and what you can do. This is how you load your personal brand. But there is one more thing you should do: carefully listen on LinkedIn. Do not just send, but also listen to your network. Scroll through your timeline and engage in the interaction. This can be done simply by being active in groups or responding to an update of one of your LinkedIn connections. Giving implies receiving. If you do not pay attention to your connections, you do not need to pay any attention to your updates. Sad, because those interactions strengthen your connections and your own reach.

The last imperative aspect of personal branding on LinkedIn is creating ambassadors. Describing what you do and what you are good at works. But when others do that for you, it really makes a difference. LinkedIn lends itself perfectly to gathering nice customer and user stories. Satisfied customers are mostly super-fans, also called advocates. Use them and ask them for reviews or recommendations if they have not already shared them. Not all satisfied customers are proactive in this, so sometimes you have to help them. The credibility of advocates is huge, so collect and cherish them!

LinkedIn is therefore an ideal platform to give your personal branding a face. If you regularly share valuable content, avoid sharing links and dare to opt for video, this will lead to a much wider range of customers. If you combine this with listening to your network, responding to others and changing followers into ambassadors through recommendations, not only will LinkedIn see you as an expert in no time at all, but so will your entire network.

A SCIENTIFIC PERSPECTIVE

Scientists have investigated the effects of personal branding and research shows that peopele can indeed increase the chances of securing a job by creating a strong personal brand[5]. They can positively stimulate the perceptions of recruiters through impression management, tactics to promote a desirable picture of themselves. Research indicates that recruiters' perceptions of a personal brand, their processing and choices made based upon this are of great importance when hiring new employees[6]. The *theory of person-environment fit* predicts that a person will have more success when applying for a job that matches his personal brand. According to this theory, there is a person-environment fit if these two match[7]. When the skills of a person match the offered job (*person-job fit*) and the vision and identity of an organisation (*person-organisation fit*), the recruiter will perceive this person as capable and skilled from objective qualifications.[8]. And when the person's personality matches that of the recruiter (person-person fit), the recruiter will recommend this person from a subjective impression[9].

How the perception of a recruiter in relation to a personal brand arises can be explained using the Processing of Commercial Media Content Model. The image above illustrates this process. When a recruiter is motivated and has time and energy for cognitive elaboration, he or she will process the personal brand in a systematic way. The personal brand is deliberately evaluated and assessed based on the quality of the actual properties. The recruiter is mainly guided by the strength of the arguments, thinking of the person-job fit and person-organisation fit, and recommends a person based on his education and experience. On the other hand, if a recruiter has neither motivation nor the extensive possibility for cognitive elaboration, a personal brand is processed via the peripheral route. The focus is on superficial cues or cues that are not directly related to the candidate's objective profile, such as source reliability, first impressions and emotions[10]. For example, the recruiter will be led by the candidate's face, clothing, or hobbies. In addition to systematic and peripheral processing, a recruiter can also automatically process a personal brand. Therefore your best bet is to stress central as well as peripheral cues in the creation of your personal brand. Automatic processing is characterised by minimal cognitive elaboration.

Someone does not deliberately pay attention to the message, but notices it unconsciously, which may result in an implicit attitude change. For example, the recruiter scrolls through a LinkedIn page and unwittingly registers a message from an applicant who is active on professional social media. When he then takes a list of applicants, he has a preference for this person by recognising the name. In psychology this is called the mere-exposure effect; people tend to judge stimuli to which they are repeatedly exposed more positively because the stimulus (in this case a personal brand) is increasingly easier to process after a number of exposures. The brain subsequently (falsely) attributes the positive feeling that is evoked by the ease with which the stimulus is processed to the stimulus (the personal brand) itself.

For people it is therefore important to match their personal brand to a *person-job fit*, *person-organisation fit* and *person-person fit*, because they all influence the recruiter via different routes and could eventually result in a recommendation. Finally, research shows that subjective impressions (person-person fit) have a significantly greater effect on the perception of a recruiter than objective qualifications (person-job fit and person-organisation fit), in that feelings often prevail over the rationale of the recruiter[11].

FUTURE AND ETHICS

Due to changes in the economy and the way of working, it is expected that building and maintaining a personal brand will become increasingly important. People change employers more often, which makes it important to maintain the personal brand permanently. The competition in the job market means that individuals need personal branding to be able to make the difference. Those who cannot fulfil all the job requirements in a vacancy must have a very good story or a strong personality. Here a personal brand contributes to this: you can show who you are as a person, making you more noticeable and distinctive from the competition. Thirdly, social media is increasingly being used worldwide and it is the most important place for personal branding: people use it to profile themselves and impress employers, and employers use them to seek candidates for a job[12].

An ethical issue that sticks to personal branding is that it could encourage narcissism. As we have seen, research suggested that Instagram usage correlates with narcissistic traits. Moreover, when anybody shows themselves continuously from a positive side, this can also have negative consequences. This could result in jealousy and feelings of uncertainty. According to *the social comparison theory*[13], people constantly compare themselves with others in order to determine how well they are doing. If someone always sees idealised images of others, this increases his or her standard of comparison[14]. Not being able to meet this high standard may cause people to become uncertain about their own (market) value.

Personal branding can have positive effects on man, however. First, because it makes certain experiences possible, which might not be there without personal branding. People, for example, are invited for interesting conversations because of their strong personal brand, helping them in their careers. Personal branding thus supports the achievement of self-actualising experiences and thereby increases someone's eudaimonic well-being, the subjective evaluation of someone's life satisfaction, and of his/her positive emotional feelings[15]. This kind of happiness has repercussions on business. It appears that employees who are given the freedom to build their personal brand are more satisfied than employees who do not have this freedom[16]. Finally, by developing their own personal brand, people learn about their personality and purpose in life and these insights will make people feel more confident and happier[17]. Think about this: someone who incorrectly ascribes certain qualifications to himself, such as lying about his education and work experience, acts unethically. But, when someone highlights his positive side and reveals his talents and passions, is that unethical?

CLASSIFICATION

★★★★★   ★★★★★   ★★★★★   ★★★★★   ★★★★★

References and notes

1   AZ Quotes. (n.d.). Gary Vaynerchuk. Retrieved from https://www.azquotes.com/quote/614786.

2   Rampersad, H. K. (2009). Authentic personal branding. Charlotte, NC: Information Age Publishing.

3   Sheldon, P., & Bryant, K. (2016). Instagram: Motives for its use and relationship to narcissism and contextual age. Computers in Human Behavior, 58, 89-97.

4   Johnson, K. (2017). The importance of personal branding in social media: Educating students to create and manage their personal brand, 4. 21-27.

5   Damnianovic, V., Matovic, V., Kostic, S. C., & Okanovic, M. (2012). The role of the LinkedIn social media in building the personal image. Management-Casopis za Teoriju i Praksu Menadzmenta, 65(1), 15–23. doi:10.7595/management.fon.2012.0036

6   Caers, R., & Castelyns, V. (2011). LinkedIn and Facebook in Belgium: The influences and biases of social network sites in recruitment and selection procedures. Social Science Computer Review, 29(4), 437–448. doi:10.1177/0894439310386567

7   Kristof-Brown, A. L., Zimmerman, R. D., & Johnson, E. C. (2005). Consequences of individuals' fit at work: A meta-analysis of person–job, person–organization, person–group, and person–supervisor fit. Personnel Psychology, 58(2), 281–342. doi:10.1111/j.1744-6570.2005.00672.x

8   Roulin, N., & Bangerter, A. (2013). Social networking websites in personnel selection: A signaling perspective on recruiters' and applicants' perceptions. Journal of Personnel Psychology, 12(3), 143–151. doi:10.1027/1866-5888/a000094

9   Davison, H. K., Maraist, C., & Bing, M. N. (2011). Friend or foe? The promise and pitfalls of using social networking sites for HR decisions. Journal of Business Psychology, 26(2), 153–159. doi: 10.1007%2Fs10869-011-9215-8

10 Gregory, C. K., Meade, A. W., & Thompson, L. F. (2013). Understanding internet recruitment via signaling theory and the elaboration likelihood model. Computers in Human Behavior, 29(5), 1949–1959. doi: 10.1016/j.chb.2013.04.013

11 Roebken, H. (2010). Similarity attracts: An analysis of recruitment decisions in academia. Educational Management Administration & Leadership, 38(4), 472–486. doi: 10.1177/1741143210368264

12 Dekay, S. (2009). Are business-oriented social networking web sites useful resources for locating passive jobseekers? Results of a recent study. Business Communication Quarterly, 72(1), 101–105. doi:10.1177/1080569908330378

13 Festinger, L. (1954). A theory of social comparison processes. Human Relations, 7, 117-140. doi: 10.11177/001872675400700202

14 Richins, M.L. (1991). Social Comparison and the Idealized Images of Advertising. Journal of Consumer Research, 18(1), 71–83. doi: 10.1086/209242

15 Riva, G., Banos, R. M., Botella, C., Wiederhold, B. K., & Gaggioli, A. (2012). Positive technology: Using interactive technologies to promote positive functioning. Cyberpsychology, Behavior, and Social Networking, 15(2), 69-77. Doi: 10.1089/cyber.2011.0139

16 Creating a personal brand is good for business (2017). Retrieved from: https://www.ttec.com/articles/creating-personal-brand-good-business

17 Huta, V. (2015). An overview of hedonic and eudaimonic well-being concepts. In L. Reinecke & M. B. Oliver (Eds.), Handbook of media use and well-being. Chapter 2. New York: Routledge. Manuscript accepted for publication on November 11, 2015.

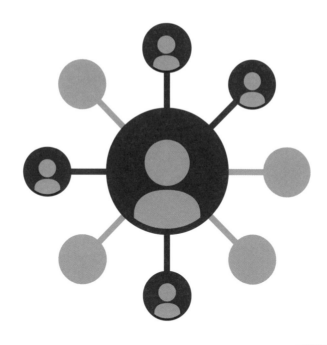

#20 INFLUENCERS

Influencers are individuals who have the power to affect the opinions or purchase decisions of others because of their real or perceived authority, knowledge, position, or relationship. They are hired by organisations because they are inspirational and more convincing than when these messages come directly from companies.

Sunday morning. You feel the warmth of the sunshine on your face as you turn around in your bed once more. You wake up slowly, craving for a coffee and a bagel. With an impulsive thrust, you relinquish the comfort of your bed and take a quick shower using your favourite shampoo that leaves your hair soft, clean, and manageable and also makes the in-shower experience ultimately pleasant. And as you stand there, and look straight in your camera, you realise once more that work has just begun.... Ellen realises that her life isn't easy as a vlogger. Her camera records most parts of her day, making her private life public. This Sunday morning at home, but also the following family outing, and the visit to the grocery store and the salsa workshop later this day. In the evening she will edit all the footage, to make her day worthwhile viewing for her followers.

DEFINITION AND KEY FEATURES

In this chapter we discuss a specific form of influencers: vloggers who engage in in-vlog advertising such as Ellen in the above example. First there were blogs and then vlogs. Bloggers want to share online articles with information (blogs) with their followers, for instance, about their daily lives. The start of YouTube in 2005 enabled people to use their camera instead of their keyboard for the sharing of video messages (vlogs). The technique is simple to use and quickly applicable. Just like blogging, anybody can be a vlogger.

A FOCUS ON IN-VLOG ADVERTISING

Vloggers are video content creators, documenting their life or a topic such as a certain hobby. The main goal of a vlog is to communicate with a wide audience on a personal level. When vloggers are involved in a financial (or product) transaction with companies they engage in in-vlog advertising. In exchange they share content, diverting traffic from their site to other fellow vloggers, in order to build a bigger audience community and achieve a greater reach of their vlogs. From now on when we use the term vloggers we refer to those vloggers engaging in in-vlog advertising.

BUILDING TRUST WITH AUDIENCES

Nowadays, vlogging is a powerful tool because it can hide the commercial nature of the message by having a vlogger show and promote a product in their highly personal, individual tone of voice, style, and time, directed specifically at their followers (people who most likely started following vloggers due to their likeability, trustworthiness, and shared interests). The audience may think that these are the vlogger's personal views and recommendations. Unable to detect the sponsorship, some in the audience may proceed to purchasing. For brand and vlogger, it is a win-win scenario: the brand communicated its message in a covert, highly engaging manner – without being the official sender. The vlogger received a product or payment in return, and posted content on their channel to keep their audience engaged.

PAID ADVERTISING, SPONSORSHIPS, AND REVENUE SHARES

Vloggers test and demonstrate new products and recommend them – a trend that has become vastly profitable for many of them, especially as brands have increased spend on this marketing tactic. In the early days of vlogging, the collaboration was based on just providing products. This has evoluated towards paid advertising, sponsorships, and revenue shares. Vloggers recieved a product or payment in return, and posted content on their channel to keep the audience engaged.

INFLUENCERS IN PRACTICE

Although vloggers seem to be a valuable method for the marketing of products and brands, there are important things to bear in mind. The key to the success of many vloggers is the trust they build with their audiences. That relationship makes them valuable for advertisers. Vloggers devote time to strengthening their ties with their followers, and to building a community around them. Some of them may even meet fans offline on organised fan days. They are popular for being themselves. Ellen, in the example above, could be the girl next door. Of utmost importance for organisations is to determine whether the reputation and authenticity of the vlogger coincide with the image of the advertised brand.

Big luxurious fashion and make-up brands often have tight relationships with their vloggers[1], but not exclusively so. Even teeth-whitening brands or fitness drink companies make heavy use of vloggers and start building a tight community of vloggers to work with. When famous vloggers interact in their communities about these brands, these brands profit from their endorsements.

STRICT RULES FOR VLOGGERS AND THEIR CONTENT.

However, due to this commercial relationship between organisations and vloggers, regulations about the etiquettes and rules on vlogging have become much stricter in recent years, forcing vloggers to disclose collaborations or otherwise face sizeable fines. These compliance requirements have come in response to calls for greater clarity from vloggers about when material in vlogs becomes advertising and how they can make that clear. Ads must obviously be identifiable as such. If a vlogger is paid to promote a product or service and an advertiser controls the message then it becomes an ad. When that happens, like all advertisers, vloggers must clearly signpost that they are advertising. Even tax authorities are tracking the behaviour of vloggers and fining those who break the rules. Social media also inflicts rules through self-regulation. For instance, Facebook provides strict rules for vloggers and their content.

However, nowadays many vloggers set a bad example, and build their channels on pranks or breaking rules, simply for the entertainment value, giving their audience quite bad ideas of what is ok and what is not. Unfortunately, this sometimes results in even higher engagement with the profile, which can lead to a larger following and the ability for vloggers to ask for higher fees for collaborations with companies.

Juliane Blasche will now describe how influencer marketing, in her view, can be used as a branding strategy, and can be considered as the new word of mouth.

REFLECTING ON INFLUENCER MARKETING

By Juliane Blasche
Digital Marketing Manager
ChargePoint

Fame always fascinated us … throughout the centuries, we wanted to know what the royals were up to, followed by Hollywood celebrities. Today, we follow the 2.0 celebrity: influencers. These people with highly engaged social media accounts can impact their audiences' opinions and (consumer) behaviours. The collective term "influencer" comprises bloggers, vloggers, YouTubers, Instagrammers, Snap-chatters, Twitter-birds, LinkedIn professionals, and more – every social media platform can give rise to new influencer types. The audience follows for various reasons, from the influencer's expertise, appearance, likeability, entertainment value, to simple curiosity.

IT'S ALL ABOUT THE FIT
Working in influencer marketing within an agency as well as a brand-promoting context, I have witnessed immense changes in a short time – and if you ask me, it will change even faster going forward. But why has influencer marketing become the next big thing to add to the marketing mix, even though its effectiveness depends on various factors and can be extremely tricky to measure, unless you promote a direct response product, and use tracking links or promotional codes? First, everyone can find their niche in social media! By

creating content on specific topics, influencers build interest-based communities. And by gathering like-minded people, influencers can quickly turn into opinion leaders in their field – which is *THE* chance for brands to organically promote products! It's all about the fit.

THE POWER OF PARASOCIAL RELATIONSHIPS

Second, the power of parasocial relationships has been established over time. Influencer marketing is truly the new word of mouth! Consider this: for most of us, a (product) recommendation from a friend will weigh more than the most elaborate, appealing, yet impersonal message. Or would you rather trust an online banner? A billboard? A TV ad featuring a celebrity? If you have no connection to the people you are advertising for, you most likely will not! We turn to trusted voices – be that a friend or the pretty, funny, attention-grabbing influencer you follow.

PRODUCT-ENDORSER-CONGRUENCY

Lastly, it's all about storytelling. If an influencer embeds a product in a highly organic (-seeming) manner, one may tend to believe they really use the product in their everyday life. And since I like and identify with that influencer, maybe I will look just as good as them in the clothes they promote or with the make-up they wear. Consequently, it is likely that I will fail to understand the sponsored nature of the influencer's content. Liking and trusting influencers thus leads exactly to what is suggested in this chapter: our persuasion knowledge is diminished. So how can communication professionals implement influencers in their strategy? In theory and in practice, influencers act as highly credible or likeable voices for specific audiences on specific channels. For brands, that means a potentially never-thought-possible degree of product-endorser-congruency!

THE FUTURE OF INFLUENCER MARKETING IS UNCERTAIN

In my view, the future of influencer marketing is uncertain. The availability of data will become even more important, yet data protection acts will follow quickly, too. Social media platforms provide in-depth audience insights into which brands will reach their intended target audience. Learning to read these insights as well as manually analysing social media profiles is a crucial skill working in the field! Otherwise, one will be tricked by "influencers" who bought their followers and engagement, thus seeming more popular than they really are, and confidently asking for higher fees for brand promotions – a trend seen a lot in 2014 to 2016. The untrained eye can rely on technology to detect fraudulent engagement or audience data – but probably, it will cost you.

But even with data and the needed skills, influencer marketing may already have peaked! Initially, vloggers and bloggers were authentic content creators. But as more brands discovered the power of this marketing mechanism, and heavily invested in it, social media accounts became filled with ads. The result? Dropping engagement rates, lower credibility, growing consumer scepticism, and finally the slow death of accounts – a pitfall many of the early influencer stars fell into.

MICRO INFLUENCERS ARE ON THE RISE

Influencers thus need to be strategic. Building a following audience and turning it into a loyal community takes time. Building trust and credibility is even harder. But once achieved, the influencer becomes the object of desire for brands. Whilst brands initially hunted for the biggest profiles, aiming to reach the largest audience possible, micro influencers (with smaller yet usually more engaged audiences) are on the rise. This is because these smaller influencers have not yet turned their social media into advertising boards. They have stayed credible and trustworthy to their still somewhat exclusive community – in contrast to those macro influencers regularly and openly promoting products. But, whether macro or micro, the key is in staying true to one's content creation roots, and to balance non- and commercial messages.

A fantastic example is Dutch-Iranian fashion blogger Negin Mirsalehi – from girl next door to Forbes 30 under 30. The highest-level luxury brands compete to appear on her profiles. She started by creating content about her utmost passion: fashion! The quality, authenticity, and aesthetics of her work catapulted her to a whooping international following. But how did she maintain that status and audience engagement over the years? She continued to stay true to herself and her "brand", declining big sums offered for brand promotions if the product was not right. Yet she makes a living out of her influencer career. How? She embeds advertising in such a natural, aesthetically pleasing way that one cannot fail to believe her – it is in line with the content she created before and made a name for herself with. Moreover, she connects her personal values with commercial messages. For example, she grew up using bees' wax and honey in the family's cosmetic routines, which she communicated to her fans within heart-warming stories about the family and her childhood. Unsurprisingly, she launched her own beauty care series with bee products. Although the audience knows they are exposed to a commercial message, they still know that Negin truly believes in and uses bee products herself, because they saw and heard it from her directly many times! It thus only makes sense that she launched products in this field. Persuasion knowledge in this case is present, but strongly diminished for the audience, simply because of the great product-endorser-fit and Negin's authenticity.

AN INFLUENCER BECOMING A POWERFUL BRAND

Although Negin is an exception to the rule, she is the perfect example of an influencer becoming a powerful brand and endorser in one, in my personal and professional opinion. She illustrates how brands should use influencers in their marketing mix without harming anyone's image, whilst benefitting from today's most innovative word-of-mouth and consumer-to-consumer marketing mechanism.

A SCIENTIFIC PERSPECTIVE

Influencer marketing has become more popular among scientists as a research subject, but the fast pace in this sphere may make it difficult to conduct reliable, timely research on the subject. What are the key mechanisms of influencer marketing and what explains their effectiveness? In the first chapter of this book we talked about the systematic avoidance of the numerous communication messages that reach us each day. As Juliane Blasche has already said, a critical remark is that the popularity of vloggers and the number of their followers does not automatically translate into effectiveness.

YOUNGSTERS AS A LOYAL AUDIENCE

A challenge for marketers is to address young target audiences and to cope with the regulations on kids' marketing. Children are often difficult to reach for organisations and they use YouTube more than any other cable network, which makes YouTube an important medium for many brands to reach them.

Vloggers are likely to grab youngsters' attention and turn them into a loyal audience. Many youngsters view popular vloggers on YouTube, on a daily basis. Youngsters process information less elaborately compared to the elderly[2], which makes them more susceptible to attempts to influence their behaviour. This is reinforced in vlogs because the persuasion attempts are sometimes hidden in them and the content is based on entertainment.

CONSUMER-TO-CONSUMER MARKETING

Social influencer marketing can be considered as consumer-to-consumer marketing. The parasocial interaction theory[3] explains the feeling of friendship between vloggers and their followers. This theory posits that most young fans of vlogs are in the phase of identity construction, that they loosen their ties with their parents, and associate more with their peers. They do not want to fall by the wayside, but how do they manage this? A vlog offers an approachable look into the lives of peers, even though most of it may be staged. How do they cope with problems, which clothes do they wear, how do they apply their make-up, what do they define as cool, how do they relate to people of all sexual orientations? Youngsters recognise the situations the vloggers are in, and learn from them about mores and values.

SKILFULLY STAGED CONTENT

Although the content of vlogs is often skilfully staged, a share of vlogs deals with the real-life issues of many youngsters. The popularity of vlogs can thus partly be explained in terms of relevance, personal identification, and parasocial relationships[4]. Youngsters feel that they are closely tied to the vloggers and that they know them personally. They consider them as close friends, and trust their advice, which shows that influencer marketing is the new word of mouth. However, vloggers do not always offer these highly impressionable followers 'the real thing'.

SIMILARITY OF THE VLOGGER'S VALUES WITH THOSE OF THEIR FOLLOWERS

Important preconditions for success are the social attractiveness and the similarity of the vlogger's values with those of their followers,[5] and their entertainment value in this highly competitive space. Furthermore, the way content is offered is exactly what youngsters want: on demand, visual, highly entertaining, and informative, and without parent state supervision. Despite these optimistic thoughts about its effectiveness, the positive effects of influencer marketing have not yet been unequivocally proven.

Back to Ellen. Because of the 'girl-next-door effect', and the fact that she shares the good as well as the bad moments in her daily life with her followers, they consider her as a trustworthy friend. They listen to her judgement repeatedly, about the quality and usability of the personal care products. It makes them think positively about these products, and wanting to buy these products, leading eventually to buying behaviour. Seeing Ellen use these products on a daily basis and on various occasions without obviously stating that the brand asked her to promote them further creates the illusion that she is a true user who bought the product herself because of truly cherishing its merits...

FUTURE AND ETHICS

In the public and scientific debate, worries are being expressed about the use of influencer marketing. It appears that not all followers know that the vloggers are paid to show and talk about products. When the product, as in product placement, is intertwined with the narrative, this may cause a low resistance in followers towards the dominant persuasive message: 'buy this product'.

A trend for the future may be that youngsters actually want to become vloggers as a full-time job! They have discovered the amount of brand promotions that vloggers conduct, the cars they buy, and the lives they lead … So the ideal lurks that, if done well, it can be a well-paying job, "doing what you love".

PERSUASION KNOWLEDGE IS ACTIVATED

One may question the added value of vloggers for companies. Vlogs are popular among youngsters, who are not fully developed in advertising literacy, which makes it difficult for them to distinguish between an honest video and a video with a commercial intent[6,7]. Therefore, the branch has developed its own ethical codes. In the Netherlands, the 'social code: YouTube'[8] is a self-regulating mechanism in which vloggers may participate voluntarily. Participating vloggers should openly state with each shown product whether they are paid for it or not.

However, this clarity raises the chance that persuasion knowledge is activated among youngsters, which may interfere with the goals of advertisers. Followers will be made conscious of the persuasive intent of the vlogger's message and may show resistance to this persuasion attempt, causing detrimental effects on the advertised brand as well as the vlog[9]. By proactively increasing persuasion knowledge, influencer marketing may lose some of its effectiveness and in turn wear out as a powerful element in the marketing mix.

Marketers are of course aware of these detrimental effects and sometimes ask vloggers to only disclose their brand with a little note in the corner of the video which can barely be seen: "ad sponsored". However, this clarity is to the advantage of vloggers who are eager to participate in this code because this reinforces their status of being open, transparent, and trustworthy, offering their followers a means to distinguish between fake and reality in vlogs.

ILLUSION OF PARASOCIAL FRIENDSHIP

One might question the nature of the admiration that followers feel for their idols. A characteristic of friendship in the eyes of Aristoteles is the giving instead of the receiving of love. What the followers receive is content, being today's form of love on demand, tailored to their taste, and directed at them. Many vloggers proactively ask their followers for suggestions on what content they should create, giving the followers the feeling of 2-way-communication.

In friendship, you wish that everything goes well with the other. We can see this in the reactions under a vlog, where we see many expressions of love towards the vloggers. Unique in the friendship with vloggers is that this online friendship is unidirectional, from the perspective of the follower. However, it feels like 2-way-communication when the vlogger engages with them, this being the key to retain them as followers. Also, by being able to send direct messages on the platforms, followers have the feeling of having a chance to communicate with the vlogger, in contrast to celebrities who are unattainable. The comment function is another option to communicate with them, although that's somewhat less direct. The messaging of vloggers is meant for a more general public and does not aim to develop friendships[10]. Nevertheless, it is part of the new decorum to tell followers in videos how much they are loved, how much the vlogger appreciates them for their attention, organising fan meetings to show gratitude even more, and that none of this (the channel) would be possible without them. This flatters the viewer and gives the illusion of a parasocial friendship.

CONTENT IS STAGED

In theory, the beauty of vlogs is in their transparency, making it possible to dive, in real time, into the personal lives of vloggers. But again, this is an illusion. All content is staged, aiming to portray a certain lifestyle that is not a true reflection. One may wonder what the impact of the staged picture and perfectly filtered content of influencers may be on the wellbeing of their sometimes very young audiences. They present themselves 'as they are', apparently with no acting, making them appear sincere and trustworthy. In order to keep these good virtues alive and to maintain a successful cooperation with vloggers, companies should openly communicate about their cooperation with vloggers, and they should carefully select the vloggers who they want to be associated with. Especially by using available data. If only 10% are Dutch, and 90% are from the US, the collaboration will most likely flop from a brand perspective.

THE RISE OF VIRTUAL VLOGGERS

Technology has enabled the creation of virtual vloggers. Miquela[11] was created by a company and has more than a million followers. She lives her own life on Instagram, just like a real influencer of flesh and blood. She hangs out on the beach, chills with friends, wears expensive clothes, makes her own music and even had a quarrel with another virtual vlogger called Bermuda. Miquela's popularity among her followers may be explained by the fact that she obviously is fake and programmed and honest about it. Marketers have their ultimate trustworthy puppet that they can manipulate in any direction they like. Is this the future of vlogging? Do we also bond with avatars influencers? Judging by the number of followers and vlog posts we are inclined to say yes. Being genuinely 'fake' might be the new realism in vlogging.

Although technologically advanced, Miquela is not really an AI-based artificially intelligent being, an AI creation. The future of influencers may be digital beings who are actually powered by AI, requiring no human involvement whatsoever. Everything would be completely computer generated, from the images they post to the captions that go with them. Machine learning technologies would then allow these virtual influencers to interact with people on social media. However, there will probably always be a human storyteller behind the virtual face, because that will help people to socially engage with the character and become friends in the long run.Again, back to Ellen. We may question her behaviour, 'sneaking in' the use of her branded personal care products in her daily life. At least she should be open and honest about it. Her followers will be aware that she is sponsored but will still follow her because of her interesting lifestyle. So, the answer to the question 'Do we think that vloggers are the brand ambassadors of the future?' is 'yes'. Provided brands and vloggers provide a perfect fit and stick to regulations.

"One of the biggest shifts in marketing is the fact that a brand's message does not have to come from the brand. Vloggers are the influencers of the 21st century."

CLASSIFICATION

★★★★★ ★★★★★ ★★★★★ ★★★★★ ★★★★★

References and notes

1   Brands that have used social influencers in the past are the watch brand Daniel Wellington, L'Oréal and Disneyland Paris.

2   Buijzen, M., Van Reijmersdal, E., & Owen, L. H. (2010). Introducing the PCMC model: an investigative framework for young people's processing of commercialized media content. Communication Theory, 2-, 427-450. doi: 10.1111/j.1468-2885.2010.01370.x.

3   Giles, D. C. (2002). Parasocial interaction: a review of the literature and a model of future research. Media Psychology, 4(3), 279-305. doi: 10.1207/S1532785XMEP0403_04.

4   Giles, D. C. (2002). Parasocial interaction: a review of the literature and a model of future research. Media Psychology, 4(3), 279-305. doi: 10.1207/S1532785XMEP0403_04.

5   Lee, J., & Watkins, B. (2016). YouTube vloggers' influence on consumer luxury brand perceptions and intentions. Journal of Business Research, 69(12), 5753-5760. doi:10.1016/j.jbusres.2016.04.171.

6   Valkenburg, P. M. (2004). Children's responses to the screen: A media psychological approach. Mahwah, NJ: Lawrence Erlbaum.

7   Rozendaal, E., & van Reijmersdal, E. (2017). Hoe kan de transparantie van reclame in online video's vergroot worden voor minderjarigen? Een literatuuronderzoek naar de effecten van vermeldingen. Internal report. Amsterdam School of Communication Research (ASCoR).

8   Retrieved from: https://www.desocialcode.nl/.

9   Van Reijmersdal, E. A., Fransen, M. L., van Noort, G., Opree, S. J., Vandeberg, L., Reusch, S., & Boerman, S. C. (2016). Effects of disclosing sponsored content in blogs: How the use of resistance strategies mediates effects on persuasion. American Behavioral Scientist, 60(12), 1458-1474.

10 Becker, M. J. (2015). Ethiek van de digitale media. Boom.

11 Retrieved from: https://www.instagram.com/lilmiquela/.

#21 NEUROMARKETING

Neuromarketing is a research method that investigates which neurological reactions occur when exposed to a marketing stimulus (e.g. advertising, packaging).

You may already know that smoking is the most important cause of cancer[1]. Probably you have seen confronting images of the (black) lungs of a smoker compared to the lungs of a non-smoker. However, did you know that stopping smoking, at whatever time of your life, reduces the risk of cancer significantly[2]? If you are planning to quit smoking, wouldn't it be great if you could predict, by looking into your head, which messages would have the most effect on you in the long term? Now, this research has been carried out, with results. You can read more about this in this chapter.

DEFINITION AND KEY FEATURES

Neuromarketing is a concept that has gained increasing recognition in recent years. The term 'neuromarketing' was introduced in 2002 by the Dutch marketing professor Ale Smidts, but research into the field had already been done in the early 90s. But what exactly is neuromarketing? Some psychologists use the term, among other things, when they talk about Cialdini's influencing principles, psychological heuristics, or other well-known terms that have nothing to do with direct measurements of the brain. The name suggests that it concerns certain activities that brands perform to sell products or services. As the founder of the term, Smidts[3] defines neuromarketing as using neuroscientific research methods to better understand consumer reactions to marketing stimuli such as commercials or packaging. In other words, neuromarketing differs from all other innovations in this book because it is not a form of marketing or communication, but a form of research! The brain could be seen as a black box that conceals the emotions and preferences of consumers and only a small part of these emotions and preferences is accessible. Neuromarketing is the window of this black box through which researchers can learn more about these emotions and preferences[4].

This branch of research arose because in recent years it has become increasingly clear that the *homo economicus* is a myth: the idea that people make decisions in life on the basis of a careful consideration of all the pros and cons. For years this thought has also been commonplace in marketing. A classic model within marketing based on this is the AIDA model[5] (the letters stand for: Attention, Interest, Desire, Action). It dates back to 1925 and describes the steps that consumers must take consecutively until they make a choice or take action. First of all, there must be attention/awareness of a product or service before the interest can be aroused by emphasising positive aspects. If the interest is aroused, this should be converted into desire; the consumer must then be convinced of why the product or service is valuable. If these steps have been completed, a consumer can act, by finding out where a product can be obtained'. We now know, however, that the sequence of these steps is not always followed in daily practice. Instead of thinking about the options before making a choice, people make all sorts of choices and then form a rationale for this choice. In psychology, this is called *self-perception*[6]. In traditional surveys of consumer behaviour, consumers often first get the chance to think, allowing them a socially desirable and/or incorrect answer. Neuromarketing, on the other hand, looks at the unconscious, emotional processes that take place in the brain on exposure to stimuli, giving it an advantage over traditional marketing (consumer) research. In addition, smaller numbers of consumers are needed to gain insights into the consumer because brain reactions are much more universal than written or spoken reactions, which makes it easier to generalise to a consumer target group[7].

METHODS IN NEUROMARKETING

Two commonly used methods in neuromarketing are EEG and fMRi and these are both forms of *neuroimaging*, research in which structures and functions of brain areas are depicted. In EEG (Electroencephalography) the electric activity of the brain is measured by means of a number of sensors on the head (like a swimming cap) while a test subject is exposed to a stimulus. The electrical activity is then converted into a graphic pattern from which, for example, the excitement of subjects can be read at different moments of a video commercial. It is a relatively coarse measurement method when it comes to determining in which specific area of the brain certain activity occurs, but it is relatively affordable and precise when it comes to measurements in time, when examining responses to moving, dynamic stimuli. In fMRI (functional Magnetic Resonance Imaging), a subject lies down in a long narrow tube, surrounded by magnets, while, for example, an advertisement is shown. When a part of the brain is stimulated, it requires oxygen and the more active a part of the brain, the more oxygen is supplied. The magnets measure the change in the amount of oxygen, and fMRI can thus be used to create a three-dimensional image of the activation in the brain regions. Because it is known from research which brain areas are involved in emotions such as anxiety, involvement, or lust, fMRI can be used to see what happens in the head in more depth than with EEG. Other methods such as eye tracking and facial expression analysis are often also included in neuromarketing, but because they do not meet the condition of direct measurement techniques of the brain, they do not comply with this.

NEUROMARKETING IN PRACTICE

As can be deduced from the increase in articles on neuromarketing in professional literature, many communication professionals are very positive about this method of marketing research. According to many communication professionals, neuro-marketing is a welcome addition to traditional research methods because it enables researchers to verify existing theories, to circumvent social desirability, and to measure unconscious processes. A study[8] that illustrates this makes a comparison between the estimated effectiveness of anti-smoking campaigns via self-reporting and the actual effectiveness of those same campaigns via neurological research using fMRI. Neuroscientist Emily Falk scanned the brains of 31 heavy smokers while watching stop-smoking movies. After seeing the videos they made an estimate of their effect on their intention to stop. They indicated to what extent they agreed with statements such as: these advertisements have convinced me, are powerful, have prompted me to think, et cetera. All of the participants stated after the programme that they planned to quit, although not everyone was convinced that he/she wouldn't smoke again. After one month it appeared that the fMRI scans had been much better able to predict who would actually stop than the self-reports! How exactly was this predicted? The participants who actually stopped showed significantly more activity in the prefrontal cortex, the brain area involved in planning, impulse control, and decision making.

BRANDS AND THE BRAIN

Another famous example that should not be missed here is McCLure's research into the emotional responses to drinking Pepsi or Coca-Cola [9]. The researchers wondered what was happening in the brains of people who have a strong preference for Coca-Cola because these two soft drinks have an almost identical chemical composition. If subjects in the experiment drank Coke without being told which brand it was, the preferences were the same for either Pepsi or Coca-Cola. But if the subjects did see what they drank, a large majority preferred Coca-Cola. The fMRI scans made clear what was going on here: the brand knowledge activated the hippocampus, an area on the inside of the brain that is named after the sea animal that resembles the form, the seahorse (Hippocampus). This area is involved in storing memories in the long-term memory. The memories of (experiences with) the brand were so powerful that they played a bigger role than the (taste of) the soft drink itself. The experiment thus demonstrates the strength of a brand's strong identity and the subsequent implicit preferences.

Now that you know that activity in certain areas of the brain can be linked to the success of a brand, you can certainly imagine that marketers would offer large sums of money to predict the impact of advertisements on the public. The commercial in which a little boy in a Darth Vader outfit calls a Volkswagen Passat to life, with the help of The Force (which gives a Jedi his power in Star Wars) is also called 'the ad that changed the Super Bowl commercials forever'. The advertisement was made especially for the Super Bowl, the best viewed and therefore the most expensive TV moment of the year in the US. Sand Research[10] was able to predict on the basis of an EEG that the commercial would make an impact. The legendary video in which the commercial is played simultaneously with the EEG can be watched online. In the video clip you can see at which moments the engagement and the emotional valence (positive/negative) of the viewer change during the viewing of the commercial.

PROS AND CONS OF NEUROMARKETING

Researchers have high expectations of neuromarketing because this research method also fits the changed media landscape. As a result of more competition, companies are increasingly making budgets available for communication and marketing, from which they naturally want to get as much profit as possible. As a result, it has become increasingly important to have media statements match the right target group and person. It is also important to use the correct elements in a message so that it receives the desired attention. Neuromarketing helps to get this attention, because an advertisement formed with this technique can trigger the right emotions and thus reach the subconscious of consumers. Some critics argue that there is a high risk that brain scans will be overestimated. For example, a brain scan can measure which parts get more blood circulation and more oxygen, but which thoughts and emotions belong to this is only interpretation. Another disadvantage is that neuromarketing research takes place in laboratories and it is not always possible to add factors that influence day-to-day practices. Think of exposure to commercial messages on television; at home you are mainly inclined to zap away or grab your smartphone to spend your time on social media during the commercial break. In addition, data acquisition and processing take a relatively long time and are relatively expensive due to the required knowledge and equipment. We believe that neuromarketing, in combination with survey research or focus groups, can give a holistic view of the interaction between people, media, and brands. Walter Limpens will now tell about his work as a researcher in neuromarketing.

REFLECTING ON NEUROMARKETING

By Walter Limpens
Founding partner
Neurensics

After I graduated in Psychology and Business Studies, I started to work at an advertising agency as a communications strategist. One of my teachers in a social psychology course told me that there were not a lot of psychologists active in the advertising world, so chances were small to work in the field. I could not understand why so few (social) psychologists were working in a field where social behaviour is so important. Nevertheless, I managed to get an internship at an advertising agency and I was dedicated to showing them the importance of psychology in advertising.

THE PSYCHOLOGY OF ADVERTISING

Soon I realised that this was not an easy task. Advertising campaigns are made by creatives, people who are very skilled in thinking out of the box and coming up with fresh and exciting ideas. However, I also noticed that they generally do not have a scientific view of how people think, make decisions, and are influenced by (mass) communication. For example, I told them that people do not really like to put a lot of energy into processing ads. This dilemma gets attention in the chapters Go Figure and Storytelling in this book. Or as Nobel laureate Daniel Kahneman says: *"Thinking is to humans as swimming is to cats, they can do it but they would prefer not to."*[11] Ok, the creatives answered, but what then is an effective way to communicate with consumers? And to be honest, I did not know. Sure, I knew how their social environment influenced people, but I did not know the ingredients of an effective advertisement. This motivated me to explore the world of neuromarketing, which eventually resulted in the founding of a neuromarketing research company in 2010. What I notice in my daily work as a research manager is that the customers that we work for, advertisers, have the same question as I had when I just started working in the advertising field: how does creative communication have an impact on people? This seems like a really simple question to answer, but it is not. Most consumers think that advertising does not influence them and that it has a greater effect on others than on themselves. (In psychology we call this the third-person effect). It nevertheless is a field where billions are spent each year. Of course this is not a complete waste of money: advertisers know that advertising works. However, just like the consumer they do not always know *what* works. That is the reason why advertisers spent a lot of money on studying the effects of their ads. But the problem with traditional forms of research is that they look at the conscious responses of consumers. Most advertisers know this is a problem and in their attempts to answer the question of whether or not their ads are effective, they make increasing use of neuromarketing studies.

However, even more important than knowing whether their ads work or not, is the question *'why?'* The learning that advertisers will get from neuromarketing research about how to optimise their current and future ads is quite different from the insights that they will normally get from traditional research methodologies like surveys, focus groups, and interviews. In the end I think that this is the power of neuromarketing and the main reason why the field has gained so much attention in the last few years.

OPTIMISING ADVERTISEMENTS USING NEUROMARKETING

To make this more concrete I will use the MRI studies that I have done for Smint Netherlands (peppermint), one of our most loyal clients, as an example. The first time we did something for Smint was in 2015. Their advertising agency made an ad in which people were watching a guy who was about to give someone mouth-to-mouth. The guy in the ad did not feel self-assured, but this all changed when he took a Smint. What we learned from our MRI study was that the ad activated a lot of negative emotions (fear, anger, and disgust). In addition, we saw in our eye-tracking analyses that the people in the ad who were watching the guy who was about to give the mouth-to-mouth attracted a lot of attention from the viewers. They looked closely at the reaction of the audience, which was not really positive: they looked fearful and showed disgust. One of the most important findings from our fMRI studies is that we automatically mirror the emotions of others in order to empathise with them. When we see someone smiling, we can feel that he or she is happy because the corresponding emotion is activated in our own brain. This also means that the depiction of negative emotions in the Smint ad unintentionally led to the activation of similar emotions in the consumers' brains. This resulted in the ad activating too much negative emotion. With this finding in mind, Smint changed the ad and replaced the bystanders with the negative facial expressions with bystanders with more positive expressions. In a subsequent

MRI study we saw that this adjustment was enough to make the ad more positive and thus more effective. For Smint this was a valuable lesson that they could not get from a traditional form of ad testing. And for them this was also the start of further exploration of what works and what does not.

Advertising mostly works via unconscious processes. Neuromarketing is capable of measuring these and that leads to the discovery of new and valuable insights. This makes ads more effective and media spending more efficient, and it increases our general knowledge about the workings of advertising. This makes neuromarketing a very interesting field to follow in the coming years.

A SCIENTIFIC PERSPECTIVE

When communication professionals talk about neuromarketing, people sometimes talk about the 'buy button' – that one piece in the brain that triggers consumers to buy things when it is activated. The underlying theory of this buying button is that purchases are driven by, on the one hand, the preferences and desires of a consumer and, on the other hand, the price that the consumer has to pay. By means of neuroimaging, the neural circuits associated with these two issues can then be localised. In one study[12] participants were instructed to make purchasing decisions in a situation where the different products were shown and then the prices, after which they were asked whether or not they wanted to buy the product. The fMRI scans showed that at the moment that someone experienced a preference for a product, the nucleus accumbens (to a greater extent) was activated, the area that plays an important role in feelings such as desire, motivation, and satisfaction. The nuclei of this area respond to the rewarding effects of behaviour. The nucleus accumbens is therefore also called the 'craving spot' or the reward centre. Decisions that promise emotional rewards, such as the purchase of an attractive product, food, social cooperation, or even the ability to punish someone[13] fire the nucleus accumbens. But if our brain were only driven by reward, we would never say 'no' to anything. That this does not happen is due to another area in the brain. If participants in the same study were shown a product and then an extraordinarily high price for this product, the insula was activated, the area that plays a role in experiencing pain. The insula becomes active in physical pain, but also in response to loss (high price). These two opposing forces drive consumer behaviour: if the reward system is stimulated more strongly than the pain system, then a consumer is actually more inclined to buy a product. If the activation of the reward system is very large, a marketer can ask for a higher price without a consumer abandoning the purchase.

Neuromarketing is a reaction to the insight that (consumer) behaviour often arises without consciousness. We may be aware of our behaviour, but most of what we do is not preceded by a conscious choice[14]. How consumers face certain brands or beliefs is also largely a result of unconscious processes. Think back to the Coca-Cola vs. Pepsi experiment. Showing the brand name had a dramatic influence on the preferences for one or the other, while blind tests did not result in an outspoken winner. To explain how attitudes and preferences arise, often dual systems are used in science. The well-known Elaboration Likelihood Model (ELM)[15] is an example of this. Such models assume that people do not always think about (persuasive) messages. According to these *dual processing models*, people think critically and arguably about things, or people use simple low-effort reasoning, heuristics (e.g.: "if many people do X, it will be fine"). The PCMC[16] model states that there is another way in which persuasive messages have an effect, namely automatically. Persuasive messages have an influence without explicit attention to or awareness of the persuasive communication. The influence is completely unconscious and therefore applies to neuromarketing, in which these unconscious processes are scrutinised.

Neuromarketing enables researchers to investigate the unconscious part of human activity, which was previously virtually unattainable for research. This means that neuromarketing can be seen as a tool within Fogg's Functional Triad [17]. Marketers can use neurotechnics to find out better and more efficiently what the best advertisements are and, in this way, achieve more success compared to traditional research methods. This then also leads to information becoming more relevant to individuals, resulting in increased attention and excitement and thus to increased attitude and behavioural change.

FUTURE AND ETHICS

No other type of research portrays unconscious processes that lead to behaviour as well as neuromarketing. Realise, however, that the same areas of the brain are not necessarily activated when a consumer is exposed in a calm environment, such as the laboratory[18], compared to the daily practice in which people are confronted with thousands of messages in busy surroundings, where they try to escape as much advertising as possible. Neuromarketing also provides insight into the brain of the average consumer, but there are individual differences, despite the fact that the reactions in the brain are for a large part universal. However, we believe that neuromarketing is a valuable addition to existing research methods because it enables marketers and researchers to gain deeper insight into decision processes that are largely unconscious. We predict that when the knowledge about the relationships between neural activity and consumer behaviour increases, the demand for and also the supply of neuromarketing will only increase. Now neuro-research is mainly only affordable for organisations with large budgets, but when the costs go down, neuromarketing will also be accessible to smaller companies.

DOES NEUROMARKETING PRESS THE BUTTON?

Do you as a consumer cheer for neuromarketing? What if the buy button is actually found one day and marketers can make irresistible advertisements for products, so that you can hardly say 'no' anymore, partly because you are not aware of the influence that this knowledge has on you? Today, many people believe in the inherently bad nature of marketing, but in spite of that, the ultimate goal of marketing is to bring together consumer demand and supply in the market. For this reason, marketers provide information designers with information, so that they can then ensure that the products meet the needs of the consumer. They are informed about the aspects that consumers value and really want. Research into the observations of marketing academics, neurologists and marketing professionals with regard to neuromarketing shows that they do not see neuromarketing as a manipulative way to sell unnecessary goods and services[19]. The main reasons for using neuromarketing are understanding consumer behaviour and how consumers make choices during a purchase process; we don't believe that the consumer is under the power of the marketer, due to neuromarketing. Even though a large part of consumer decisions happens unconsciously, unconsciously is not the same as unwanted. The buy button, the balance of the reward and pain system, the nucleus accumbens and the insula, show marketers what people want. The subconscious buys nothing that we do not want.

ETHICAL RESPONSIBILITY OF NEUROMARKETING COMPANIES

Although we believe that neuromarketing does not pose a major threat to free will, we are dealing with two ethical issues. The first issue concerns the role played by the nucleus accumbens, the area that responds to the rewarding effects of behaviour. Research[20] shows that compulsive buyers have significantly more activity in the nucleus accumbens during the buying decision phase. The urge to buy is even greater with them than with non-compulsive buyers. In addition, compulsive buyers have less activity in the insula in a buying decision phase. In other words, with them the urge to buy is bigger and the mechanism that keeps them from buying is actually less effective. It is important that vulnerable groups are taken into account in marketing because they are less able to protect themselves. In our opinion, this is a social responsibility of marketers. The second ethical issue concerns neuromarketing for a completely different purpose than selling products, namely politics. A democracy benefits if citizens are well informed about the issues of a political party so that they can form independent opinions and can cast an independent vote. The New York Times[21] reported on neuropolitical consultancies, agencies that provide advice to politicians and on political campaigns, based on neurological research. You can imagine that it is not conducive to the independent political decision making of citizens. The Neuromarketing Science & Business Association (NMSBA) has developed an ethical code that organisations must comply with if they want to join. The association was established as a step towards international standards for the use of neuroscientific methods to investigate the communication campaigns of both commercial organisations and government institutions. The code stipulates, among other things, that neuromarketing cannot be used for political purposes. Furthermore, it is not allowed to conduct research among vulnerable groups and participants may withdraw at all times and the research may not be started before the participants are fully informed about the techniques.

Due to the increasing interest in the unconscious processes that lead to behaviour, neuromarketing will be a future-proof research method. The way in which the research will be conducted and used for consumer insights will to a large extent be determined by the ethical debate.

CLASSIFICATION

★★★★★ ★★★★★ ★★★★★ ★★★★★ ★★★★★

References and notes

1   Gandini, S., Botteri, E., Iodice, S., Boniol, M., Lowenfels, A. B., Maisonneuve, P., & Boyle, P. (2008). Tobacco smoking and cancer: A metaanalysis. International journal of cancer, 122(1), 155-164.

2   Hart C, Gruer L, & Bauld L.(2013). Does smoking reduction in midlife reduce mortality risk? Results of 2 long-term prospective cohort studies of men and women in Scotland. Am J Epidemiol., 178(5), 770-779. doi:10.1093/aje/kwt038.

3   Smidts, A. (2002). Kijken in het brein: Over de mogelijkheden van neuromarketing. ERIM Report Series Reference No. EIA-2002-012-MKT. Available at SSRN: https://ssrn.com/abstract=1098540

4   Fortunato, V. C. R., Giraldi, J. M. E., & Oliveira, J. H. C. (2014). A review of studies on neuromarketing: Practical results, techniques, contributions and limitations. Journal of Management Research, 6(2), 201-220.

5   E.K. Strong (1925). Theories of selling, Journal of Applied Psychology, 9, 75-86.

6   Bem, D. J. (1972). Self-perception theory. Advances in Experimental Social Psychology, 6, 1-62. doi: 10.1016/S0065-2601(08)60024-6

7   Pradeep, A. K. (2010). The buying brain : Secrets of selling to the subconscious mind, Hoboken, NJ: Wiley.

8   Falk, E. B., Berkman, E. T., & Lieberman, M. D. (2012). From neural responses to population behavior: neural focus group predicts population-level media effects. Psuchol Schi., 23(5), 439-445.

9   McClure, S. Li, J., Tomlin, D., Cypert, K.S., Montague, Montague, P.R. (2004). Neural correlates of behavioral preference for culturally familiar drinks, Neuron, 44(2), 379-387.

10 http://www.sandsresearch.com/little-darth-video.html

11 Kahneman, D. (2011). Thinking, fast and slow. New York: Farrar, Straus and Giroux.

12 Knutson, B., Rick, S., Wimmer, G.E., Prelec, D., & Loewenstein, G. (2007). Neural predictors of purchases, Neuron, 53(1), 147-56.

13 Carter, R. M., Macinnes, J. J., Huettel, S. A., & Adcock, R. A. (2009). Activation in the VTA and nucleus accumbens increases in anticipation of both gains and losses. Frontiers in Behavioral Neuroscience, 3, 21. doi:10.3389/neuro.08.021.2009

14 Dijksterhuis, A., Chartrand, T. L., & Aarts, H. (2007). Effects of priming and perception on social behavior and goal pursuit. In J. A. Bargh (Ed.), Frontiers of social psychology. Social psychology and the unconscious: The automaticity of higher mental processes (pp. 51-131). New York: Psychology Press.

15 Petty (1986). Communication and persuasion: central and peripheral routes to attitude change. Springer-Verlag, New York.

16 Buijzen, M., Van Reijmersdal, E.A., & Owen, L.H. (2010). Introducing the PCMC model: An investigative framework for young people's processing of commercial media content. Communication Theory, 20, 427-450.

17 Fogg, B. J., Cuellar, G., & Danielson, D. (2002). Motivating, influencing, and persuading users. In J. Jacko & A. Sears (Eds.), The human-computer interaction handbook: Fundamentals, evolving technologies and emerging applications (pp. 133-147). Hillsdale, NJ: Erlbaum.

18 Lee, N., Broderick, A. J., & Chamberlain, L. (2007). What is 'neuromarketing'? A discussion and agenda for future research. International Journal of Psychophysiology, 63(2), 199-204. http://dx.doi.org/10.1016/j.ijpsycho.2006.03.007

19 Eser, Z., Isin, F. B., & Tolon, M. (2011). Perceptions of marketing academics, neurologists, and marketing professionals about neuromarketing. Journal of Marketing Management, 27, 854-868.

20 Raab, G. & Elger, C.E., Neuner, M., & Weber, B. (2011). A neurological study of compulsive buying behaviour. J Consum Policy. 34. 401-413. 10.1007/s10603-0119168-3.

21 https://www.nytimes.com/2015/11/04/world/americas/neuropolitics-where-campaigns-try to-read-your-mind.html

Search...

#22 SEARCH ENGINE MARKETING

Search Engine Marketing is a form of digital marketing, paid and unpaid, that aims to increase the prominence of a website on search engines with the objective of leading more visitors to this website.

In 1945, the technical scientist Vannevar Bush described the problem of the accessibility of the increasing amount of scientific information and the problems that this entails. Before the rise of the internet, information was stored, for example, as a book or report or another paper medium, and the medium could be located in a house or library in another country. In his view, this was a problem because a lot of information was therefore not accessible to everyone and therefore had no value. For this he devised a device, the Memex, and introduced it with the words: *"Consider a future device for individual use, which is a sort of mechanised private file and library. It needs a name, and, to coin one at random, 'memex' will do. A memex is a device in which an individual stores all his books, records, and communications, and which is mechanised so that it may be consulted with exceeding speed and flexibility. It is an enlarged intimate supplement to his memory[1]"*. The Memex (which is the abbreviation for Memory Extender) would behave as an extension of the individual human memory and an unprecedented amount of image and text material could be stored in the memex. The problem that Bush pointed out in 1945 is still a relevant issue. The amount of information that comes in the form of photos, videos, and texts on the internet every day is bigger today than yesterday. Search engines help us to bring order to that huge amount of data, and if you want people to find your information online, it is important to know more about how these engines work.

DEFINITION AND KEY FEATURES

Today, search engines like Google, Bing, Yahoo Baidu (China) are smarter than ever; machine learning is sorting all sorts of information on the web and search engines even understand human speech. Just ask your Google Assistant for 'leather dining room chairs' by talking to it and you will get a series of suggestions. However, it was not always that easy to navigate on the internet. There was a time when you had to enter the exact wording of a website to find it. Since the turn of the millennium, internet users have been using more and more search engines to get to a website. Voice Search is much younger than searching on the basis of textual queries and it is speculated that it is just the beginning of a new era in searching. What is certain is that search engines have taken a prominent place in the online world and are used to search for all sorts of information on the internet: from people, places and news to events. The search engine plays a crucial role as a medium for organisations to get in touch with their target customers and to build their image because it is often the starting point of people's online orientation. In internet marketing, how organisations can achieve a high ranking in search results on the basis of certain keywords or phrases is therefore an issue of much interest. Search Engine Marketing increases the prominence in search engines. It is less important to be findable for as many people as possible, as it is to be findable for the right people, who, for example, are potential customers and therefore relevant to the approach.

Within search engine marketing, a distinction can be made between search engine optimisation (SEO) and search engine advertising (SEA). One important difference between these two variants is that SEO belongs to the owned media (a medium that is within one's own control) of an organisation, where SEA falls under paid media.

INCREASING TRAFFIC TO THE WEBSITE WITHOUT PAYING

The first unpaid form (SEO) is all about finding words, phrases, and visuals on a website, blog, or other online content with a search engines and, once found, they get the highest possible ranking in the organic search results. In other words: what the algorithm of the search engine considers important for the entered search terms. An algorithm is nothing more than a series of calculations to solve a problem. Search engines use an algorithm to determine a sequence of search results based on the search terms. The output of a search engine is also called SERP, which stands for Search Engine Result Page. The exact algorithm of Google (and many other search engines) is a big secret and changes continuously without anyone noticing because the success of the search engine depends on it. Nevertheless, through experimentation and testing it is possible to point out some important factors to get as high as possible in the ranking. The first factor is the popularity of a specific search. How often people search for specific words is important because the more often a (combination of) words is searched for, the higher these will be in the ranking. Secondly, creating good, fun, and relevant content for the right target groups by writing blogs with a specific focus, for example, is important. If people click on a link coming from the search engine, it is crucial that the information on this page matches their interests because they otherwise will leave the page quickly. In internet marketing terms, they bounce. If the content is in line with their expectations, visitors will not leave the page directly, which will positively influence the ranking. Besides appealing to popularity, relevance, and specificity, it is important that the content is accessible to read (or view or listen). By writing in an attractive way and editing texts in such a way that they are easy to read, the threshold will be lower to read and stay longer on the web page. In addition, it helps if content is written in a unique way, with distinctive keywords. Search engines try to filter out duplicative content as much as possible because they do not want to show things that are too similar (the same texts, the same pictures) because users generally do not like having a whole list of sites with all the same content. And last, for online presence, it is essential that websites are suitable for mobile devices. In many countries, the number of smartphones has exceeded the number of desktop computers. Google applies a mobile first index[2] that first indexes mobile versions and then desktop versions of websites.

SEARCH ENGINE ADVERTISING

In addition to SEO, an advertiser could pay a search engine to have an advertisement that appears on the result page when a user searches for a particular term. 'Google AdWords' and 'Yahoo! Search Marketing' are two major SEA programs that are used and here, advertisers bid against competitors who want to link the same words and phrases to their ads. How high a certain advertisement is placed in the search engine depends on two important factors: how much money an organisation is willing to pay for each click on the advertisement and what the click-through ratio (CTR) is. The CTR is based on the number of people clicking on the ad divided by the number of people who see the ad in the search results. The SEA providers are constantly working to improve their services in order to respond to both the wishes of the user and the paying organisations.

SEARCH ENGINE MARKETING IN PRACTICE

According to experts, the main effect of search engine marketing is to get higher in the result pages, in order to generate structurally more visitors. Search engine advertising is becoming increasingly important because internet users click more frequently on the paid positions of Google's result page and advertisers start paying more for the top positions[3]. Effects are directly measurable for marketers because they can track how many people click on an advertisement and whether this leads to buying a product, requesting a brochure, or watching a video. If optimisation is not applied, this may cause visitors to miss out because the website cannot be found and the competition runs off with potential customers.

DEPENDENCY ON GOOGLE

The most popular search engine worldwide is Google and in 2018 it had a market share above 90%[4]. Compared to other search engines like Bing, Yahoo! and Baidu (China), the reach of Google is very large. Many companies therefore use search engine marketing on Google to increase the visibility of their website. The tools that Google offers to measure data, such as the conversion rate, and to set up effective advertisements (Analytics and Adwords) are also very clear and easy to use, making advertising on Google attractive. However, even though Google's market share is large and can be an effective channel for relevant traffic, some practitioners believe it is good to not be completely dependent on Google and search engine marketing for a couple of reasons.

Firstly, search engine marketing is relatively expensive according to some, even if a company only does SEO. Months of work have to be invested in online research into the niche market in which a marketer wants to compete, to get to know the weaknesses of the competing parties as an input for a successful SEO campaign[5]. After that, the right keywords must be integrated into the web content in a strategic way. Some say that it is more difficult for small companies to compete with large businesses. The more paid ads are shown on Google, the further the organic search will move to the bottom of the page and this would reduce the visibility of smaller companies. And then Google itself is sometimes a competitor because Google comes up with initiatives with which they compete with organic (unpaid) results. An example of this is the functionality that the weather forecast shows when a user, for example, types in 'weather in Toronto'. A lot of practitioners also claim that the paid ads on Google over the years take up more and more space on the results page, causing the organic results to disappear further.

It should be clear that search engine marketing is of great value for those who want to be found online, but the critical sounds show that it is a complex business. The algorithms of search engines are constantly changing, especially because online devices are increasingly integrating into our lifestyle and we are now interacting with devices in a different way than a few years ago. Just think about the rise in voice search, which is used by many users to avoid typing[6]. The former Senior Vice President of Google once said: *"Google will keep reinventing itself to give you all you need for a simple and intuitive experience. At some point, pulling out a smartphone to do a search will feel as archaic as a dial-up modem"*. As we have seen in the chapter about voice, the input is different when we speak to our devices than when we type. Marloes Smit will now elaborate on a strategy to effectively target users of search engines.

CATCH THE FISH WITH CUSTOM INTENT AUDIENCES

By Marloes Smit
Founder & Senior PPC specialist
Buro Foss

I compare online advertisements to bait in a pond full of fish. It's all about the consumer taking your bait and not someone else's. In order to catch as many 'fish' as possible, two things are relevant: which bait does the fish like and when is it hungry? For years, online advertising using keywords was the best and only method to attract more visitors to a site. Advertisers paid when a visitor clicked on an advertisement, also known as Pay-Per-Click (PPC). It is important for PPC specialists to ensure that as many consumers as possible use an advertisement to buy, for example, an airline ticket online. The campaigns must 'convert', as it's called in our business. The specialists keep a close eye on the overall costs of a campaign, working on this every day: what does a click (the bait) cost and how many clicks (bait) do I need for a conversion? In other words: how much do I need to get enough fish to bite?

CLICKBAIT
In this game, Google AdWords and other advertising platforms provide the metaphorical fish bowl. If the consumers are the fish and the specialists are the anglers, then Google AdWords and its associates take care of the water. Until now, large advertising platforms were designed mainly to create online campaigns that would be shown according to search results. These campaigns were built by specialists on the basis of keyword research. Using keywords, consumer searches were matched and advertisements were shown. The campaigns that performed the best and yielded the highest conversion rates were those that achieved the highest search positions through an adequate budget. Keywords, advertisements and landing

page structures were also optimally designed for these campaigns. But what the anglers didn't yet know was when the fish were actually hungry. An internet user looking for garden furniture does not necessarily have the current intention to buy garden furniture. Because of this, an advertiser might waste his bait.

For online advertisers, it has become increasingly important to reach internet users with the right message at the right time. An overload of online messages and the increase in smartphone use constantly exposes people to messages that advertisers have sent out into the world. Consumers are increasingly accustomed to buying things online almost immediately (if necessary) and with almost no effort. Advertisers have to deal with demanding and impatient consumers, as well as many more anglers. Platforms like Google AdWords (nowadays called Google Ads) are continuously developing their fishing waters. Smarter ways to reach consumers are being developed.

Audience targeting is one of today's exciting trends in PPC marketing. Until recently, this trend offered limited opportunities. Think, for instance, of retargeting, one of the more well-known and effective examples of audience targeting that has been around for some time. This method targets those who have visited your website. The specialist then chooses, for example, to follow visitors who have not yet bought anything. In such a case, these visitors will see the advertisement on sites they visit afterwards. You could imagine this: you want to surprise your partner with a city trip and do preliminary research on a website. Therefore you use the tablet you both use. Next, you and your partner only get ads related to hotels in Prague. With this form of online advertising, it is still not known whether the consumer is truly ready for a purchase.

ADVANCED TARGETING

Since 2017, Google has been adding new audience targeting capabilities to Google Ads. In our opinion, Custom Intent Audience targeting is the most important and most effective. Through this, a specialist can reach a target group that has an above-average intention to buy or use certain products or services. These 'fish' leave a trail on the internet that indicates that they really want to bite. They have passed the research phase, the period in which they wanted to know whether a product or service was something for them. They want to buy. It's now the specialist's job to make the 'hungry fish' take their bait. The specialist knows that the consumer is one step ahead in their customer journey and that they intend to take action. How does one get that knowledge? Google assembles groups of people based on their online activities. Using the Google Display Network, consisting of millions of websites on which you can place advertisements, the specialist can achieve better results through these Custom Intent Audiences. For this form of targeting, Google collects data based on the online behaviour of users on all kinds of websites and in apps. Now, you can use not only the behavioural data from one particular website, as in remarketing, but can also approach a new target group using the data that Google collects. In this way, Google maps out a new potential customer group that does not yet know your specific site. PPC specialists can use this information, in combination with approximately 10-15 keywords, URLs, or apps, to compose a very specific target group and launch a good Custom Intent campaign. Google groups keywords that belong together in context, such as 'backpack', 'hiking boots' and 'sleeping bag', and matches these groups of keywords to websites that fit.

Google has collected a wealth of information about consumers in its fish bowl. This enables specialists to work more precisely with data. Custom Intent Audiences are currently one of the most valuable methods for internet marketers to reach the right target group at the right time. It is becoming easier to present the bait not only in the right fish bowl but also at the time that the fish wants to bite. By cleverly using this form of targeting, PPC specialists can reel in the fish at exactly the right moment: as soon as the float moves!

A SCIENTIFIC PERSPECTIVE

The starting point in the search process, in which people use devices to find usable information on the web, lies with the person who is looking for information. In other words, the information finder is in the lead, at least it is a feeling of control that is automatically evoked when a user gives input and gets output. This is a crucial aspect for the operation of search engine marketing. A consumer who is looking for a loan for the renovation of his or her home goes online for research and starts by consulting a search engine. Because the consumer plays an active role in the search process, Search Engine Marketing creates a stronger interaction between advertiser and user than via traditional less interactive advertising media. The contact is initiated by the consumer, who takes an active and often critical attitude. Based on the framework of people's processing or commercialised media content[7], the cognitive resources allocated by the user will be high due to the highly personal relevance of the information. After all, the user has searched for the information himself. Depending on the extent to which the displayed links and the information they contain require cognitive effort, the degree of elaboration in the processing of the information will normally be high, but this depends on the search query. When it comes to a more complicated or serious search, such as the loan for the rebuilding, the resources required are greater than for a simple search, like a drugstore nearby. In general, due to the degree of engagement, the information obtained through search engines will be processed critically and systematically. This critical processing is a conscious process, with attention and motivation, and it ensures that advertised messages are noticed faster. It is important to note, however, that the user will be more critical and will discard worthless information more quickly because of this state of mind.

SEARCH, EMOTION, AND MEMORY

A study[8] in which not only the cognitive response, but also the emotional response was investigated when people searched online for information, showed that the cognitive and emotional impact of online content is greatest when it is acquired by searching, compared to random online surfing, without the use of a search engine. The researchers recorded the heart rate and skin conductivity of participants who selected news stories according to whether or not a headline matched a predetermined interest (searching), and those who selected their stories with no search criteria by simply choosing interesting headlines. They found that searching caused a greater emotional impact when they searched for the information compared to surfing a news website, without an engine. Moreover, they found that the information was better memorised and understood when the users conducted specific searches for information. Content that satisfies the existing information need of web users therefore produces stronger emotional reactions.

EXTERNALISATION OF KNOWLEDGE

Seen from Fogg's Functional Triad[9], it is clear that search engines function as a tool in particular. This function influences attitude and behaviour by simplifying a complicated process to a few clicks with the cursor, influencing decision making and providing information to the user. A characteristic of innovations as a tool is that they increase the self-efficacy of individuals through the simplification of complex processes. This means that technique increases the confidence of a person in their own ability to successfully exert influence on his or her environment, for example by accomplishing a particular task or by solving a problem. In another study[10] participants were asked to assess their ability to answer questions like 'How does a zipper work?' after they had the opportunity to search the internet for the answers to these questions. In another condition, the participants were instructed not to use a search engine but to go directly to the website scientificamerican.com for the information. The participants who actively searched the internet assessed themselves to be better able to give a good explanation. The search for explanations online led to increased self-assessed knowledge, even if both groups had access to the same content. A higher assessment of own knowledge was also observed when an internet search was unsuccessful and did not lead to the answer to the question. A series of such follow-up experiments by the researchers shows that the active search on the internet inflates our sense of the knowledge we actually possess, because we find it difficult to recognise to what extent we base ourselves on external sources of information. Because the internet covers an incredible breadth of content and search engines make it so easy to get to the right information, the illusion of our own knowledge becomes extra large.

FUTURE AND ETHICS

2.5 Exabyte of data[11] is added to the internet each day. To put it into perspective, this is 90 years of High Definition videos, each day. Every two years the amount of data on the internet at least doubles. Imagine how complicated it would be to surf the web if there were no search engines. Because of the exponentially increasing amount of data on the web, search engines will become even more important. Companies obviously want internet users to reach their own website and not the competitor's.

CONFLICTING INTERESTS OF SEARCH

An ethical discussion that can be discussed here relates to the conflicting interests of search engines and advertisers. The purpose of search engines is to offer content that is as meaningful as possible, and that matches the user's way of searching, to earn big money. That is because the better a search engine performs on gratifying information needs, the more often people use the search engine and the more advertisers could earn through advertising. The goal of advertisers, on the other hand, is to get as high as possible in the Search Engine Result Pages, in any way whatsoever. An ethical argument against search engine marketing is that it uses tricks that serve a different interest than providing the right content to the right consumer, think of spamming or using misleading texts that direct internet users to wrong websites. The monitoring of that ethical side of the case happens in part by search engines themselves. Misuse of certain methods to score high is punished by the fact that search engines apply their algorithms to these strategies. One of the old school and now outdated techniques to get higher in the search results is called keyword stuffing, where non-relevant keywords are put into a metatag. Metatags are tags that can be placed in web pages and contain extra information for search engines so that search engines can find the pages better. By placing an excess of keywords on a webpage in an unnatural way, influence could be exerted on the search engine output. Many metatags, however, have become obsolete through the Google algorithm.

PERSONALISATION OF SEARCH

Another ethical issue concerns how search engine providers collect information from their users and then exploit it to advertisers in order to display personalised searches. You could think about searches queries as signposts that direct search engines to the right information. On the other hand, searches give very personal information about the user because they reveal interests, passions, needs, and fears. Google compiles search logs from its users and this goes far beyond merely routing to the right information when you realise what Google knows about you[12].

An engine that competes with Google is named Duckduckgo and it claims on the basis of its own research[13] that even in Incognito mode, users don't escape the following algorithms from Google. Duckduckgo, on the other hand, does not maintain a profile of its users, allowing different users to see exactly the same results with the same query. With this, the search engine bypasses the filter bubble, the tunnel vision that is caused by using some search engines by displaying results based on previous searches and thus implicitly confirming the user's life vision. Deviating results that are incongruent with previous searches are shown less quickly by algorithms that rely on search history. By not tracking search history, Duckduckgo is less sensitive to privacy. On the other hand, it can also be convenient if a search engine knows what information you prefer and adjusts the results as well as the advertisements. In our view, it is good to experiment with different search engines and think about the goals you have for using a search engine so you could adapt your search strategy to it. That way you become more aware of your online behaviour; learn to know your search engines, and you will process information in a more critical way and make yourself less vulnerable to unwanted influence.

SEARCH AND BRAIN FUNCTION

Finally, from the perspective of positive technology, one experiment showed[14] that internet search activity stimulates the brain function in middle-aged adults. In this study, half of the adults had experience with search engines and the other half not at all.

The participants performed two tasks: reading a text from a book and conducting searches on the internet. In both tasks, fMRI scans were made to show the brain activity during these two tasks. All participants showed significant brain activity during the book-reading task, demonstrating use of the brain regions controlling reading, memory, and language. In the task where the participants searched online for different types of information, a significant difference was visible in the brain activity of the two groups. While during the book-reading task the same brain activity was recorded for all participants, the more experienced internet search group registered activity in the frontal, temporal, and cingulate areas of the brain, which are responsible for complex reasoning and decision making. Above that, when the participants searched the internet, more neural circuits were activated than while reading, but only with those with online search experience. This shows that technology could contribute to brain functions.

In conclusion, search engines and search engine marketing are a double-edged sword; they facilitate search processes for the user and are a means for companies to approach the right people. Searching with search engines also maintains important brain functions. But remember to be aware of the traces you leave on the internet through searches and how stakeholders use them.

CLASSIFICATION

★★★★★ ★★★★★ ★★★★★ ★★★★★ ★★★★★

References and notes

1   Vannevar, B. (1945). As we may think. The Atlantic Monthly. 176 (1), p.101–108.

2   Retrieved from: https://webmasters.googleblog.com/2018/03/rolling-out-mobile-first-indexing.html

3   Retrieved from: https://www.smartinsights.com/search-engine-marketing/search-engine-statistics/

4   Retrieved from: http://gs.statcounter.com/search-engine-market-share

5   Retrieved from: https://www.seohermit.com/articles/why-is-seo-so-expensive/

6   Retrieved from: https://www.searchenginejournal.com/death-organic-search-know/189625/

7   Buijzen, M., Van Reijmersdal, E.A., & Owen, L.H. (2010). Introducing the PCMC model: An investigative framework for young people's processing of commercial media content. Communication Theory, 20, 427-450. doi:10.1111/j.1468-2885.2010.01370.x

8   Wise, K., Kim, H. J., & Kim, J. (2009). The effect of searching versus surfing on cognitive and emotional responses to online news. Journal of Media Psychology, 21(2), 49-59.

9   Fogg, B. J., Cuellar, G., & Danielson, D. (2002). Motivating, influencing, and persuading users. In J. Jacko & A. Sears (Eds.), The human-computer interaction handbook: Fundamentals, evolving technologies and emerging applications (pp. 133-147). Hillsdale, NJ: Erlbaum.

10 Fisher, M., Goddu, M., & Keil, F. (2015). Searching for explanations: How the Internet inflates estimates of internal knowledge. Journal of Experimental Psychology: General, 144 (3): 674 DOI: 10.1037/xge0000070

11 Retrieved from: https://www.emc.com/leadership/digital-universe/2014iview/executive-summary.htm

12 Tene, O. (2007). What Google knows: Privacy and internet search engines. SSRN Electronic Journal. 10.2139/ssrn.1021490.

13 Retrieved from: https://spreadprivacy.com/google-filter-bubble-study/

14 Small, W., Moody, T., Siddarth, P., & Bookheimer, S. (2009). Your brain on Google: Patterns of cerebral activation during internet searching. The American Journal of Geriatric Psychiatry: official journal of the American Association for Geriatric Psychiatry, 17, 116-26. 10.1097/JGP.0b013e3181953a02.

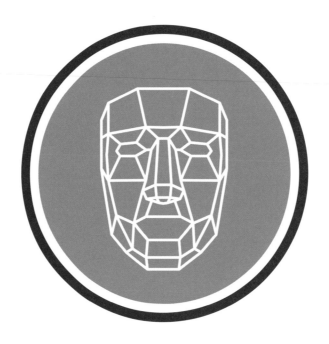

#23 FACIAL RECOGNITION

Facial recognition is a technology capable of identifying or verifying a person from a digital image or video.

Angela is anxiously waiting in the interrogation room. Paperwork has just been done, fingerprints have been taken, her face, eyes, and even her total body were scanned. Now she has to answer all sorts of anxiety-evoking questions, and these answers are thoroughly checked. Then the final redeeming words of the immigration officer that Angela was waiting for: our decision is that you may enter our country. Have a nice holiday!

DEFINITION AND KEY FEATURES

In the above example we touch upon a dilemma that is often associated with facial recognition: giving up your privacy in exchange for relevance. When you want to enter a country for a holiday, nobody will refuse a facial recognition and total body scan procedure, because the relevancy is clear: after approval, you can enter the country; without approval, you have to fly back home on the first available plane. The higher goal is also obvious: to safeguard a country from criminal activities. So you submit, wait in line, accept the scanning procedures and sometimes are interrogated a bit more, like Angela. Besides, you know in advance that you are going to be scanned, and are prepared to undergo it. This knowledge is also important and helps to resonate.

A FACE IS UNIQUE LIKE A THUMBPRINT

In this final innovation in this book we focus on facial recognition, an innovation that appeals to the imagination of many people. Facial recognition is an innovation that uses biometric software to map an individual's facial features mathematically and it stores the data as a faceprint. The software uses algorithms to compare a live capture or digital image to the stored faceprint in order to verify an individual's identity[1]. Machine-learning enables facial patterns to be analysed and compared with facial features stored in a database, such as facial muscles, the distance between the viewers' eyes or the shape of the eyebrows, the width of the nose, length of the jaw line, shape of the cheekbone and even facial movements. This comparison happens in real time.

Thus, this technology is capable of recognising the most personal and unique part of the human body. Just like a fingerprint, a face is unique, and even more important than the body in judgements of physical attractiveness[2]. It is fascinating that a technology exists that can recognise your face out of billions.

FROM SIMPLE RECOGNITION OF A FACE TO DETERMINATION OF A PERSON'S IDENTITY

We will present four examples in which, respectively, facial recognition varies from the simple recognition of a face itself to the more complicated determination of a person's identity. In the first example, recognition does not go further than the rough features of a face. A campaign about domestic violence on an interactive billboard was just based on the recognition of faces being faces. The billboard showed a maltreated woman. After software detected the face of a person, it said: "if you can see this, you can change this". The more passers-by saw the billboard, the faster her wounds healed. In this example, no privacy issues are involved because no data are stored or used.

Unique in this specific example is that a digital technique (facial recognition) is used in an offline context (billboard) to establish an interaction with people. When people pass by, these billboards have a stopping power and a surprise effect, because of their real-time character.

CAMPAIGN FOR WOMEN'S RIGHTS

In the second example, facial recognition software spots people's age and gender, not revealing the identity of people. In a bus shelter, the message in a campaign for women's rights was adjusted to gender. Women saw a video that encouraged them to take action for oppressed women. Men just saw a message, no video, stating: "We are choosing to show our advert only to girls to give you a glimpse of what life would be like without choices". Again in this example, privacy issues are not a real issue because no data are stored.

TAGGING INDIVIDUALS IN PHOTOGRAPHS

The next example many people have experience with. Social media uses facial recognition software to tag individuals in photographs. Each time an individual is tagged in a photograph, the software stores information about that person's facial characteristics. Once enough data has been collected, the software can use that information to identify a specific individual's face when it appears in a new photograph. Privacy issues may be involved because faces of people are stored and compared.

CONNECTING FACES TO SOCIAL MEDIA

In a last example, facial recognition recognises your face, after which a connection is made to your personal social media, using algorithms to analyse your lifestyle in order to offer personalised information, in real time. This of course raises questions about privacy issues, which we will discuss later.

FACIAL RECOGNITION IN PRACTICE

Facial recognition is becoming a widespread phenomenon used in several disciplines such as the security sector, marketing, and health. It was first used in the security sector when people crossed borders or entered football stadiums. Travellers experience these security checks as a time-consuming activity that is part of their holiday. But sometimes this is creatively solved. In cooperation with Emirates, Dubai's International Airport has created a walk-in video tunnel, capable of displaying changing landscapes, such as an aquarium, a desert, or simply advertisements. The aim of these varied landscapes is to keep visitors entertained and to encourage them to look at different sections, allowing the 80 inbuilt cameras to view the faces of travellers from various angles and identify them accordingly through facial recognition and iris scanning. At the end of the tunnel, visitors will either pass through or be stopped for further checks (like Angela), at a quick pace.

FACIAL RECOGNITION ENABLES MARKETERS TO HYPERTARGET

Nowadays, marketers have high hopes of facial recognition. Compared to the previously discussed innovations in this book, facial expression analysis is most capable of targeting people and approaching them in real time (see chapter about real-time communication). Marketers are offered a new way to interact with, and get attention from, consumers to sell their products and services. Especially in places where people are waiting or standing in front of a shop window display. Marketers can craft tailored messages based on, for instance, age, gender, skin, mood, viewing direction, moment of the day and even people's buying history. The coffee company Douwe Egberts detected people yawning, offering them a free cup of coffee for an energy boost. Virgin Mobile introduced a short interactive ad, which detected user blinks to serve as "clicks" to advance a story, and changed the story based on the user's eye movements.

THE USAGE OF FACIAL RECOGNITION IN HEALTH

Not only in marketing and the security sector but also in healthcare, facial expression analysis proves to be beneficial. A specific example is a walking stick with facial recognition for blind people that can recognise faces from ten metres away, so they can greet the people by their name. Or a 'cause-and-effect' health app, showing people how they will look if they continue their bad food habits, changing them into fat people.

In the next paragraph, Natasja Bogers and Jacqueline Martinali will discuss the merits of facial-expression analysis. This is a technique that does not focus on determining the identity of people but instead on assessing their emotions. It does not register data of people per se, as is mostly the case for facial recognition.

WHY YOU WANT TO KNOW IF YOUR CUSTOMERS ARE BORED, AND HOW TO FIND OUT

By Natasja Bogers & Jacqueline Martinali
Marketing Communications Specialists
Noldus Information Technology

Emotions run through everything in our everyday life. Your emotions define your mood and your behaviour. When you feel happy, you are more likely to have a good day in the office and enjoy the things you do. It might also make you more receptive to that billboard you saw at the bus stop on your way to work. If you are moody or even bored while watching an advertisement, chances are that you are not very interested in the product, let alone want to buy it. No wonder researchers, advertisers, and marketers are interested in these emotions. They play a key role in non-verbal communication and are essential in understanding human behaviour. This is the same reason why many marketing conferences are filled with talks about advertising effectiveness or the most persuasive texts for packaging design. This general interest in emotions is one of the reasons why facial-expression analysis is often used in consumer and behaviour research, because facial expressions often mirror the emotions that people experience. Data about emotions provide crucial insights that allow researchers to explain complex human behaviours in greater depth.

THE ADDED VALUE OF FACIAL-EXPRESSION SOFTWARE

The question is: how to get hold of these data? You can always just ask a person. However, this is unlikely to get honest, objective, replies. People usually find it very difficult to comment on their own emotions and state of mind. Self-reported emotions do not necessarily mirror what a person is actually feeling at that moment. Besides that, asking how someone feels also means you get an 'after the fact' reply, while the real-time emotions are what advertisers, for instance, want to know, because they can customise their ads to the real-time emotions of members of their target group. Facial-expression analysis software[3] is an addition as a research tool in consumer behaviour research, as it helps to collect valuable real-time data.

Based on the original basic emotions defined by Paul Ekman[4], effective facial-expression software automatically determines the presence and intensity of happiness, sadness, anger, surprise, fear, disgust, and contempt, as well as neutral emotions. This software is only effective when validated by using several human coders[5], reaching a high degree of agreement concerning Ekman's basic emotions. Using validated facial-expression software will ensure better understanding of human-human, human-machine, and human-product interactions.

PREDICTING CONSUMER BEHAVIOUR BY DETERMINING AFFECTIVE ATTITUDES

While facial-expression software has already been able to detect basic emotions, it should also be able to figure out affective attitudes. Attitudes in general are dispositions to evaluate objects, groups, events, or symbols in a negative or positive way. They include three different components: affective attitudes or evaluations (feelings/emotions), cognitions (thoughts, beliefs, and knowledge), and actions (past behaviours or experiences). Let's look closer at affective attitudes: the feelings or emotions that are something evoked, such as engagement, boredom, sympathy, or even hate. These complex emotional states differ from the basic emotions described by Ekman. The strength with which an attitude is experienced is often a good predictor of behaviour. The stronger the attitude, the more likely it should lead to behaviour. So knowing about people's attitudes can help predict their behaviour. This means valuable information for behaviour researchers and marketers, as this can help in predicting whether people will buy a product or service after seeing an advertisement. Advertisers might also measure the type of affective reactions towards their advertising campaigns in order to optimise them. This may even happen in real time. For instance, a Spanish theatre related the entrance fee, paid after the performance, to the number of smiles of each visitor. When people smiled less, the entrance fee was lowered.

With state-of the art facial-expression analysis software, emotions of test participants can be examined even further, as that software should be able to measure three commonly used affective attitudes: 'interest', 'boredom', and 'confusion'. To estimate these affective attitudes, the intensities of a number of action units, which are actions of individual facial muscles or groups of muscles, are determined.

FOCUS ON THE RELEVANT ATTITUDES

Because of the increasing interest in automatically measuring affective states, more investments have been made in further developing facial-expression software. Nowadays it is even possible to allow users to specify their own 'custom expressions'. So if you need to know, for example, if your test participants feel embarrassed, attracted, or excited by watching your advertisement, you can design your own algorithms by combining expressions and action units into a new self-defined state. Such 'do it yourself' expressions can make all the difference in the success of the launch of a new product or website. In all, the future looks bright for facial-expression software for a variety of purposes.

A SCIENTIFIC PERSPECTIVE

Although the professional industry has been speculating about the effects of facial recognition, communication science has only recently started to research this innovation.

The chances are high that people will devote attention to the tailored messages based on facial recognition and that they will process the information based on facial recognition analyses systematically, with a high level of elaboration. Such information is very 'close' to them and thus potentially highly relevant to them[6]. When the offered information is highly relevant, aligning with the goals of consumers, coming to them at the right time at the right place, it serves as a tool, facilitating choices, making life easier[7].

PEOPLE'S NEED FOR UNIQUENESS

The level of processing will depend on the context in which the message is received. For instance, when people receive a personalised message after passing a billboard they will not always be motivated to process that information because it interferes with their daily routine, walking from A to B at a certain pace. When people are aware of the attempt to persuade them, they might counteract and even dissociate from the offer[8]. People's privacy concerns will influence the effectiveness of the information sent after facial recognition. The more people experience privacy concerns, the less they will appreciate the tailor-made offerings, because they will feel violated in their privacy. A way that organisations can avoid this risk is to be transparent about how the data were collected and to assure people that they will treat their data with respect[9]. Lastly, the acceptance of the message will be related to people's need for uniqueness[10], a personality trait that differs between people. People who feel very unique may be more sensitive to – and feel attracted to – tailor-made offerings than people who do not feel that unique.

The increase in the adoption of facial-expression analysis and facial-recognition technology across a variety of sectors may seem like science fiction. Nowadays it might help to improve consumers' day-to-day lives – in terms of security, healthcare, commerce, and convenience.

FACIAL RECOGNITION AND ULTRA-TARGETED ADVERTISING

The technique will improve to perfection in the near future, reducing mistakes in identifying people and their emotions. As the technology improves, we'll no doubt see it further incorporated into situations that would have seemed unimaginable years ago. In the near future, struggling to find a password will certainly be a thing of the past and a simple nod to a cashier will be sufficient to pay for your groceries.

Facial-recognition technology may lead to ultra-targeted advertising, made possible by the widespread use of social media. In marketing, facial-expression analysis seems to offer advantages for marketers as well as consumers. Marketers use facial-expression analysis to tailor their messages to the right consumers, thus making their offerings more meaningful and more persuasive[11], increasing the chance of sales. The advantage for consumers is that they will only be exposed to relevant messages based on their personal needs and wants[12].

A POWERFUL AD TOOL OR PRIVACY NIGHTMARE?

Although there is a lot of positive attention paid to the possibilities of facial recognition, it is also heavily debated. Most people find the idea of facial recognition creepy because they value their privacy. Creepy in the sense that facial recognition enables the storage of data about you while you do not know who uses these data and for what purposes. Ultra-targeted advertising especially might arouse feelings of privacy violation. People will get the uncanny feeling that companies know much more about them than preferred. Therefore, some people might be eager to scrutinise each persuasion attempt that makes use of facial recognition, for the simple reason that they do not know which personal data were used to make the offering.

A shortcoming of facial expression analysis is that, just like neuromarketing, it will never be fully capable of detecting *why* people are showing an emotional response, making the gained insights, for instance towards an advertising campaign, somewhat subjective.

BOUNDARIES FOR INSTITUTIONS FOR USE AND STORAGE OF PERSONAL DATA

Just as with other privacy issues, the solution lies in making clear agreements around transparency and informed consent. When organisations use facial recognition for safety reasons, in healthcare or in marketing, they should ensure that only gender and age are analysed, for instance to give them personalised information or so that they can use aggregated instead of individual data. And, of course, people should have consented to certain institutions using their data. There have to be strict regulations for institutions about what personal data they are allowed to capture and store.

Finally, we would like you to think about the following provocative issue: go back to Angela in the introduction to our chapter. As we all know, she also knew that at the border her identity was checked using facial recognition. But did she also know that, as a next step, her emotions betrayed something related to safety? Who is to decide that facial expression analysis should, or should not, happen at the border?

In short, facial recognition is seen as a promising development. There are shortcomings, which are mostly privacy related, and the future will show whether or not these issues can be solved in an agreeable way for all parties involved.

CLASSIFICATION

★★★★★　　★★★★★　　★★★★★　　★★★★★　　★★★★★

References and notes

1　Retrieved from: https://searchenterpriseai.techtarget.com/definition/facial-recognition

2　Zebrowitz, L. (2018). Reading faces: Window to the soul? Routledge.

3　Facial-expressions analysis software such as FaceReader developed by our company.

4　Ekman P., Friesen W.V. & Hager J.C. (2002). The facial action coding system. Second edition. Salt Lake City: Research Nexus eBook. London: Weidenfeld & Nicolson.

5　Lewinski, P.; den Uyl, T.M. & Butler, C. (2014). Automated facial coding: validation of basic emotions and FACS AUs in FaceReader. Journal of Neuroscience, Psychology, and Economics, 7(4), 227-236.

6　Buijzen, M., Van Reijmersdal, E.A., & Owen, L.H. (2010). Introducing the PCMC model: An investigative framework for young people's processing of commercial media content. Communication Theory, 20, 427-450. doi:10.1111/j.1468-2885.2010.01370.x

7　Fogg, B. J., Cuellar, G., & Danielson, D. (2002). Motivating, influencing, and persuading users. In J. Jacko & A. Sears (Eds.), The human-computer interaction handbook: Fundamentals, evolving technologies and emerging applications (pp. 133-147). Hillsdale, NJ: Erlbaum.

8　Friestad, M., & Wright, P. (1994). The persuasion knowledge model: How people cope with persuasion attempts. Journal of Consumer Research, 1-31.

9　Aguirre, E., Mahr, D., Grewal, D., de Ruyter, K., & Wetzels, M. (2015). Unraveling the personalization paradox: The effect of information collection and trust-building strategies on online advertisement effectiveness. Journal of Retailing, 91(1), 34-49. doi:10.1016/j.jretai.2014.09.005.

10　Tian, K. T., Bearden, W.O., & Hunter, G.L. (2001). Consumers' need for uniqueness: scale development and validation. Journal of Consumer Research, 28, 50-66.

11　Maslowska, E., Putte, B. V. D., & Smit, E. G. (2011). The effectiveness of personalized email newsletters and the role of personal characteristics. Cyberpsychology, Behavior, and Social Networking, 14(12), 765-770.

12　Lewinski, P., Fransen, M. L., & Tan, E.S.H. (2014). Predicting advertising effectiveness by facial expressions in response to amusing persuasive stimuli. Journal of Neuroscience, Psychology, and Economics, doi: 10.1037/npe0000012.

VISIONS OF THE FUTURE

In this final chapter we give the floor to experts who share their view of the future with us. Interestingly they all mention different game changers and their contributions combined will give us a comprehensive window on 'what is next'.

Lotte Willemsen emphasises that AI-driven agents will rapidly emerge in our networked society. She discusses what the consequences of this major change are for digital communication.

Wrapping things up, *Aurelie Valtat* makes a case for digital influencers being the game-changers of the future, offering both reputational and sales benefits at a reasonable cost. She issues a warning over a new form of digital divide that may emerge.

Marnix van Gisbergen challenges us, claiming that virtual reality will unavoidably be part of our lives. He explains how current technologies are being used to transform VR into a mass medium, even to the extent of becoming the dominant medium within a media-convergence-driven society.

Finally, *Justien Marseille* takes us to the year 2049 when, surprisingly, the state of communication technology may well be biological. She proposes new lines of ethical algorithms and how we can safeguard our privacy. She concludes with a statement: As the digital revolution comes closer to maturation, the only certainty is that new radical evolutions lie ahead.

SAY HI TO AI

Lotte M. Willemsen
Professor in Applied Science
Creating010, Rotterdam University of Applied Science

In the next ten years, the Web of the People (people connected with each other through social media), will quickly turn into the Web of the World (smart objects connected with each other through the internet of things), and eventually also the Web of Agents (intelligent agents equipped with artificial intelligence (AI)[1,2]. This means that people and AI-driven agents such as conversational assistants, chatbots, and voice assistants are all likely to interact with each other in communication networks. How AI will impact our profession is difficult to predict, but I strongly believe that we can plan for it. This begins with asking questions about the current applications of AI as already witnessed in society today.

CAN PEOPLE RELATE WITH NON-HUMAN ENTITIES?

The emergence of AI-driven agents in our networked society does come with intriguing questions. What types of content and conversations can be effectively created and shared by intelligent, non-human entities? How can we differentiate 'real' from 'real fake', when the boundaries between human and non-human, and physical and digital, are fading away? What is real to start with? And can people relate with non-human entities, even when they are aware of the fact that they are not made of flesh and blood, but bits and bytes?

DEMARCATION BETWEEN HUMAN AND NON-HUMAN

Academic research shows that it is common for people to attribute human characteristics such as senses, emotions, and a free will to non-human entities, a process that is also known as anthropomorphism. Due to this process, we believe plants to be thirsty, computers to be confused, and navigation systems to be stubborn. This unconscious process is often consciously prompted in users by means of communications and design. Take for example the all-electric, partially 3D-printed, autonomous vehicle that has been produced by Local Motors to offer a sustainable transportation option for cities, hospitals, campuses, and entertainment districts. The car has been given a human name (Olli), a human voice, and a grille resembling a smiling face. The reason is simple: research shows that we are more prone to trust something when it looks human[3]. However it may also be misleading to equip AI-systems with human appearances, because humans might expect more than the system may be able to offer. This is why ethicists argue for not giving robots an appearance that is too humanlike. These is of critical importance for technologies that intend to replace humans in performing complex tasks. When consumers interact with the autonomous vehicle Olli, it is obvious that Olli is an object.

COMPUTER-GENERATED INFLUENCERS

The demarcation between human and non-human may be less obvious for other types of creations. One such creation is Lil Miquela, already introduced in the chapter on influencers, an Instagram user with 1.5 billion followers who models for clothing brands such as Prada, and uses her fame to promote songs but also political ideologies such as Black Lives Matter. Anyone who takes a closer look will learn that Miquela is nothing more than a computer-generated character produced as parts of a digital arts project. Yet, this does not discourage people from following, interacting and bonding with 'her', as evidenced by comments such as "I am in love with u ❤" underneath Miquela's photos.

To many users, Miquela is as real as other flesh-and-blood influencers, who use filters to brush out human imperfections and editing apps to embellish their selfies. "I am confused, so are you a robot or not?" are comments that followers regularly post in response to Lil Miquela, who relies on storytelling techniques to create an authentic persona. For organisations that are seeking influential persona to promote their goods and services, the non-human nature of Miquela may be a benefit rather than a shortcoming. Everything that Miquela does, says, and posts is carefully staged, planned, and crafted, thereby giving sponsors more control over the actions of a computer-generated influencer than a real influencer. Hence, brands seem less susceptible to reputation scandals when they are endorsed by computer-generated influencers.

Do consumers deserve to know whether the entities that inspire, inform, entertain, or serve us are human or not? From an ethical point of view, the right answer to this question would probably be 'yes'. The creators of Lil Miquela are transparent about the non-human nature of their creation. The same holds for the creators of many bots that can be found on Twitter. For example, the Twitter bioof @TrumpSideKik informs that this account belongs to an AI duplicate of the president, that learns to speak like the real Donald Trump by using comments from his official Twitter account. And on Fox Business you will find a disclosure underneath news stories about stock markets and sports games: "This story was generated by Automated Insights", informing readers that AI was used to analyse data, come up with story ideas, and even write sentences.

From a business points of view, the right answer to this question would probably be 'yes' as well. If people find out that a previously deemed human agent appears to be non-human, they may feel misled, or maybe even worse, 'uncanny'. There is a fine line between realistic and unrealistic creations, which if breached causes uncanny feelings or revulsion in people[4]. To prevent such 'uncanny valley' effects from happening, Autodesk gave purple eyes to 'Ava', an AI-driven assistant that appears on its website and will later be placed in Autodesk software. Her appearance looks remarkably lifelike, as does her behaviour. This is made possible by her ability to analyse facial expressions and voices for the presence of emotions like joy, sadness, and frustration. Real-time knowledge of a person's emotional state allows Ava to respond with a natural emotional reaction on her face in return.

SOFT SKILLS ARE IMMENSELY VALUABLE FOR AN AI-DRIVEN FUTURE

What do these examples teach us about our own role in tomorrow's networked society? Will we still be relevant, when the Web of People shifts to the Web of Agents? If AI is the future, do we need to disrupt ourselves, and focus on learning skills such as Science, Technology, Engineering, and Mathematics (STEM)? Of course, it is never a bad idea to learn new skills, but the soft skills that communication professionals have acquired as part of their study and training are immensely valuable for an AI-driven future. AI-driven agents are developed by humans, and as the various examples in this contribution show, most of them are intended to behave like humans and to influence humans. Hence, skills such as persuasive writing, which is very useful for writing scripts for AI, good communications, empathy, and ethical decision making are of pivotal importance to ensure that AI will resonate on a human level, and will be free of the unethical consequences that this nascent technology may bring. Indeed, tech companies from Silicon Valley state that STEM skills aren't the most important skills[5]. This is supported by research showing that the most important predictors of career success at tech companies such as Google are abilities such as communication skills and the insights of others[6], as these skills are achieved after a lot of effort and training, I follow Philip J. Hanlon, President of Dartmouth College, in his plea to stop using the word "soft skills" and instead refer to these abilities as "power skills".

Concluding, AI-driven agents will be important communicators in our networked society. Yet, communication professionals are imperative for developing and training AI-driven agents that are truly effective.

References and notes

1   Duivestein, S., & Bloem, J. (2011). We the web: Defusing the big data frenzy. Retrieved from: https://www.ict-books.com/topics/digital/vint-report-we-the-web-lowres-pdf1-en-info.

2   Duivestein, S. (2016). In de toekomst heeft iedereen een digitale butler [Everyone will have a digital butler in the future]. Retrieved from: https://www.marketingfacts.nl/berichten/in-de-toekomst-heeft-iedereen-een-digitale-butler

3   Waytz, A., Heafner, J., & Epley, N. (2014). The mind in the machine: Anthropomorphism increases trust in an autonomous vehicle. Journal of Experimental Social Psychology, 52, 113-117.

4   Gray, K., & Wegner, D. M. (2012). Feeling robots and human zombies: Mind perception and the uncanny valley. Cognition, 125(1), 125-130.

5   Shen, L. (2018, October 3). Want to work on AI? Study philosophy or communications, execs say. Fortune. Retrieved from http://fortune.com/2018/10/02/ai-philosophy-communications-technology/

6   Agarwal, A. (2018, October 2). Data reveals why the 'soft' in 'soft skills' is a major misnomer. Forbes. Retrieved from https://www.forbes.com/sites/anantagarwal/2018/10/02/data-reveals-why-the-soft-in-soft-skills-is-a-major-misnomer/#c7808c66f7b0

FUTURE OF DIGITAL INFLUENCING

By Aurelie Valtat
Head of Digital Presence and Internal Communication
European Commission, DG International Cooperation and Development

In hindsight, word-of-mouth remains - even if not face to face - the most effective way of shaping consumer or employee behaviour. As a result, new forms of influence have emerged online, now that a majority of people are active on one or more social networks.

MICRO-INFLUENCERS ARE THE FASTEST GROWING SEGMENT

Digital influencers have become a boon for many companies, offering both reputational and sales benefits at a reasonable cost. These influencers are not limited to real-world celebrities; in fact, digital influencers with large numbers of followers (above 100,000) whose fame started online remain the most sought-after group. Although as of yet there are no studies to support this view, I believe that this is mainly due to the fact that these influencers are digital natives.

Micro-influencers, however, are the fastest growing segment, with bloggers and vloggers flocking to networks for their own "15 minutes of fame"[1]. Marketers have jumped on the bandwagon and are now wooing this audience for sponsored content and brand ambassadorship contracts. Watch out for micro-influencer marketing in the coming years. As authenticity and trustworthiness remain the top qualities that followers look for in an influencer, those who once rose to fame thanks to these qualities are now losing out on juicy advertising contracts because of their openly marketed and less 'authentic' content.

MARKET OF EMPLOYEE AMBASSADOR SOFTWARE

Consumer-to-consumer (C2C) marketing, as influencer marketing is also called, is not limited to marketing communications. More and more corporate and internal communicators are exploring how to build rapport with digital influencers, both large and small. The benefits for a brand's reputation of third-party endorsements from YouTubers or influential Instagrammers seem important enough to justify significant ad budgets being diverted to them, despite the lack of clear evidence from research about the real reputational benefits one can expect from influencer marketing.

Even internal communications have fallen prey to the lure of (micro) influencer marketing with the recent arrival on the market of employee ambassador software. How do these applications work? They leverage the personal connections of employees on social media to spread positive corporate messages. More and more internal blogs feature staff with interesting insights into the company's life, rather than the traditional CEO blog, in an attempt to be more authentic and to generate more empathy for company decisions.

Despite its bright future, a number of obstacles are looming ahead for digital influencing as we know it today: the lack of research evidence, market saturation, ethical and legal considerations, and in-app evolutions.

LACK OF RESEARCH EVIDENCE

Despite its appeal to marketers and communicators, influencer marketing is a field where, surprisingly, little research has been undertaken. This has led to unsatisfactory results when it comes to measuring its effectiveness in terms of brand reputation and sales conversion. And even where past successes have consolidated the good collaboration between a brand and an online influencer, one is never immune from a sudden personality or lifestyle change, impacting the fit between the two brands. This unreliability of digital influencers, as opposed to non-human advertising means, may explain the lack of available research in this new field of marketing.

A growing number of digital influencers make their living from influencer marketing, which in turn attracts a growing number of users trying to become digital influencers. This market saturation will make it ever more difficult, even for micro-influencers, to retain brand attention.

ETHICAL AND LEGAL CONSIDERATIONS

Recent data breaches and fake political news scandals forced Facebook in 2018 to revisit its personal data management set-up and to be more transparent about who sponsors political content on its platform. As digital influencers continue to subtly "sell" the brands that pay them on their channels using storytelling and visual tricks, more and more questions will arise regarding the transparency of their relationship with sponsors and brands. Today, too few followers realise that the content they are seeing is actually promoted.

As the competition for brand attention increases among digital influencers who are quickly learning to take advantage of the algorithm of the platform they are using[2], platforms themselves will be tempted to offer specific advantages to retain influencers and keep them happy. This is already the case with Instagram where accounts with more than 10,000 followers enjoy perks not available to other accounts. Another possible route for future in-app improvements could be shared benefits from the monetisation of a given transaction between the influencer and the app itself.

A NEW FORM OF DIGITAL DIVIDE WILL EMERGE

While technologies such as artificial intelligence, virtual reality, and face recognition will no doubt have a direct and significant impact on marketing in the near future, mediated communications through the use of digital influencers is not likely to disappear. The success of relationships between brands, companies and influencers will however depend just as much on the proper use of data and the right ethical approach as on a more intangible skill, which is identifying the right fit between a company's brand and that of the influencer and maintaining that fit over time, despite the evolving nature of the influencer's own status.

The impact that such a race to influence will have on younger generations is yet unknown. One can imagine that a new form of digital divide will emerge, one where those who master online influence will be able to leverage their skills to generate significant personal benefits at the expense of the influence of "digital illiterates". This may in turn possibly perpetuate, or on the contrary disrupt, existing patterns of real-world influence among societal groups.

References and notes
1   Adapted from Andy Warhol's expression coined in 1968.
2   Cotter, K. (2018). Playing the visibility game: How digital influencers and algorithms negotiate influence on Instagram. New Media & Society, 1461444818815684.

DIGITAL DÉJÀ VU KNOWN AS VIRTUAL REALITY

By Marnix S. van Gisbergen
Professor Digital Media Concepts
Breda University of Applied Sciences

Let us start with two assignments before reading this chapter. First, mention a 'new' medium that has recently appeared. An easy task probably (and otherwise read this book). However, now mention a medium that has disappeared. This seems a simple request, but as you may now have noticed, it is not. It is actually quite difficult to mention a medium that has truly disappeared. You might accidentally come up with an example that still exists, such as the fax, introduced around 1850 and still used by means of digital transmissions and standalone machines. Or you may come up with an example that has only recently ceased production and as such is still present among audiences (e.g. the video cassette recorder, the manufacturing of which stopped in 2016). Other examples that pop up might not have disappeared but have been 'eaten' by another medium (e.g. virtual fax machines can be downloaded on your smartphone) or 'changed' so much we call them something different (e.g. the term 'video' seems to have disappeared for recording devices, even though we sometimes still refer to online films as 'online videos'). Media, especially the so-called mass media like radio, television, and the internet, all seem to have survived the rise of new media. So what are the chances that Virtual Reality (VR) or Augmented Reality (AR) will disappear[1]?

VR RECURRENCE

We can safely argue that VR and AR will not disappear, despite recent sceptical articles that refer to the decline of VR[2]. We will spend a significant proportion of our time inside a mediated digital VR. However, the question is how much time and with what purpose? Due to the increasing number of media, the selection of a medium becomes increasingly more complex and important, especially as we do not suddenly get more time to spend on media and budgets for organisations do not increase with the same speed as new media arise. Hence, the key question is: what kind of role will VR have? What is the added value of VR compared to other media?

VR ADOPTION

There are two main routes through which VR can become part of our daily mediated lives. The first route is to become a mainstream (mass) medium, used by many people. A second route is a more aggressive one, in which VR will even become the dominant medium, integrating existing media into its core existence. Currently the industry is working hard for the adoption of VR as a (mass) medium. This adoption depends on developments within five dimensions: 1 *Channel* (improvements in VR hardware and technologies); 2 *Creation* (the ease of producing VR content); 3 *Content* (to have and easily find and access content); 4 *Connection* (ease of sharing and communicating within VR content), and 5 *Cost reductions*[3]. Within these developments, the main question is: "What will VR add to existing media?" Currently the main benefit is the unique experiences of being in a mediated simulation that 'feels real', as discussed in the chapter Virtual Reality. Research indicates indeed that VR has an added value in creating immersive experiences compared to other media. However, currently VR is far from being a mass medium. Only a few VR devices have been sold in comparison with other media. For instance, 3M PlayStation VR headsets were sold between 2016 and 2018, which means that around 4% of PlayStation 4 owners have one[4]. In addition, VR is being used mainly as a solitary medium, despite many social VR possibilities and technical developments. Current world records do not reveal VR as a mass medium yet. The World Book of Records mentions a record of 1,867 users who simultaneously viewed a three-minute 360[0] VR experience (March, 2017) and 2,340 people who used VR displays simultaneously across multiple venues in China in October 2018[5].

VR CONVERGENCE

The second road deals with media convergence. Convergence is seen as the coming together of two things[6]. On the one hand, media convergence refers to the merging of different media into one 'super' medium. On the other hand, it refers to a process where different media still exist but have connected content that may even originate from one overall media ecosystem[7] – one medium with several manifestations (mediamorphoses). The question is whether VR will play the dominant role within this convergence. When we look at the developments within the four technology dimensions (sensory, location, interaction and control), it seems like VR holds some good cards[8]. Within the sensory dimension, we see improved technologies. Take for instance the newly (February 2019) released VR headset that runs at human-eye resolution[9]. In addition, new senses like smell are being added by means of new VR technologies[10]. Also, new technologies appear that stimulate touch, making use of vibrating actuators, haptic feedback systems, and electrical impulses to stimulate skin receptors and nerve endings to an extent where pain and pleasure are directly communicated to the brain[11]. These forms of Transcranial Direct Current Stimulation (or tDCS) are very new when it comes to VR[12]. A current popular example of how this could look is the Azanaband. This is a prototyped device that sends pulses through your body via a device worn round the neck; it was used to promote a Channel 4 new series 'Kiss me first'.

Within the interaction dimension, digital media twins are created and existing media are connected with the VR environment. A new Microsoft filed patent shows for instance the possibility of tethering your smartphone through the VR headset[13]. The location tracking moves beyond body tracking and already includes voice and direct brain control[14] as well as foveated rendering and eye tracking to interact within the VR world. In addition, we see the blending of VR with AR in order to ensure the interaction between the real and virtual worlds. Although of course the question remains whether we can see a real convergence, as the benefit of interacting with the real world might also jeopardise the virtual experience.

Within the manipulation dimension, technologies are utilised ranging from improved Motion Capturing technologies to advanced 3D scanning studios, and from photogrammetry to volumetric video, creating real looking and behaving avatars. Fascinating examples are the digital humans created at Soul Machines together with IBM/Watson[15] and the Siren project with, among others, Epic Games[16]. Technology is ultimately moving towards the creation of your digital self, or even a better digital extension, as discussed in the chapter Virtual Reality. The question is: how many of these developments do we need to make VR a mass or dominant media? Research also shows that more realism does not always lead to more realistic (VR) behaviour and increased experiences[17]. It can even alienate us due to uncanny effect reasons, a topic discussed in the chapter Robots. However, despite the aforementioned technical developments, we at the same time are witnessing user rejection behaviour towards VR.

VR REWARD-EFFORT PARADOX

It seems that we are dealing right now with a VR reward-effort paradox. On the one hand, VR appears to provide us with the ultimate freedom to experience the most realistic mediated experience. The reward to use VR is often explained in terms of a unique experience based on presence, realism, naturalness, and engagement. On the other hand, this is not offered to us in a seamless manner. Using VR is complicated and no medium today exists that asks so much of our attention and (processing) effort. VR seems to be the most demanding medium of all media that, contrary to other media and AR, currently does not allow us to connect with the non-mediated reality and with other media. Despite the fact that many books and movies describe a VR-driven society (e.g., the Lawnmower Man, the Matrix, Tron, Total Recall and the recently released movie Ready Player One), it is not easy to be in VR. There might be limits to the time we are able to spend inside VR, despite current world records of a 42-hour non-stop game marathon and a 50-hour non-stop 360o VR movie-viewing session[18]. As one of the record holders explains: *"Being completely immersed for such a long time was a huge mental strain. It was also physically demanding but an incredibly forward-looking experience"*[19]. This creates a catch-22 context. Do we want, and allow for, huge investments in a medium that demands so much of us with the promise of transforming it into a medium that will set us free?

The reward to actually let yourself be transported into a virtual world, and put on those helmets, must be very high – at least more satisfying than the digital experiences created through other media. So while more research is needed to answer this question, the real answer to whether the reward is worth the effort, is to stop reading this print medium, and start experiencing VR yourself.

References and notes

1 Out of practical laziness we do assume you have read Chapters Virtual reality and Augmented reality concerning what VR and AR entails.

2 Windsor, R. (2018, September 06). Virtual reality: Steep decline is more than a hiccup. Forbes. Retrieved from: https://www.forbes.com/sites/richardwindsoreurope/2018/09/06/virtual-reality-steep-decline-is-more-than-a-hiccup/

3 Van Gisbergen, S. M. (2016) How rearranging a media puzzle, brings virtual reality into being. NHTV Breda University of Applied Sciences. ISBN 978-90-819011-8-5.

4 Lang, W. (2018, August 08). PlayStation VR passes 3 million units sold. Road to VR. Retrieved from: https://www.roadtovr.com/playstation-vr-3-million-units-sold-sales-figures-install-base/

5 www.guinnessworldrecords.com

6 Wilkonson, J., & Grant, A. E. (Eds). (2009). Understanding media convergence: The state of the field. Oxford University Press.

7 Jenkins, H. (2004). The cultural logic of media convergence. International Journal of Cultural Studies, 7(1), 33-43.

8 Van Gisbergen, S. M. (2016) How rearranging a media puzzle, brings virtual reality into being. NHTV Breda University of Applied Sciences. ISBN 978-90-819011-8-5.

9 Retrieved from: www.varjo.com.

10 Retrieved from: www.feelreal.com.

11 For an overview see: Stone, Z. (2018, April 01). Haptic controllers bring real pain to VR games. Wired. Retrieved from: https://www.wired.com/story/haptic-controllers-for-vr-bring-real-pain-to-games/

12 Lee, S. J., & Chun, M. H. (2014). Combination transcranial direct current stimulation and virtual reality therapy for upper extremity training in patients with subacute stroke. Archives of Physical Medicine and Rehabilitation, 95(3), 431-438.

13 Carlton, B. (2019, February 01). Newly revealed Microsoft patent points towards HoloLens 2. VR Scout. Retrieved from: https://vrscout.com/news/microsoft-patent-hololens-2-device/.

14 Lécuyer, A., Lotte, F., Reilly, R. B., Leeb, R., Hirose, M., & Slater, M. (2008). Brain-computer interfaces, virtual reality, and videogames. Computer, 41(10), 66-72.

15 Retrieved from: www.soulmachines.com.

16 Alvarez, E. (2019, March 14). With 'Siren,' unreal engine blurs the line between CGI and reality. Retrieved from: https://www.engadget.com/2018/03/22/siren-epic-games-unreal-engine-vicon/.

17 Van Gisbergen, M. S., Kovacs, M. H., Campos, F., van der Heeft, M., & Vugts, V. (2018). What we don't know. The effect of realism in virtual reality on experience and behaviour. In In T. Jung & M. C. tom Dieck (Eds.), Augmented reality and virtual reality (pp. 45-57). Cham: Springer International Publishing

18 www.guinnessworldrecords.com.

19 Stephenson, K. (2017, April 17). Cyberlink Corp sets new virtual reality viewing marathon record. Retrieved from: http://www.guinnessworldrecords.com/news/2017/4/cyberlink-corp-sets-new-virtual-reality-record-469072.

IN 2049 COMMUNICATION MAY WELL BE BIOLOGICAL

By Justien H. Marseille
Futurist / Senior Lecturer
The Future Institute / Creating 010, Rotterdam University of Applied Sciences

In this final contribution, we will be looking ahead towards possible scenarios for the future of digital communication: how will we, for example in the year 2049, look back upon today's cutting-edge innovations? Fields of research and developments such as persuasion profiling or real-time communication now seem very innovative, perhaps even a bit odd. Thirty years from now, they may well have become the 'new normal'.

HORSELESS CARRIAGE SYNDROME

As we look ahead into the future, we would be wise to remember Marshall McLuhan's 'horse-less carriage syndrome': the tendency to build the future, using today's new technology, to address the needs of the past. In the case of information technology, algorithms that focus mainly on targeting advertisements and maximising relevance for audiences are based upon the assumption that in the future, increasing the dissemination of messages will still be the norm. However, we should also consider the possibility that changes in media usage and social-media culture will shift the demand from spreading more messages and reaching wider audiences, to curating the resulting overload of information. Using digital technology to continue doing what we have always done, would thus amount to designing a future 'with all other things being equal'. In doing so, we overlook the possibilities of disruptive change and underestimate the impact of paradigm shifts. The future will result from changes within a complex tangle of political, economic, social, technological, legal, and environmental forces. Seeing technology as anything more than one of these forces is like reinventing the carriage without considering the long-term effects of mass transportation. The digital revolution is not about providing better ways of sustaining old habits; it is about using innovative technologies to reinvent the ways in which we can address the core values behind these habits – such as the need to belong, to be safe, and to stand out. We cannot consider the future without questioning the past.

TECHNOLOGY MAY BECOME DOMINATED BY BIOLOGY

Besides focusing on how innovation can bring about positive change, we should also consider possible transformations in what we currently believe to be normal. The future beyond the digital revolution will result from an exploration of paradigm shifts made possible through innovation: will it be a world in which more information leads to better distribution and less scarcity? A world in which big data and machine learning gradually make the future as predictable as the weather? Looking ahead at what is still a constantly changing future, some possible developments may seem out of place in a publication on digital communication such as this one; consider for example the discovery of the wood wide web (to which we shall return later), or research in the field of brain-to-brain communication, potentially heralding an era in which technology may become dominated by biology. We should also be mindful of the changing nature of the communication process, and of the need for a response to the increasing amount of messages and noise resulting from the explosion in the number of broadcasters.

TRUTH FILTERS

Ours is an age of overwhelming noise amplified by algorithms. Curators are becoming a rare and valuable commodity. Messages spread through social media are endlessly echoed in the form of retweets, likes and nudges, driven by algorithms. Though the original messages may have been sent to targeted recipients, their echoes become noise by the time they have reached a public that has no means of filtering truth from falsehood, amusement from influence. During the past decade, the ever-changing media landscape has seen an increasing concentration of institutional mass media[1], accompanied by an explosion of micro-media channels (i.e. media run by individual users, including social media and blogs) with an estimated 2.9 billion individual broadcasters in 2019.[2] The distinctions between commercial, personal, and persuasive communication have become increasingly blurred, as have the boundaries between advertising, fake news, and civic reporting. This should lead to a renewed focus on gatekeeping and contextual editing: user reviews and curatorial algorithms (which Facebook and Google for instance are already experimenting with) are but a first step towards unravelling the noise.

NEW LINE OF ETHICAL ALGORITHMS

We should thus expect the development of a whole new line of 'ethical' algorithms that address the need for demarcating and curating content, rather than merely enabling broadcasters to further refine their strategies of behavioural targeting. This new ethical curator could, for instance, track the origin of the content and put it into context, making the path of 'influencers' visible to the receiver, or facilitate the further development of technological 'truth filters', which identify the original broadcaster, their motivations, and the interests behind the message. The focus will then shift from spreading to checking. Currently we do this mostly through human peers; a move towards algorithms can help further establish who the original broadcaster of the message was, which parties have contributed to its dissemination, and which lobbying system has contributed to the opinions being presented. This would entail a

shift in the focus and use of algorithms, from reaching an ever-wider audience, to filtering and excluding unwanted noise. At some point in the early 21st century, we stopped paying for news and other information; by 2049, we may well have to pay in order to shield ourselves from the influence of unwanted information.

SAFEGUARDING PRIVACY

A crucial next step will be to reconsider the core value of the gatekeeping role in the information process. This step may be driven by industry requirements, cultural needs, or international legislation. Should our privacy be safeguarded on a collective scale, or rather through individuals' privilege-based control of access to their data? Beyond the political question of whose responsibility this should be, a more immediate question may be how technology might enable different solutions. Blockchain technology seems a good candidate for the second, individual approach. The principle behind the blockchain is a decentralised protocol for recording each step of a transaction or other communication process. The blockchain hype has so far been mainly associated with the world of finance. As it hits the broader field of communication, the technology can be used to reveal which message has been transmitted by whom, and with which intentions. For example, experiments have already been conducted in using blockchains to simplify the process of arriving at legal and regulatory decisions regarding the collection, storage, and sharing of sensitive data[3].

NATURE-DRIVEN

The explosive increase in the number of broadcasters, and the ensuing need to somehow distinguish what is relevant and true from all the noise, next leads us to the question of whether digital communication is really the most suitable medium for this job. Increasingly, nature itself seems an excellent information carrier for the future. Brain-to-brain and brain-to-machine communication are entering the field of serious exploration, ranging from operating machines by thought, to setting up social networks without the use of verbal communication, and remotely exploring physical locations[4,5,6]. In the field of commercial communications, such technologies could replace profile-based targeting by just letting people think about having a Coke. Conversely, they could enable post-Babylonian scenarios for sharing and teaching without the need for verbal communication.

We should thus be considering more seriously the possibility that the future of communications will be less technology driven, and more nature driven. A valuable concept in this regard is the wood wide web, a network of mycorrhiza, fungi, and roots providing a collaborative structure that helps plants and trees maintain a healthy living environment. The network distributes not only information (even warning neighbouring organisms of dangers) but also resources such as sugar, nitrogen, and phosphorus[7]. Another interesting concept is 'information foraging': by 2049, we will have developed interfaces that allow us to 'read' each other, thus explicitly articulating information which we now experience on an intuitive level, in much the same way as a predator 'reads' the value of its potential prey[8].

Regardless of whether advances in communication technology will be driven by machines or by living organisms, the discussion about the motivations behind communication is likely to go on escalating. How long will we tolerate our minds being distracted by messages aiming to persuade us to do, buy, or think things that are not related to our own wishes and needs? The question for the future should thus not be how to better disseminate content in order to gain more influence, but rather how to collect wisdom and truth for the benefit of the commons.

TOTAL TRANSPARENCY

The digital revolution will continue to bring about considerable challenges in the near (and distant) future, with a huge societal impact. We must consider how we, as a society, wish to further incorporate digital communication into our economy and democracy, keeping in mind that the digital revolution includes much more than only communication: by enabling new models of distribution, it also changes the basic paradigm of our economy. Sharing information about what is scarce or abundant, when and where, undermines the very foundations of traditional economic powers. As we enter a future of ubiquitous digital communication and total transparency, we should also be preparing for a society in which the common purpose becomes the individual purpose. In this new paradigm, branding and marketing would be less interesting pursuits than finding the most valuable solution. Machine learning would then focus less on profiling-based persuasion, and more on promoting truth and predicting real needs. Chatbots could develop from mere marketing instruments to become teachers, guides, or even companions.

Change is the one thing we can count on. As the digital revolution comes closer to maturation, the only certainty is that new radical evolutions lie ahead.

References and notes

1 Retrieved from: http://www.globalissues.org/article/159/media-conglomerates-mergers-concentration-of-ownership

2 Retrieved from: https://www.statista.com/statistics/278414/number-of-worldwide-social-network-users/

3 Zyskind, G., Nathan, O., & Pentland, A. (2015). Enigma: Decentralized computation platform with guaranteed privacy. arXiv preprint arXiv:1506.03471.

4 A Direct Brain-to-Brain Interface in Humans. Retrieved from: https://journals.plos.org/plosone/article?id=10.1371/journal.pone.0111332

5 BrainNet: A multi-person brain-to-brain interface for direct collaboration between brains. https://arxiv.org/abs/1809.08632

6 Retrieved from: https://www.cnbc.com/2017/07/07/this-inventor-is-developing-technology-that-could-enable-telepathy.html

7 Simard, E. P., Ward, E. M., Siegel, R., & Jemal, A. (2012). Cancers with increasing incidence trends in the United States: 1999 through 2008. CA: a cancer journal for clinicians, 62(2), 118-128.

8 Pirolli, P., & Card, S. (1999). Information foraging. Psychological review, 106(4), 643.

CLOSURE

After discussing 23 innovations that matter in our opinion, where do we stand and how we can advance? Less than 25 years ago we were introduced to the 'World Wide Web', social media made their entrance, digital communication got lightning fast and computers became smarter, enabling hyper targeting, among other things. Also, the smartphone has become a jack-of-all-trades, accommodating a plethora of functionalities, such as for augmented reality purposes, and in just one portable device. In this drastically changed media landscape, a big challenge for organisations is to send the right messages to the right person at the right time at the right place, in the right way, accounting for people's privacy. We summarise two of the major changes that are central to all you have read in the previous chapters and their consequences for society, organisations, and science.

SO WHERE DO WE STAND AND HOW TO ADVANCE

The digital media landscape seems to be developing in two contradictory directions. With more competition shouting for our attention, more channels to reach us, constant availability, precise targeting, and striking communication techniques, the intrusiveness of mediated communication has increased dramatically. Location-based advertising is an example of an intrinsically intrusive medium. Even when you have given organisations the permission to push messages to your smartphone directly at your location (so-called 'opt-in'), these messages may still be experienced as intrusive when they actually show up on the display of your smartphone. On the other hand, developments such as the rise of social media, but also consumer-initiated innovations such as online reviewing and viral communication, give people a voice and a choice again. Another example is voice assistants. Their service is initiated by the consumer and is therefore not intrusive. We believe that consumer-initiated communication is the future. Already, people use the tricks and tools they have, such as ad-blockers, to regain control over the flood of messages.

INTERCONNECTED MEDIA AND THE REWIRED BRAIN

Machines have become smart. No doubt about that. The term 'smart', as in smart phones, smart computers, smart speakers, and smart systems, will become empty and redundant because soon all devises will have become smart and interconnected in our networked society. On the one hand, technology does not develop that fast. We, for instance, tend to overestimate the capacities of human-looking robots. It may take considerable time before computers will actually behave and act like humans.

Furthermore, smart algorithms are being developed but they are not interconnected on a large scale yet. On the other hand, technology in other devices does develop fast, such as in chatbots, voice assistants, and wearables. These devices will become self-learning and thus more powerful. That power may become an ethical issue.

In 1964, the philosopher Marshall McLuhan wrote that once technology is invented, it will be hard to uninvent it. The evolution of media and mankind go hand in hand. Computer-based technologies create parallel realities. In addition to the physical reality, you can escape into virtual worlds for entertainment purposes. In virtual simulations you can gain experience to overcome fear of heights. Interactive narrative technologies in serious games, using machine learning to determine the most engaging outline of the story, mean that people become even more absorbed in stories. Virtual reality is the ultimate form in which people shut off from the physical world. With their goggles on, they immerse themselves completely in virtuality. Augmented reality brings realities together by adding virtual layers to the physical world. Gamification is the integration of virtual elements into everyday reality. This paradigm was previously called real virtuality. In other words, media not only represent reality. Media realise reality.

Using neuromarketing and facial expression analysis, we uncover the impact of media messages in the short term. But also in the long term, media messages shape us at the biological level. We have seen that our intelligent capabilities and even our brain structure evolve under the influence of media. We outsource knowledge and overestimate our internal knowledge. We become better able to process and memorise fast images and develop visual skills such as iconic representation, spatial orientation, and spatial visualisation. Research among middle-aged adults suggests that experience with internet searching may alter the brain's responsiveness in the neural circuits controlling complex reasoning and decision making.

BUILDING A DIGITALLY LITERATE SOCIETY

The fact that people get more powerful and machines are getting smarter underscores the importance of digital literacy. Governments, organisations, and citizens have to become digitally literate in our digital society. They have to develop new media skills and become aware of contemporary digital language. Schools play an important role in educating children so that they become digital-literate citizens. They may help children to attain both new literacy skills, such as how to distinguish between fiction and reality, as these will blend in the future, learning how to programme, and how to recognise subtle less obvious branded content such as in-vlog advertising, and literacy skills such as 'reading' stories, and story-telling in traditional as well as new media.

Education should focus on the risks of excessive technology use, and the positive and negative effects of social media on child and adolescent mental health, from peer-to-peer support to cyberbullying. Education might facilitate the use of innovations such as serious gaming. Various games have been proven to achieve learning effects, but questions arise over how youngsters are incited to play these games as they are obviously less sexy than the games that they play for fun. Additionally, parenting and family life in the digital age might change and parents should get the right tools to raise their children in the digital age.

BECOMING AWARE OF AI-RELATED MORAL DILEMMAS

A subtopic of digital literacy is AI literacy. The access of AI to media, strategies, branding, and methods gives rise to speculations. No doubt, AI is a highly dynamic area integrating multiple disciplines and methods and it is already an important driving force in organisations, with machine learning and big data as its necessary fuel. Ethically, the question is not whether AI-rendered innovations such as behavioural targeting are good or bad, but how they are used and under which circumstances, and how society, advertisers, and consumers alike, may benefit optimally. AI in itself will not solve communication problems, or act intuitively like humans can (not yet, anyway), or be a driving force in creating enduring friendships with devices; it will probably not take over the world. At least not in the near future. For now, it is important that people become more aware of AI and what it can mean for society, enabling them to participate in the public debate. For instance, whether it is ethically responsible to make use of people's persuasion profiles, or even their facial expressions and unconscious processes for the collection of data. Where to draw the line?

AVOIDING PRIVACY FATIGUE

Lastly, a specific subtopic of digital literacy is of course privacy literacy. Our data are stored in places we cannot control, such as voice assistants saving audio recordings of users. These data are sometimes sold to parties we have never known the existence of, as in real-time bidding systems. A new age of data privacy has started, with the introduction of several privacy laws around the globe such as the General Data Protection Regulation (GDPR). The chase for privacy demands continues, and the request for trustworthy data-driven offers will be on the rise, leading us into a new era of Willingness To Share Data (WTSD)[1].

People should be reinstated as the gatekeepers of their own data, deciding themselves which data can be used for which purposes. This implies a change in people's mindset, based on knowledge many do not yet have. However, nowadays people's autonomy is reduced to a click, which decides whether to accept cookies and privacy regulations, or not. We should cautiously focus on how users of digital technology can be helped to behave responsibly to treasure their privacy, not making them weary of privacy rules because they experience privacy regulation overload. Research has shown that privacy fatigue is a multi-dimensional concept including exhaustion and cynicism and that it has a significant effect on privacy-coping behaviours. Privacy fatigue has an even stronger impact on disengagement behaviour than privacy concerns[2]. Therefore, we should determine whether people want to hand control over to the system, instating strict privacy laws, or whether they prefer to be in control themselves, actively choosing levels of privacy control.

Organisations have to realise that they play an important role in making people privacy-savy. And that they do not own people's data. They must find out how to behave according to privacy rules, in order to regain the trust of their most important stakeholders: the people they want to reach with their messages. As an example, there is nothing wrong when at the border people are informed about what is happening with their data. There is plenty of time to implement this transparency when they are waiting in line to cross the border.

REORIENTATION OF COMMUNICATION-RELATED STUDIES

The changes in the digital landscape call for a reorientation of communication studies. The goal of these studies is to prepare students for working in the field. In order to do that, the studies need to accommodate the opportunities and challenges introduced by, for instance, increasingly intelligent machines, autonomous decision-making systems, and smart devices[3]. Historically, the discipline of communication has accommodated new technology by interpreting these innovations as a medium of human interaction and message exchange. With the rise of digital media – starting with the 'traditional' computer – in the latter half of the 20th century, computer-mediated communication (CMC) was developed. In this transition, the need for new communication theories became evident. In CMC, the computer was understood and investigated as a more-or-less neutral channel of message transfer and instrument of human interaction. This formalisation neglected the fact that the computer, unlike previous technological advancements, also occupies the position of participant in communicative exchanges. Especially in its newest forms, such as voice assistants, chatbots and robots, and the rise of AI. Thus, communication studies need to rework their basic framework in order to address and accommodate the unique technological challenges and opportunities of the 21st century.

COOPERATING MULTIDISCIPLINARY TEAMS, FROM THEORY TO PRACTICE

How should we cope with the challenges that media innovations pose to us? Major questions about the applicability of media innovations should be tackled in multi-disciplinary teams as these innovations will almost always render issues of an ethical, law, communication, psychology, and AI nature. In these teams, practitioners and scientists should both have a say, just like in this book. This way, scientists keep track of the inventive and thoughtful applications that practitioners develop and are thus more up-to-date, and practitioners keep a keen eye on the insights rendered by scientific research, that they can use as the foundation of new developments and communication. Just think of the tremendous possibilities of these combined efforts, for instance for gamification and for virtual and augmented reality, for clinical benefits, for instance to get rid of anxieties. And the role of automated assessment fuelled by big data and strengthened by AI, offering big opportunities to detect diseases at an early stage, for instance by wearables.

IN 2049 WE ARE LOOKING BACK AT 2019 … WITH A SMILE ON OUR FACES?

We started and ended our book with biology. In the first chapter, Gabi Schaap described in his contribution 'the Digital Brain' how digital innovations affect our brain in the long term. Our brain is already adapting to the new reality that awaits us, and technology is already taking over some of our brain functions, whereas other functions are evolving. In the last contribution in our book, Justien Marseille remarked that technology may become dominated by biology. Therefore, science and practice should keep focusing on the impact of digital innovations on humanity: on cognition, learning, decision-making behaviour and in a broader sense on whether innovations add to our mental and physical health and well-being.

So how will people in 2049 look back at 2019? Will they laugh at how awkward and naïve we were, sharing all our data with thousands of people? Will communication indeed become more biologically based? We simply do not know. We do believe that machines are getting better at understanding us humans, we are getting better at understanding them, and that both sides are getting better by working together. Humans and machines will work side by side. Computers will help to augment humans with technology. Also, technology does not exist on its own; it is the result of human effort, so it will continue serving humans. We are in control and should keep it that way. But that is just the start. What we do with it is just as important. What goals do these innovations help us achieve? We should not innovate just for innovation's sake, only to respond to the unmet needs of users, organisations, and society. Will all these digital innovations make us happier, better informed, and healthier? We believe they will.

Concerning the future, we have no doubts that fascinating innovations will be developed and will merge into media of a higher order that may be beyond our imagination. Therefore, in an analogy with the unpredictability of life in general, we would like to end our book with the following positively framed saying from a beautiful movie:

"Life is like a box of chocolates. You never know what you're gonna get."

Forrest Gump, 1994

ACKNOWLEDGEMENTS

We, the authors, owe a big 'thank you' to a lot of people without whom this book would not have been realised.

Firstly, experts from national and international organisations who all contributed to the book and had to divulge all their knowledge in just a few pages: Marcel Becker, Fleur Willemijn van Beinum, Juliane Blasche, Natasja Bogers, Marjolein Bongers, Loes Brouwers, Pascal Cramer, Niels Cuijpers, Hans van Dam, Donna Davis, Pratik Dholakiya, Marnix van Gisbergen, Jan Heuvel, Maurits Kaptein, Gerrit Kuyntjes, Maarten Lens-FitzGerald, Ralf van Lieshout, Walter Limpens, Justien Marseille, Jacqueline Martinali, Jeroen van Mastrigt, Edwin Metselaar, Maarten Molenaar, Marc Oosterhout, Nathalie Peters, Kelly Philipse, Elizabeth Press, Gabi Schaap, Marloes Smit, Aurelie Valtat, Lotte Willemsen, and Gonny van der Zwaag.

A special thanks to Guda van Noort for being so kind to write the preface of our book.

We would like to thank the students who have enrolled in the course 'Innovations in Communication' for the Master's in Communication Science at Radboud University, who have inspired us tremendously by following this course, asking critical questions, and writing their assignments. And Simone de Droog, co-developer of the course 'Innovations in Communication' when it all started.

A big thank you to the people who directed us to expert-colleagues who contributed to our book: Paul Aelen, Margot Bohaty, Loes Brouwers, Maarten-Lenz Fitzgerald, Erik Hensel Olaf Igesz, Edwin Metselaar, Adriaan Monshauwer, David Phillips, and Michiel Veugelers. Thank you Jeroen van der Most for allowing us to publish one of your beautiful AI-inspired paintings.

In particular we like to thank those who were so kind to review several chapters and give us valuable suggestions for improvement: Fleur Willemijn van Beinum, Paul van der Bijl, Tibor Bosse, Moniek Buijzen, Lisa Cedrone, Marnix van Gisbergen, Jan Heuvel, Evelien Heyselaar, Marlotte Ketelaar, Joline Ketelaar, Shuang Li, Karoline Snip, Marjolein Snip, and Pim Verheyke who has read and 'structified' several chapters of the book! Thanks to the people who have been willing to review a chapter: Paul Aelen, Erik van den Berge, Kevin van Geest, Margot van der Goot, Tim van der Kallen, Gero

Lange, Sari Nijssen, Esther Rozendaal, Anne-Roos Smink, Hans Theuws, Addy Weijers, and Maizie May Wythe.

Furthermore, we thank Bionda Dias from BIS Publishers for her faith in our idea and the decision to publish our book ... with just a few pages more than initially agreed upon, and Sara van de Ven for making sure our book reached you, the reader. We thank Lex Dirkse for the tailor-made illustrations and Jan van Zomeren for the design of the cover and interior of the book.

Additionally, we thank 'Stadsbrasserie de Utrechter' in Utrecht, the Netherlands, for hosting our numerous Writing Weekends, amidst hordes of people, crying children, and awful first dates, but also great food and mellow music to fuel our creative writing process.

We would like to devote this book to our families, for their love, devotion, and unlimited patience in the process of writing this book.

Paul Ketelaar

Jan Aarts

Sanne Demir

References and notes

1   https://duckduckgo.com/

2   Choi, H., Park, J., & Jung, Y. (2018). The role of privacy fatigue in online privacy behavior. Computers in Human Behavior, 81, 42-51.

3   Gunkel, D. J. (2012). Communication and artificial intelligence: Opportunities and challenges for the 21st century. Communication+ 1, 1(1), 1-25.

AUTHORS

Paul Ketelaar (PhD, 1960, The Hague, The Netherlands) is a senior assistant professor of Communication and Influence at the Behavioural Science Institute, Radboud University Nijmegen in the Netherlands. His research focuses mainly on the effectiveness of digital innovations such as personalised communication, virtual and augmented reality in healthcare and commerce, and privacy-related issues. In addition to his research and educational activities, Paul aims to bridge the academy-society divide. He blogs about digital innovations for Bitescience Communication and media, and SWOCC. He owns the agency Ketelaar Communications and is a matchmaker between young professionals and the communication field. He is a jury member of the yearly European Digital Communication Awards. He is a semi-professional photographer, inspiring leader of focus-group sessions and a dedicated volunteer worker and member of the board of Foundation Dhampus, a foundation promoting and facilitating dental care in rural areas of Nepal and Mongolia.

Jan Aarts (MSc, 1989, Ammerzoden, The Netherlands) works as a Research Manager at DVJ Insights, a research agency in Utrecht. DVJ Insights won the MOA award in 2018 for the best Marketing Research and Analytics Agency of the year. He studied Communication Science at the Radboud University of Nijmegen to obtain a Master's degree in Media and Persuasion. Jan graduated with honours. His skills and affinity for the practice of mediated communication and the science of persuasive media intertwine when he studies the effects of a variety of international brand, public and advertising campaigns. Because of his involvement in communication research as well as practice, he is the chairman of the commission Professionalisation of Communication Science at Radboud University, Nijmegen. During the release of this book, Jan has been nominated for the Young Talent Award by the MOA, Expertise Center for Marketing-insights, Research & Analytics.

Sanne Demir (MSc, 1995, Gouda, The Netherlands) is Insights Manager at one of The Netherlands' top advertising agencies, N=5, in Amsterdam. She is passionate about stories, emotions, and why we do what we do. She obtained a Master's degree in Communication Science at the Radboud University of Nijmegen with a specialisation in Communication and Influence. During her studies, she won the 'Professor Stappers Award' for best research paper. Now, she puts theories about communication and influence into practice on a daily basis, does several types of research to gain qualitative strategic insights into brands and their target audiences, and helps renowned brands to position themselves in the market and create convincing brand stories. She also applied her knowledge to a local venue 'So What!?' in Gouda, where she was responsible for their marketing. This was a volunteer job, just as every other job at 'So What!?' Is fulfilled by volunteers – which makes it a special project, with challenges and victories that are different to other organisations.